Cross-Cultural
Business Negotiations

Cross-Cultural Business Negotiations

Donald W. Hendon,
Rebecca Angeles Hendon, and Paul Herbig

Q

Quorum Books
Westport, Connecticut • London

Library of Congress Cataloging-in-Publication Data

Hendon, Donald W.
  Cross-cultural business negotiations / Donald W. Hendon, Rebecca
Angeles Hendon, and Paul Herbig.
      p.   cm.
  Includes bibliographical references and index.
  ISBN 1–56720–064–8 (alk. paper)
  1. Negotiation in business—Social aspects.   2. Intercultural
communication.   I. Hendon, Rebecca Angeles.   II. Herbig, Paul A.
III. Title.
  HD58.6.H458   1996
  658.4—dc20   96–3619

British Library Cataloguing in Publication Data is available.

Library of Congress Catalog Card Number: 95–3619
ISBN: 1–56720–064–8

First published in 1996

Quorum Books, 88 Post Road West, Westport, CT 06881
An imprint of Greenwood Publishing Group, Inc.

Printed in the United States of America

The paper used in this book complies with the
Permanent Paper Standard issued by the National
Information Standards Organization (Z39.48–1984).

10 9 8 7 6 5 4 3 2 1

Dedicated to the memory of Hugh Kramer (April 17, 1929–December 24, 1995), Professor of Marketing at the University of Hawaii-Manoa: A close friend, esteemed colleague, respected academician, well-loved professor, lifelong student of the marketing sciences, and devoted husband and father.

Contents

Introduction

When two people communicate, they rarely talk about precisely the same subject, for effective meaning is flavored by each person's own cognitive world and cultural conditioning. Negotiation is the process by which at least two parties try to reach an agreement on matters of mutual interest. The negotiation process proceeds as an interplay of perception, information processing, and reaction, all of which turn on images of reality (accurate or not), on implicit assumptions regarding the issue being negotiated, and on an underlying matrix of conventional wisdom, beliefs, and social expectations. Negotiations involve two dimensions: a matter of substance and the process. The latter is rarely a matter of relevance when negotiations are conducted within the same cultural setting. Only when dealing with someone from another country with a different cultural background does process usually become a critical barrier to substance; in such settings process first needs to be established before substantive negotiations can commence. This becomes more apparent when the negotiation process is international, when cultural differences must be bridged.

When negotiating internationally, this translates into anticipating culturally related ideas that are most likely to be understood by a person of a given culture. Discussions are frequently impeded because the two sides seem to be pursuing different paths of logic; in any cross-cultural context, the potential for misunderstanding and talking past each other is great. Negotiating internationally almost certainly means having to cope with new and inconsistent information, usually accompanied by new behavior, social environments, and even sights and smells. The greater the cultural differences, the more likely barriers to communication and misunderstandings become.

When one takes the seemingly simple process of negotiations into a cross-cultural context, it becomes even more complex and complications tend to grow exponentially. It is naive indeed to venture into international negotiation with the belief that "after all, people are pretty much alike everywhere and behave much as we do." Even if they wear the same clothes you do, speak English as well as (or even better than) you, and prefer many of the comforts and attributes of American life (food, hotels, sports), it would be foolish to view a member of another culture as a brother in spirit. That negotiation style you use so effectively at home can be ineffective and inappropriate when dealing with people from another cultural background; in fact its use can often result in more harm than gain. Heightened sensitivity, more attention to detail, and perhaps even changes in basic behavioral patterns are required when working in another culture.

Members of one culture may focus on different aspects of an agreement (e.g., legal, financial) than may members of another culture (personal, relationships). The implementation of a business agreement may be stressed in one culture, while the range and prevention of practical problems may be emphasized in another culture. In some cultures, the attention of people is directed more toward the specific details of the agreement (documenting the agreement), while other cultures may focus on how the promises can be kept (process and implementation). Americans negotiate a contract; the Japanese negotiate a personal relationship. Culture forces people to view and value differently the many social interactions inherent in fashioning any agreement. Negotiations can easily break down because of a lack of understanding of the cultural component of the negotiation process. Negotiators who take the time to understand the approach that the other parties are likely to use and to adapt their own styles to that one are likely to be more effective negotiators.

American and Russian people are not similar; their ethical attitudes do not coincide: they evaluate behavior differently. What an American may consider normative, positive behavior (negotiating and reaching a compromise with an enemy), a Russian perceives as showing cowardice, weakness, and unworthiness; the word "deal" has a strong negative connotation, even today in contemporary Russia. Similarly, for Russians, compromise has negative connotation; principles are supposed to be inviolable and compromise is a matter of integrity (The Russians are not alone here: a Mexican will not compromise as a matter of honor, dignity, and integrity; likewise, an Arab fears loss of manliness if he compromises.) A negotiation is treated as a whole without concessions. At the Strategic Arms Limitation Talks (SALT) talks, the Americans thought they had an agreement (meaning conclusive commitment), while the Russians said it was an understanding (meaning an expression of mutual viewpoint or attitude). When the Americans thought they had an understanding, the Russians said it was a procedural matter, meaning they had agreed to a process for conducting the negotiation.

Different cultural systems can produce divergent negotiating styles—styles shaped by each nation's culture, geography, history, and political system. Unless you see the world through the other's eyes (no matter how similar they appear to you), you may not be seeing or hearing the same. No one can usually avoid bringing along his or her own cultural assumptions, images, and prejudices or other attitudinal baggage into any negotiating situation. The way one succeeds in cross-cultural negotiations is by fully understanding others, using that understanding to one's own advantage to realize what each party wants from the negotiations, and to turn the negotiations into a win-win situation for both sides.

A few potential problems often encountered during a cross-cultural negotiation include (Frank, 1992):

1. Insufficient understanding of different ways of thinking.
2. Insufficient attention to the necessity to save face.
3. Insufficient knowledge of the host country—including history, culture, government, status of business, image of foreigners.
4. Insufficient recognition of political or other criteria.
5. Insufficient recognition of the decision-making process.
6. Insufficient understanding of the role of personal relations and personalities.
7. Insufficient allocation of time for negotiations.

Over two-thirds of U.S.-Japanese negotiation efforts fail even though both sides want to reach a successful business agreement (The U.S. Department of Commerce is even more pessimistic; it estimates that for every successful American negotiation with the Japanese, there are twenty-five failures.) In fact, these numbers hold true for most cross-cultural meetings. Often barriers to a successful agreement are of a cultural nature rather than of an economical or legal nature. Since each side perceives the other from its own ethnocentric background and experience, often neither side fully comprehends why the negotiations failed. It is precisely this lack of knowledge concerning the culture and the "alien" and "unnatural" expectations of the other side that hinders effective negotiation with those from another culture.

In cross-cultural negotiations, many of the rules taught and used domestically may not apply—especially when they may not be culturally acceptable to the other party. For most Western negotiators this includes the concepts of give and take, of bargaining, and even of compromise. The stereotypical, common Western ideal of a persuasive communicator—highly skilled in debate, able to overcome objections with verbal flair, an energetic extrovert—may be regarded by members of other cultures as unnecessarily aggressive, superficial, insincere, even vulgar and repressive. To other Americans, the valued American traits of directness and frankness show evidence of good intentions and personal convictions. To an American it is complimentary to be called straightforward and aggressive. This is not necessarily so, however, for members of other cultures. To describe a person as "aggressive" is a derogatory characterization to a British citizen. To the Japanese, those very same traits indicate lack of confidence in one's convictions and insincerity. Instead, terms such as thoughtful, cooperative, considerate, and respectful instill positives in the Japanese and many Asian cultures.

Domestically, the study of negotiation tends to encompass business relationships between parties, tactics, bargaining strategies, contingency positions, and so on. However, in a cross-cultural context, besides the usual rules of negotiation, one has to be wary of fine nuances in relationships and practices and how they are perceived and executed by members of the other culture. The two business negotiators are separated from each other not only by physical features, a totally different language, and business etiquette, but also by a different way to perceive the world, to define business goals, to express thinking and feeling, to show or hide motivation and interests. From the other party's perspective, for example, to some cultures Americans may appear aggressive and rude, while to others, those very same Americans appear calm and uninterested.

It is our intent, in this book, to present a tutorial on cross-cultural negotiation and to provide specific, detailed examples on how to negotiate with other cultures.

1

What:
The Art of Negotiations

The word "negotiations" stems from the Roman word *negotiari* meaning "to carry on business" and is derived from the Latin root words *neg* (not) and *otium* (ease or leisure). Obviously it was as true for the ancient Romans as it is for most businesspersons of today that negotiations and business involves hard work. A modern definition of negotiation is two or more parties with common (and conflicting) interests who enter into a process of interaction with the goal of reaching an agreement (preferably of mutual benefit). John Kenneth Galbraith said "Sex apart, negotiation is the most common and problematic involvement of one person with another, and the two activities are not unrelated." Negotiations is a decision-making process that provides opportunities for the parties to exchange commitments or promises through which they will resolve their disagreements and reach a settlement. A negotiation is two or more parties striving to agree when their objectives do not coincide.

Negotiation consists of two distinct processes: creating value and claiming value. Creating value is a cooperative process whereby the parties in the negotiation seek to realize the full potential benefit of the relationship. Claiming value is essentially a competitive process. The key to creating value is finding interests that the parties have in common or that complement each other, then reconciling and expanding upon these interests to create a win-win situation. Parties at the negotiating table are interdependent. Their goals are locked together. A seller cannot exist without a buyer. The purpose of a negotiation is a joint decision-making process through which the parties create a mutually acceptable settlement. The objective is to pursue a win-win situation for both parties.

Negotiations take place within the context of the four Cs: common interest, conflicting interests, compromise, and criteria (Moran and Stripp, 1991). Common interest considers the fact that each party in the negotiation shares, has, or wants something that the other party has or does. Without a common goal, there would be no need for negotiation. Conflict occurs when people have separate but conflicting interests. Areas of conflicting interests could include payment, distribution, profits, contractual responsibilities, and quality. Compromise involves resolving areas of disagreement. Although a win-win negotiated settlement would be best for both parties, the compromises that are negotiated may not produce the result. The criteria include the conditions under which the negotiations take place. The negotiation process has few rules of procedure. Rules of procedure are as much a product of negotiation as the issues. Over time, the four Cs change and the information, know-how, and alternatives available to the negotiating international company and the host country also change, resulting in a fresh interpretation of the four Cs, the environment, and the perspective. In essence, negotiation takes place within the context of the political, economic, social, and cultural systems of a country.

The theory of the negotiation process includes the following dimensions: (1) bargainer characteristics, (2) situational constraints, (3) the process of bargaining, and (4) negotiation outcomes. This theory is based on actors who share certain values and beliefs based on their culture. These actors function in business and economic situations that also have cultural influences, and they act in certain culturally inscribed ways. We bargain when:

1. A conflict of interest exists between two or more parties; that is, what one wants is not necessarily what the other one wants.
2. A fixed or set of rules or procedures for resolving the conflict does not exist, or the parties prefer to work outside of a set of rules to invent their own solution to the conflict.
3. The parties, at least for the moment, prefer to search for agreement rather than to fight openly, to have one side capitulate, to permanently break off contact, or to take their dispute to a higher authority to resolve it.

In summary, negotiations primarily consists of five aspects: (1) goals: motivating the parties to enter; (2) the process of negotiating that involves communications and actions; (3) outcomes; (4) preexisting background factors of cultural traditions and relations; and (5) specific situational conditions under which the negotiation is conducted.

IMPORTANCE OF NEGOTIATIONS

A typical senior manager in an American business spends at least twenty percent of his or her working day negotiating. The percentage of time spent negotiating by executives involved in international business is even higher. Three major obstacles exist in most negotiations: the fear of conceding too much, the fear of losing face, and the belief that "We are more reasonable than they are." This belief is based on egotism (of course, we are more reasonable than they are) and by the natural tendency to feel that our position is correct, while they have taken their position because they are irrational or want to gain a bargaining advantage. This belief also affects perceptions of concessions; ours were real, while theirs were just "cutting away fat."

An example of the importance of negotiations is Rolls Royce. Its negotiators desperately wanted the engine contract for Lockheed's L-1011 airliner. Despite repeated warnings from their own engineers, they made concession after concession. They ended up with a contract that any rational engineer would have know was ridiculous. They agreed to go well beyond the existing state-of-the-art on a low-margin, fixed-price contract. When the nearly inevitable cost overruns occurred, they found that they were selling each engine for substantially less than it cost to build. This contract (and various other mistakes) literally drove Rolls Royce, a famous name and a fine engineering firm, into bankruptcy. The Lockheed negotiators naturally felt they had negotiated very well. However, they had actually made an extremely costly mistake. By driving the price so low, they bankrupted a key supplier, could not meet their commitments to their own customers, and ultimately lost $2.5 billion on the L-1011. The moral is quite clear—if a deal is too good for any side, it is probably bad for both of them. Experience by itself is insufficient unless it is transformed into expertise.

Arbitration is another form of negotiation and one of the most widely used methods of settling disputes. It is basically a process where two groups or persons agree to submit the dispute to a non-aligned third person and further agree that they will carry out that third person's decisions. Arbitration avoids going to court and the uncertainties of an unknown legal system. International arbitration has a time-tested set of rules and procedures to govern the arbitration, the organization to manage the proceedings, and an established group of experienced arbitrators.

STAGES OF NEGOTIATIONS

The stages through which negotiations proceed include:

1. *Initial Planning and Fact Finding*: This stage occurs prior to leaving or beginning the negotiations. As information is power, the more information you can obtain about the other side, the better. This should begin well before any negotiations commence and should involve learning about the organization, history, and negotiating styles of the other side. One should also identify all the potential issues to be discussed, prioritize the issues, establish a settlement range, and develop the strategies and tactics to be used during the negotiating session. If it is at all possible, one should assemble the team before the negotiations start and conduct all preliminary discussions, individual assignments, and team organization prior to leaving.

2. *Orientation at the Site Prior to the Negotiations*: Time should be given to adjust to the negotiations location before any meeting commences. This is to get over any jet lag, anxiety, or culture shock that might occur to the team members at the negotiations site. The negotiating site should be viewed and all arrangements and equipment necessary should be tested and guaranteed prior to the meeting. One should meet with local representatives for cultural and site-specific information and any recent data prior to the meeting. If necessary, team building, and strategy planning, and consensus building should be performed or confirmed at the site before the commencement of the negotiation itself.

3. *Non-task*: This stage establishes relationships among the negotiating parties. Information specific to the issue under negotiation is not considered; rather, the parties seek to get to know each other first. Credibility and trust must first be present before commitments can be made and accepted. When trust is low or non-existent in a relationship, the parties find it difficult to communicate their expectations. The basic job of all negotiators is to create doubts and uncertainties in the minds of others as to the viability of the other parties' positions. Nonetheless, negotiators must create trust and confidence in the minds of others to provide a basis for relationship building. Untrusted negotiators do not get far. When communication is problematic, parties do not listen effectively to each other. Ineffective listening creates problems in understanding. Ineffective listening makes education of the positions impossible.

4. *Task-Related Exchange of Information*: This stage provides information directly connected to the issue under negotiations. Each party explains its needs and preferences. The initial focus should be on

reconciling interests rather than taking positions or making demands. Objectives should be introduced followed by discussion of merits of each. In every negotiation the participants have different points of view and different objectives. Positions are adopted by negotiators to advance their own interests. Focusing on the position rather than the interest is confusing the means with the ends. Negotiation can take place both on the official table as well as away from the negotiating table. One of the most common mistakes in the negotiating process is failing to obtain relevant or missing information by not asking the right questions. By asking questions it is possible to update available information and test your strategy. Knowing what information is missing helps rational negotiators maximize their interests. Rational negotiators should assess each situation separately and develop appropriate strategies.

5.   *Resistance*: If you encounter no resistance, this usually means no interest on the part of other side. As long as there is resistance, there is interest. Knowing the source of the resistance allows one to work on overcoming their objections.

6. *Reformulation of Strategies*: When negotiations were first set, a negotiating strategy was planned. As you proceed and gather new data and insights, one will probably have to reassess earlier strategies. Goals, strategies, objectives, and tactics are situational. No plan should be cast in concrete.

7. *Hard Bargaining and Decision Making*: One should be concentrating on meeting the needs of both sides, not just the formal positions being stated. One should attempt to invent options for mutual gain that will result in a win-win outcome. Estimates are that between seventy and ninety percent of concessions occur during the the last ten percent of the time allowed. In many cases the opening bid is ritualistically extreme because the negotiator expects to back down.

8. *Persuasion*: One should be focusing on efforts to modify the views of other parties and sway them to our way of thinking. Persuasion is often intertwined with other stages. The best form of persuasion is self-persuasion. People are more likely to be convinced by reasons they discovered themselves than by reasons pointed out to them by others. Guide the other side through questions or observations to his or her own original conclusion or insight. You give face when you allow the other negotiator to achieve a result that is consistent with his or her principles or previous statements and action, in other words, making a person look good. A proposed agreement is more likely to be accepted if it allows all parties involved in the negotiation process to justify their existence by contributing to the result in some way.

9. *Concessions*:   Concessions are usually needed to reach an agreement. Each side frequently must give up some things; both sides give and take and compromise. In any negotiation, there is the possibility of a settlement that gives each party something it wants, without significant cost or loss to the other side. The discovery of these options breaks the win-lose deadlock that may have initially existed, and opens new opportunities for the parties to mutually accomplish their objectives. The tactics of a tie-in will not work if the opponent is asked to surrender more than he expects to receive. Counterdemands are requests for a redistribution in one's favor, either on an issue related to the one raised by the opponent or possibly on a quite unrelated issue. They are essential, not only to permit oneself to be flexible without incurring a net loss, but also to protect oneself against mediators who simply split the difference between the opposing proposals—as most mediators are prone to do.

10. *Agreement*: Agreement is the culmination of the negotiating process. One must work out the details of the negotiation and ensure understanding; parties to a negotiation may agree to the same solution for entirely different reasons. Ratification of agreement must be performed by necessary powers on both sides (negotiations also occur between team members and their respective decision makers). One must always remember the concept of BATNA: "Best Alternative to a Negotiated Agreement." Sometimes no agreement is the better alternative to an unfair and onesided agreement.

11. *Follow-up*: Effective follow-up is an opportunity for relationship building. Negotiators who have an effective ongoing relationship will be able to agree to disagree and not have the disagreement negatively affect their relationship.

THE SUCCESSFUL NEGOTIATOR

Win-win negotiators see deal making as a collaborative effort and problem-solving process; by way of contrast, win-lose negotiators view it as confrontational. Skilled negotiators have observant minds, sound judgment, a tranquil and patient nature, an appreciation for humor. They also refuse to be distracted by pleasures or frivolous amusements; are always ready to listen with attention to those whom they meet; have an open, genial, civil, and agreeable manner of speaking; provide quick replies to unforeseen surprises or comments; can discover how their counterparts are feeling and thinking; and have sufficient mind control to resist the temptation to speak before thinking. Negotiators should thoroughly understand the purpose of the negotiations before going overseas. Negotiators should know both the intent and parameters of their company's wishes prior to leaving. Good negotiators should also know the history, culture, laws, customs, and government of the country they are dealing with as well as have some knowledge of the particular counterparts they will be working with.

The complete negotiator, according to seventeenth- and eighteenth-century manuals on diplomacy, should have a quick mind but unlimited patience, know how to dissemble without being a liar, inspire trust without trusting others, be modest but assertive, charm others without succumbing to their charm, and possess plenty of money and a beautiful wife while remaining indifferent to all temptations of riches and women. It is easy to add to this garland of virtue, but difficult in the real world to judge a good negotiator from a bad one. One cannot evaluate a negotiator merely by asking how close he came to realizing the aims of his government; for if he came close, he may owe his success to modest aims or favorable conditions rather than to his skill. Nor can one be sure that he has done well just because his gains and losses compare favorably with those of the opponent; for it is an essential task to negotiators to change the evaluation of gains and losses.

A good negotiator should be realistic, yes, but not in the sense of accepting an outcome as being determined by the balance of forces without tying to reinterpret this "balance" in his favor. Instead of taking a situation for granted, he should be realistic in recognizing that his opponent's evaluations as well as his own are constantly adrift, that issues are not created by nature but by himself and by his opponent, and that there are as many ways of negotiating from weakness as well as from strength.

A good negotiator should also be flexible—not by being without a firm position but utilizing both firm and flexible proposals. He should be flexible in his tactics by discriminating between occasions when it pays to adhere to rules of accommodation and when it does not. He must distinguish between situations where it would be disastrous to make a threat and from others where it is essential to threaten or even to bluff. He must know when to humor the personal quirks of his opponent and when to ignore them. He must be willing to disregard propaganda losses at one time and to negotiate merely for propaganda at another time. He must be prepared to follow domestic opinion at home as well as to encourage a new consensus both in his government and in his country.

A good negotiator should be patient—though not primarily in order to sit in Geneva for months at a time hearing the opponent repeat speeches and repeating his own. He should be patient in working for seemingly lost causes, because by doing so he may slowly change the opponent's views and objectives. He should be patient to live with conflict and uncertainty and know that he may have succeeded even if (or precisely because) his negotiations failed. Above all, he must maintain the will to win. Wise negotiators know that the best deal is one that is good for both sides. If the agreement is mutually beneficial, both sides have an incentive to maintain it. It is better to recognize the possibility of renegotiation at the outset and set down a clear framework with which to conduct the process. In short, the successful negotiator must recognize the possibility of redoing the deal, but controlling the process.

Every negotiator must decide how open and honest to be about personal preferences and needs, and how much to trust the other party. The dilemma of honesty and openness suggests that if a negotiator is completely open and honest about what he wants, or will settle for, he many not do as well as if he bluffs or fights harder for a better settlement. On the other hand, if he is deceptive and dishonest about what he really wants or will settle for, the parties could never come to an agreement that would be workable. Most negotiators resolve this dilemma by being very careful and guarded at the beginning of negotiation, and revealing more of their true needs as they can come to trust the other side. Similarly, the dilemma of trust suggests that a negotiator has an equal problem in knowing how much to trust this opponent's ability that his opponent is lying or bluffing, and our negotiator could give away too much. On the other hand, if the negotiator believes nothing his opponent says, once again the parties could never come to agreement. Most negotiators resolve this dilemma by probing their opponent's statements for truthfulness, and for evidence that they will be true to their word.

Negotiators as members of society are led easily into attitudes of cultural bias. The only way to overcome that bias is to create awareness of one's own cultural system by understanding how other people behave in another system. Negotiators should respect and appreciate the ways and customs of the host country and attempt to adapt as well as possible to make the host at ease. Negotiators should not criticize the host country's form of government or personal conduct of government officials. They should always praise that which is praiseworthy without affection and flattery. Negotiators should single out the good points of the country and avoid mentioning the bad points. Good negotiators will never make promises that they cannot keep or negotiate in bad faith. Any concession gained dishonestly will have an uncertain result because the deceived party will have a longstanding desire for vengeance. Negotiators should emphasize mutual benefit and mutual advantage. The secret of success is to point out the common advantages to both parties and to link these advantages so that they appear to be equally balanced.

The negotiator who, from his knowledge of his opposer's culture and his sensitivity to it, can adapt his behavior to the situation and serve the interests of the interaction. The more and better the communication, the greater the amount of information shared or extracted, and the greater the build-up of trust, the more likely is the possibility of creating the satisfaction that negotiators are exchanging at the end of the day. In order to be effective the negotiator must be constantly alert to the distinctive qualities of the people with whom he is negotiating. He has to appreciate the meaning of their actions so as not to mislead or be misled by them, and to make his own points in a way that promotes advantageous outcomes. Effective negotiators operate as detectives searching for clues to the values and interests of their counterparts. They avoid assumptions about partner concerns; they look for what does matter to the partner rather than what should matter. Other attributes of a successful, complete negotiator include: having outstanding communication skills; being persistent; having flexibility, tact, open mindedness, subject knowledge; being willing to take risks; having physical stamina, self-confidence, decisiveness, creativity, willingness to listen, self- control, and a long-run outlook; and being sensitive to the interests and needs of others.

THE ROLE OF NEGOTIATIONS IN THE WESTERN CULTURE

Negotiation is emphasized and given higher status in the United States and many Western cultures than in other cultures. To an American, negotiation is the least troublesome method of settling disputes. The culture emphasizes dialogue, mediation and compromise as a means to resolving conflict between two parties in a dispute. Negotiations may be exploratory and serve to formulate viewpoints and delineate areas of agreement of convention. Or it may aim at working out practical arrangements. The success of negotiation depends upon whether (a) the issue is negotiable (that is, you can sell your car but not your child); (b) the negotiators are interested not only in taking but also in giving and are able to exchange value for value, and compromise; or (c) negotiating parties trust each other to some extent—if they didn't, a plethora of safety provisions would render the "agreement" unworkable.

Several cultural reasons exist for this emphasis. First, Americans emphasize bargaining to counteract its culture's extreme emphasis upon problem solving. Americans are natural problem solvers. The American culture values and encourages qualities such as openness, objectivity, fairness, cooperation, reason, and mutual trust. Second, when there is little or no conflict, you can usually get good results by acting naturally. But when interests conflict, or the other side uses bargaining tactics, you must act in unnatural, perhaps even distasteful ways.

Third, bargaining is where the money is. Too many companies have inadequate profit levels; too many billions of dollars in bad loans will have to be written off; and too many bad deals have been made. One reason for these bad deals is that Americans tend to be naive. They tend to be trusting and objective even when they should be tougher and more skeptical. In fact, the Russians, Arabs, Japanese, and members of other non-Western cultures often regard Americans as naive fools for problem solving when they are bargaining, for trusting them when they are unquestionably lying. The best negotiations are between two sincere problem solvers, and it would be extremely foolish to shift toward bargaining when the other side is being open, honest, and cooperative. But it is suicidal to be open, honest, and trusting when the other side is obviously lying and exploiting. Yet that is exactly what Americans have done, again, and again, and again.

John Maynard Keynes, the great economist, made this point brilliantly in his analysis of the Versailles negotiations that ended World War I. He definitely sympathized with Woodrow Wilson's ideals, but regarded him as a naive fool, a preacher playing poker with card sharks. The cynical French and British prime ministers manipulated Wilson into agreements that protected their short-term interests, but, as Keynes predicted, had disastrous long-term effects on everyone—Germany's ruinous inflation, the Great Depression, and World War II.

A fourth reason for emphasizing pure bargaining is that you cannot get much of the help you need. Numerous books and courses exist on joint problem solving, but barely any seriously discuss pure bargaining. In fact, many popular books on negotiations essentially ignore conflict. They pander to people's discomfort with conflict by pretending it does not exist, leading one to believe that all negotiations can be win-win. Tell that to a trade negotiator who is trying to ensure that an American car costs as much in Seoul as a Korean one costs in New York.

We can never forget that conflict is a fact of life and that ignoring it is dangerous. Nor will we overlook the obvious fact that people do lie while negotiating and that excessive trust can lead to disaster. If your opening offer is too generous, you may leave lots of money on the table, or it may raise expectations to unrealistic levels, or have insufficient bargaining room. On the other hand, if you are too ambitious, the other side may reject your offer out of hand, become angry and rigid, or even break off the negotiations.

Because of their culture, most Americans care more about the second set of dangers; they are afraid of offending or irritating the other side. They may therefore make overly generous first offers. For example, they frequently submit proposals that contain only modest profits. The subsequent negotiations reduce this profit still further and may even drive the deal below the breakeven point. One way to reduce the danger is to get the other side to make the first offer. You can then see whether the other side intends to be realistic and reasonable. If possible, plan ways to get them to make that first offer.

NEGOTIATIONS INTERNATIONALLY

The unique characteristic of international versus domestic business negotiations is that international negotiations are influenced by a wide diversity of environments. These require changing perspectives that determine the selection of appropriate tactics and strategies of the negotiations to be adopted (e.g., concepts of what is right, reasonable, or appropriate, expectations, mood, and reference to one's own cultural values). Negotiators must develop a broad perspective that includes the larger context within which they negotiate (e.g., similar and related projects, reactions of political and economic interest groups).

The Arabs want direct, face-to-face discussions, but tend not to bring open disagreements into a formal session. In fact, rather than say that they disagree, many Arabs will say they agree, but then take actions that gently hint that they do not agree at all. They hope that the other party will get the message. In Algeria, an American consultant once said: "My clients never disagree with my recommendations. They just do not try to implement the ones they dislike."

The Japanese are willing to meet face-to-face, but they also use third parties much more frequently than do Americans. They like to have that buffer. They are also so uncomfortable with open conflict that they hardly ever express it directly. They talk around it, or do not react at all, or give indirect hints that they disagree. In fact, they hardly ever say no directly; one must infer it from the way they say yes. In Tokyo, the running joke (though true) is the Japanese have twenty ways to say "No" without having to say it.

In Japan and the Arab countries, the direct negotiations are combined with social activities. One purpose of these activities is to demonstrate hospitality. Another, more serious purpose is to determine whether you are the sort of person with whom they want to do business. An easy way to create a bad impression is to discuss business at the wrong time. That is, the social process can be as important as the negotiations process. Good manners are very important to the Japanese, and they are so subtle that they have a novel way of punishing boors.

The Russians tend to regard negotiations as debates. They are so ideologically oriented that giving and taking are seen as immoral, a compromise of their principles. Instead of trading concessions, they restate their original position, with all of the arguments supporting it. This process can continue indefinitely; they keep repeating themselves until the other side sees the errors of its position and accepts the Russian position (or, more likely, just tires out).

Table 1.1 provides a set of intercultural implications of negotiations.

Table 1.1
Intercultural Implications of Negotiations

Negotiation is...	Intercultural Implications
• a situation.	• The appreciation of cultural differences is essential in cross-cultural situations.
• mutual understanding.	• A conscious endeavor to manage cultural differences is required.
• communication.	• Both parties must be in a position to communicate clearly and overcome cultural barriers to effective communication.
• need satisfaction.	• One must ascertain expectations and then work for their achievements.
• compromise or settlement.	• One must narrow down differences and emphasize commonalities of interest.
• a deal.	• Both written and unwritten aspects of negotiation are important
• a bargaining process	• One must be prepared to give and take.
• anticipation.	• You must familiarize yourself with management styles and assumptions of others to anticipate their moves.
• persuasion.	• You must establish your credibility and be soft while not losing your grip on the problem.
• achieving consensus.	• You must reduce differences to reach an agreement.
• practicing empathy	• You must appreciate problems and limitations of your "opponents."
• searching for alternatives.	• You should be systematic and simple (don't try to impress others with complex models).
• conflict management	• It is possible to manage conflicting interests.
• winning.	• It can create problems and generate bad feelings.
• a means of getting what you want from others.	• It also means giving what others expect of you.
• gaining the favor of people from whom you want nothing.	• It is easier to gain favors while acting in a genuine and rational manner.
• managing power and information.	• You should know in advance the limitations of your power; gain information while managing the process of negotiation.
• time and opportunity management.	• Timely actions based on opportunity analysis provide the needed edge in highly competitive situations.
• selling.	• You should create the need first.
• the least troublesome method of settling disputes.	• The use of intercultural negotiating styles, modes, and skills is important.

2

Why 1 : International Negotiations

The impact of international business on American companies has been considerably understated. With two-way trade in goods and services amounting to well over $1 trillion (nearly $1.5 trillion) and over twenty percent of the U.S. GDP in 1995, no part of the economy is sacrosanct and can avoid the international dimension. Over seventy percent of American firms are actively competing against foreign-based firms. If an American firm is not competing against a foreign firm, chances are it is either being supplied by or selling to foreign-based firms. Foreign direct investment in the United States has reached over $400 billion and continues to increase year by year. Foreign direct investment (FDI) by U.S. multinationals exceeds even that tremendous amount, and continues to increase. In the 1990s, the only firms that will be exempt from dealing with foreign entities, either U.S.-based affiliates or foreign customers, suppliers, or competitors will be those firms that are out of business or are going out of business. The playing field for business is now the globe. Businesses of all sizes must search the world for customers and suppliers.

As the proportion of foreign to domestic trade increases, so does the frequency of business negotiations among people from different countries and cultures. International trade has multiplied twenty fold over the last twenty years; similar increases in the future are not unexpected. The world is definitely shrinking and trade is helping to shrink it. Experts estimate that over fifty percent of an international manager's time is spent negotiating. At the forefront of international business opportunities are the agreements between firms. Agreements are the most important international documents that must be negotiated between all firms of different nationalities. Since implementation has become increasingly time-consuming, difficult and complex, cross-cultural negotiations have begun to take on increasing importance to the globalizing firm. Every sale or purchase has its negotiation aspect and every negotiation presents opportunities and dangers for both parties. International negotiations are fast becoming a fact of life for a growing number of U.S.-based firms. Failure to negotiate effectively can undo careful planning; operating across national cultures often magnifies negotiation problems.

Points important in international (cross-cultural) negotiations that are normally unimportant in domestic negotiations and could become barriers to global deal include (Salacuse, 1991): (1) negotiating environment, (2) cultural and subcultural differences (It is important to know whether you are negotiating with a Hindu or a Moslem in India, with an Moslem or Copy in Egypt, or with a Kongo or Muluba in Zaire.), (3) ideological differences, (4) foreign bureaucracy, (5) foreign laws and governments, (6) financial insecurity due to international monetary factors, and (7) political instability and sudden political and economic changes. Barriers increase the risk of failure and lengthen the time it takes to arrive at a deal. Many foreign governments must be convinced that a deal is consistent with their country's overall economic priorities before they will enter into discussions.

An important dimension to cross-cultural negotiations is culture shock. Culture shock occurs when a person finds himself in a place where all his norms are challenged and are no longer correct; entire sets of values, rules, and attitudes are different. Culture shock can incapacitate a visitor, make him or her withdraw from contact with other persons, feel confused, become excessively concerned about his health, and refuse to eat any local food. If seriously disoriented, visitors can actually fall physically ill. Depression is a common result of culture shock; alcoholism is the condition must likely to occur as a result of a bout of culture shock.

Familiar psychological clues that normally help an individual to function in society (as provided by his or her host culture) are suddenly withdrawn and replaced by new ones that are strange or incomprehensible. The effects of culture shock vary from individual to individual. It is common for people to suffer from anxiety, confusion, and apathy when they are first immersed in an unfamiliar environment. The emotional stress of the situation can easily lead to emotional and intellectual withdrawal. Culture shock has been known to cause violent aggressive behavior in previously docile personalities. One of the most effective means to resolving culture shock is to recognize its occurrence, understand why it is occurring and that it is a natural reaction to unusual phenomena. By one's doing so, one can be aware of its existence and able to counter it if and when it does occur.

CULTURAL INFLUENCES IN NEGOTIATIONS

All human interactions are, by definition, intercultural. When two individuals meet, it is an intercultural encounter since they both have different (sometimes drastically different, if not opposite) ways to perceive, discover, and create reality. All negotiations are therefore intercultural. Negotiations with a boss, spouse, child, friend, fellow employee, union representative, official from a foreign country, and so on are all interculturally loaded. In some countries, negotiating is present in practically every transaction, from settling a taxi fare to buying bread. Intercultural negotiations do not only exist because people who think, feel, and behave differently have to reach agreements on practical matters such as how to produce, consume, organize, and distribute power, and grant rewards, but because of the very nature of the challenging, unpredictable, and contradictory world we live in. We are forced to negotiate. In every negotiation (domestic or international), the participants have different points of view and different objectives.

When you are negotiating with someone from your own country, it is often truly possible to expedite communications by making reasonable cultural assumptions. The situation reverses itself when two cultures are involved. Making assumptions about another culture is often counterproductive since it can too often lead to misunderstandings and miscommunications. The international negotiator must be careful not to allow cultural stereotypes to determine his or her relations with local businesspersons. Needs, values, interests, and expectations may differ dramatically. It is like the proverbial fish out of water: When in water, a fish is unaware of any possible alternate environments; the water surrounding the fish is all it knows of the universe; hence, the whole universe must be made of water. Only when the fish is removed from the water does it perceive a different environment.

What gives a person his or her identity no matter where he or she was born is his or her culture—the total communication framework. Culture is a set of shared and enduring meanings, values, and beliefs that characterize national, ethnic, or other groups and orient their behavior. Culture directs judgment and opinion, describes the criteria for what is good or bad. Language structures reality and orders experience. Culture is the property of a society, it is acquired through acculturation or socialization by the individual from the society, and it subsumes every area of social life. The language of an individual significantly influences his or her perceptions and thoughts. Culture may be an obstacle to the extent that cultural stereotypes and differences distort signals and cause misunderstandings.

National negotiating styles combine culture, history, political system, and economic status. Some cultures are likely to search for compromise, while others will strive for consensus, and still others will fight until surrender is achieved. Some cultures prefer a deductive approach: first agree on principles and later these principles can be applied to particular issues. Other cultures think inductively: deal with problems at hand and principles will develop.

Culture impacts negotiation in four ways: by conditioning one's perception of reality; by blocking out information inconsistent or unfamiliar with culturally grounded assumptions; by projecting meaning onto the other party's words and actions; and by impelling the ethnocentric observer to an incorrect attribution of motive. Culture affects the range of strategies that negotiators develop as well as the many ways they are tactically implemented. The Israeli preference for direct forms of communication and the Egyptian preference for indirect forms exacerbate relations between the two countries. The Egyptians interpreted Israeli directness as aggression and were insulted; the Israelis viewed Egyptian indirectness with impatience and viewed it as insincere. Negotiators are likely to assess foreign cultures through their own cultural lenses, to interpret and judge other cultures by their own standards.

Nations tend to have a national character that influences the types of goals and processes the society pursues in negotiations. This character is called culture. A cultural dimension exists in the way negotiators view the negotiation process. In international negotiations, you bring to the negotiating table the values, beliefs, and background interference of your culture and normally will unconsciously use those elements in both the presentation and interpretation of the data. Culture naturally influences members' negotiations—through their conceptualizations of the process, the ends they target, the means they use, and the expectations they hold of counterparts' behavior. Ample evidence exists that such negotiation rules and practices vary across cultures. Thus cross-cultural negotiators bring into contact unfamiliar and potentially conflicting sets of categories, rules, plans, and behaviors. The cross-cultural negotiator cannot take common knowledge and practices for granted. Difficulties sometimes arise from the different expectations negotiators have regarding the social setting of the negotiation. These patterns can extend to styles of decision making (the way officials and executives structure their negotiation communication systems and reach institutional decisions) and logical reasoning (the way issues are conceptualized, the way evidence and new information are used or the way one point seems to lead to the next, paying more attention to some arguments than others, giving different weight to legal, technical, or personal relations). Culture influences negotiation through its effects on communications. Intercultural differences may cause misperceptions and misunderstandings.

DIMENSIONS OF CULTURE

Beliefs and behaviors differ between cultures because each develops its own means for coping with life. Culture has been defined as "the collective programming of the mind which distinguishes members of one human group from another" (Hofstede, 1984: 21). Hofstede devised four cultural dimensions that explained much of the differences between cultures. These four dimensions are masculinity/femininity, uncertainty avoidance, power distance and individualism.

Masculine cultures typically value assertiveness, independence, task orientation and self-achievement (traditional "masculine" characteristics) while feminine cultures value cooperation, nurturing, relationships solidarity with the less fortunate, modesty and quality of life (traditional "feminine" characteristics). Masculine societies tend to have a more rigid division of sex roles. Masculine cultures subscribe to "live-to-work" while feminine societies subscribe to "work-to-live." The competitiveness and assertiveness embedded in masculinity may result in individuals perceiving the negotiation situation in win-lose terms. Masculinity is related to assertiveness and competitiveness while femininity is related to empathy and social relations. A more distributive process is expected in masculine societies, where the party with the most competitive behavior is likely to gain more. The most masculine country is Japan, followed by Latin American countries. The most feminine societies are Scandinavian countries.

Uncertainty avoidance refers to the degree to which one feels uncomfortable in risky and ambiguous (uncertain, unpredictable) situations. It favors conformity and safe behavior, and tolerates deviant ideas. In high uncertainty-avoidance cultures, people tend to avoid uncertain situations while in low uncertainty-avoidance cultures, people are generally more comfortable with ambiguous uncertain situations and are more accepting of risk. Low risk-avoiders require much less information, have fewer people involved in the decision making, and can act quickly. High risk-avoidance cultures tend to have many formal bureaucratic rules, rely on rituals, standards, and formulas, and trust only family and friends. People in low uncertainty-avoidance societies dislike hierarchy and typically find it inefficient and destructive. In weak uncertainty-avoidance cultures, deviance and new ideas are more highly tolerated. Uncertainty avoidance may lead to focus on the obvious competitive and positional aspects of negotiation and may hinder the exchange of information on interests and the development of creative proposals. A problem solving orientation is likely to be found in cultures characterized by low uncertainty avoidance and low power distance. The United States, the Scandinavian nations, Hong Kong, and Singapore all have low uncertainty avoidance.

Power distance refers to the acceptance of authority differences between people; the difference between those who hold power and those affected by power. In low power distance, one strives for power equalization and justice while high power-distance cultures are status conscious and respectful of age and seniority. In high power-distance cultures, outward forms of status such as protocol, formality, and hierarchy are considered important. Decisions regarding reward and redress of grievances are usually based on personal judgments made by power holders. Power distance implies a willingness to accept that the party that comes out most forcefully gets a larger share of the benefit than the other party. A low power-distance culture values competence over seniority with resulting consultative management style. Low power-distance cultures include the Anglo-American, Scandinavian, and Germanic cultures. High power-distance cultures are Latin American, South Asian, and Arab cultures. Low masculinity and low power distance may be related to the sharing of information and the offering of multiple proposals as well as more cooperative and creative behavior. High masculinity and high power distance may result in competitive behavior, threats, and negative reactions.

In individualistic cultures, a tendency exists to put task before relationship and to value independence highly. Individuals in individualistic cultures are expected to take care of themselves, to value the needs of the individual over that of the collective—the group, community, or society. These individuals are self-actualized, self-motivated and any relationships are defined by self-interest. Collectivism implies in-group solidarity, loyalty, and strong perceived interdependence among individuals. Relationships are based on mutual self-interest and dependent on the success of the group. Collectivist cultures emphasize face, protecting others' self-image while individualistic cultures emphasize protecting one's own self-image and freedom from imposition. Collectivist cultures define themselves in terms of their membership within groups, sharply distinguishing ingroups from outgroups.

Maintaining the integrity of ingroups is stressed so that cooperation, conflict avoidance, solidarity, and conformity dominate the culture. Individualistic cultures tend to value open conflict while collectivist societies tend to minimize conflict. Individualistic cultures tend to have linear logic while collectivist societies tend to stress abstract, general agreements over concrete, specific issues. Collectivist arguments tend to contain appeals to the emotion and imagery.

Collectivist negotiators tend to assume that details can be worked out in the future if the negotiators can agree on generalities. Collectivist societies tend to use more solution-oriented strategies than do individualist societies, who are prone to use more controlling strategies. Collectivist societies show more concern for the needs of the other party and focus more on group goals than do individualist societies. Members from individualist societies expect the other side's negotiators to have the ability to make decisions unilaterally, a trait difficult, if not impossible, to find in collectivist societies. Members from collectivist societies are annoyed to find individualist culture negotiating members promoting their own positions, decisions, and ideas, sometimes evenly openly contradicting one another. The United States, United Kingdom, Netherlands, France, and the Scandinavian countries are highly individualistic. Latin American and Asian countries tend to be highly collectivist.

CROSS-CULTURAL NEGOTIATION VARIABLES

A knowledge of the other side's culture allows a negotiator to communicate, to understand, to plan, and to anticipate more effectively. In addition to the conventional preparation for any negotiation, the need for extensive study of the culture(s) can not be overstressed. This should include reading about the history and customs of the country in question and discussion with others who have had experience dealing with citizens of the foreign country. The focus of these preparations should be on the culture, not the language. However, cultural stereotypes should be avoided. Although a particular approach to negotiations with a culture should be followed, sufficient flexibility should be available. Planning is crucial. Implementation is even more important; the best laid plans often go wrong. We should know sufficiently, if not intimately, about the cultures of the people with whom we are going to negotiate. Some things that are going to be irritants should be avoided. Other items that are likely to facilitate the process should be utilized effectively.

The process of international business negotiation is considered to be influenced by two groups of variables:

1. Background factors, which includes the parties objectives, often categorized as being common, conflicting, or complementary. Other aspects include third parties involved, such as consultants, agents, and the respective government. The position of the market (seller's vs. buyer's) and finally, the skills and experience of the negotiators.

2. Atmosphere variables, which can often include those as perceived cooperation/conflict—that the parties have something to negotiate for and something to negotiate about; power and dependence—that one of the parties gains more power in the relationship; and perceived distance—that the parties are unable to understand each other. Finally, the expectations of both sides, long-term expectations of the true deals or benefits and short-term expectations concerning the prospects of the present deal.

Weiss (1993) identified twelve variables in the negotiations process which will lead to understand negotiating styles better. These include:

Basic Concept. Different groups view the purpose and process of negotiation differently. Negotiation may be seen as a conflict in which one side wins and another loses, as a competition to identify who is best or as a collaborative process to formulate some undertaking. The winner of a negotiation in some countries is the one who gains the most concessions, regardless of the value of the concessions. Americans tend to see negotiations as a competitive process; the Japanese see it as a collaborative endeavor.

Criteria for Selecting Negotiators. Different groups choose negotiators on the basis of a variety of factors. Negotiators may be selected on the basis of their previous experience, their status (or relationship with the powers that are), knowledge of a particular subject, or personal attributes, such as trustworthiness. Americans tend to select negotiators on the basis of ability and experience; the Japanese look for high-status negotiators.

Issues Stressed. Different groups stress different aspects of the negotiations. Some groups stress substantive issues directly related to the agreement while others stress relationships. Americans tend to stress substantive issues (price, delivery, quality), while the Japanese are more concerned with building relationships.

Protocol. Different groups have their own particular etiquette associated with the negotiation process and their adherence to protocol varies according to its perceived importance. Protocol factors that should be considered are gift giving, entertainment, dress codes, seating arrangements, numbers of negotiators, timing of breaks, and planned duration of the process of negotiations. Degree of formality or informality is an important component of protocol that should be assessed. Americans tend to be informal; the Japanese are conservative and formal.

Communications. Different groups communicate in different ways and are more comfortable with one or another form of communications. Some groups rely on verbal communications, others on nonverbal such as gestures, space, and silence. Some groups rely on one method, others mixed. The more varied the methods of communications, the more complex is the communications context and the more care must be given to understanding this context. Americans tend to be verbal; Japanese often use periods of silence and use extensive non-verbal means in their communications.

Nature of Persuasive Arguments. Different groups attempt to persuade others and are persuaded by the use of a variety of different types of arguments. Some rely on facts and logical arguments, others on tradition and the way things were done in the past, still others on intuition or emotion and others on the beliefs associated with a particular religion or philosophy. Americans emphasize empirical information and rational arguments; the Japanese rely more on sensitivity and intuition.

Role of the Individual. Individuals play different roles in different societies. In some groups, the individual is seen as very important and a particular individual's success or failure can depend on the outcome of the negotiation process. In other groups, individuals are subordinate to the home negotiating party and personal ambitions are contained. Still others may view the entire group as consisting of all negotiation parties, both home and host and are most concerned with achieving overall success. Americans are individualistic; the Japanese are collectivist and rely on the group as a whole in the negotiations process.

Basis for Trust. Trust is a necessity if groups are going to work together to their mutual benefit and all groups seek to establish trust with the other parties in the negotiation process. Each group may, however, establish trust on a different basis. Some groups look to past experience and past records, others rely on intuition and emotion and still others are most comfortable when sanctions exist to guarantee performance. Americans look to the past record of those with whom they are negotiating and trust in sanctions; the Japanese are more concerned with the relationships that have been built with their counterparts.

Risk-taking Propensity. Negotiations involve a degree of risk because the final outcome is unknown when the negotiations begin. Different groups view uncertainty and risk as relatively desirable or undesirable. Some groups are therefore open to new ideas and unexpected suggestions whereas others prefer to remain within the expected boundaries and accustomed agreements. Americans tend to take risks and accept uncertainty; the Japanese are more risk averse.

View of Time. The value of time differs from one group to another. Some people view time as limited and something to be used wisely. Punctuality, agenda, and specified timeframes are important to them. Others view time as plentiful and always available; therefore they are more likely to expect negotiations to progress slowly and to be flexible about schedules. Americans view time as a scarce commodity that must be maximized so as not to be wasted; the Japanese view time in the long term.

Decision-making Systems. Decisions are made differently in different groups. They may be made by individuals or by the group as a whole. Within a group, participants may defer to the person of highest status or to the most senior group member. Alternatively, some groups accept the decision of the majority of the group members. Other groups seek consensus among group members and will not make a decision until all members have agreed.

Form of Agreement. In some cultures, written agreements are expected; in others verbal agreements or a handshake is accepted. In some cultures, agreements are detailed and set out as many points as possible, discussing contingencies and potential events; in others, broad general agreements are preferred with details to be worked out as they arise. In some cultures, agreements are expected to be legally binding; in others, there is little faith in legal contracts and much more emphasis is placed on a person's obligation to keep his or her word.

To augment his or her own capabilities, a business negotiator can employ cultural experts, translators, outside attorneys, financial advisors, or technical experts who have at least moderate and preferably high familiarity with both the counterpart's and the negotiator's cultures. These experts serve two distinguishable roles, as "agents" who replace the negotiator at the negotiating table or as "advisers" who provide information and recommend sources of action to the negotiator. The use of go-betweens, middlemen, brokers, and other intermediaries is a common practice within many cultures one should consider since it represents a potentially effective approach to cross-cultural negotiation as well. Use of such bicultural brokers increases significantly one's chances for success.

Fisher (1980) identified five major considerations that should be addressed before negotiating with persons from another culture: the players and the situation (find out how negotiators and negotiating teams are selected and the background of the players), decision-making styles (the way members of the other negotiating team reach a decision), national character (differences in culture), cultural noise (anything that would distract or interfere with the message being communicated), and the use of interpreters and translators (gives one more time to think about statements but it may not convey full intended message). Moran and Stripp (1991:92) indicate four components that affect the outcome of intercultural negotiations: Policy (basic concept of negotiation, selection of negotiators, role of individuals, concern with protocol), interaction (complexity of language, nature of persuasion), deliberation (bases of trust, risk-taking propensity, internal decision-making function), and outcome (form of satisfactory agreement).

Casse and Deol (1985) provide the list of factors that must be considered when negotiating internationally: appreciation of cultural differences, conscious endeavor to manage cultural differences, communicate clearly and effectively, narrow down difference and emphasize commonalities, both written and unwritten aspects of negotiations are important, familiarize yourself with management styles and assumptions of other side, establish your credibility, reduce differences to reach an agreement, appreciate the problems and limitations of the other side, be systematic and simple, manage conflicting interests, and create the need first.

Moran and Harris (1991) propose four communicative negotiating styles. They argue that negotiators around the globe differ in terms of cultural conditioning regarding the nature of negotiation, trust, problem solving, importance of protocol, selection of negotiation team, and view of the decision-making process.

Normative. Concentrates on creating a harmonious relationship between bargainers.This style requires attention to self and other emotions and values. Appeals to emotions to reach a fair deal.

Intuitive. Imagination solves problems. Intuitive negotiators look to the future, offer creative solutions, draw attention to prospective opportunities being created in present agreements, and follow their inspirations of the moment.

Analytic. Logical analysis leads to universally true conclusions. This involves forming reasons, drawing conclusions, identifying cause and effect, and weighing the pros and cons.

Factual. Points out facts and details in a neutral way, keeps track of what has been said, and clarifies the issues.

THE CROSS-CULTURAL NEGOTIATION PROCESS

According to Graham, Intercultural negotiations consists of four major processes (Graham, 1984, 1986; Graham and Andrews, 1987; Graham and Gronhaugr, 1989):

- Non-task sounding (rapport)
- Task-related exchange of information
- Persuasion, compromise,
- Concessions and agreement

Although all negotiations include these four aspects, strategies, tactics, content, duration, and sequence spent in each phase, emphasis and importance of phase differ between cultures. Non-task sounding focuses on establishing a relationship among the negotiating parties. During this stage, information specific to the issue under negotiation is not considered; rather, the parties seek to get to know each other. Task-related exchange of information focuses on providing information directly connected to the issue under negotiation. During this stage, each party explains its needs and preferences. Persuasion focuses on efforts to modify the views of the other parties and sway them to "our" way of thinking. This stage of negotiations is often intertwined with other stages (i.e., persuasion goes on while exchanging information and making concessions). Concessions and agreement is the culmination of the negotiation process at which an agreement is reached. To reach an agreement that is mutually acceptable, each side frequently must give up some things; concessions by both sides are usually necessary.

Negotiations can easily break down because of a lack of understanding of the cultural component of the negotiations process. Negotiators who take the time to understand the approach that the other parties are likely to use and to adapt their own styles to that one are likely to be more effective negotiators. It is worth the time to investigate those differences prior to entering into a negotiation situation.

CROSS-CULTURAL NEGOTIATIONS: SUCCESS AND FAILURE

Bargaining means many different things to different people from different cultures. If one does not bargain aggressively with Arabs, one is considered naive. In traditional Arab culture, the bargaining, the haggling, the give-and-take, serves many functions, not the least being the opportunity for both sides to get to know each others as individuals. The process of bargaining is meant to establish personal relationships built on a mutual perception of virtue, honesty, and personal merit. The process of extended bargaining is a vehicle for developing the critical personal relationship. For the Japanese, bargaining too soon can be a sign of untrustworthiness. Yet the Scandinavians are uncomfortable with much bargaining at all. Basic differences in the expectations of the negotiations process must be understood and accepted prior to entering into serious negotiations with others from a different cultural background.

The American business negotiator who arrives in China hoping to establish rapport by presenting his host with a gift of a fine clock creates a problem before negotiations begin. Clocks are inappropriate gifts in China because they are associated with death. An American businessman who once presented a clock to the daughter of his Chinese counterpart on the occasion of her marriage not only failed to establish a rapport, his insult led to the termination of the business relationship. The Arab businessman who insists on giving his Japanese counterpart gifts of greater value than those he receives harms the alliance before it even begins to form.

A ten-year license agreement was signed between North American-based Cummins Engine Company Ltd. and China National Technical Import Corporation. Much of the success of the early negotiations was attributed to the careful selection of the negotiation team. Cummins insisted that its people have the ability to reach across cultural lines and close intercultural gaps. It also had at least one member who could understand the language and thinking of his Chinese counterparts. This expertise, along with his ability to listen carefully, saved the negotiations. When misunderstandings occurred because of poor translation, this team member assisted in resolving conflicts. For example, when one Chinese negotiator used the word "strategy," the Cummins side assumed that far-reaching strategic decisions had been made by the Chinese, when in fact the term was being used more loosely than interpreted. Throughout the negotiations, misunderstandings of mannerisms, habits, and word choice were resolved by attending to cultural differences.

Effective international negotiators understand that negotiation, first and foremost, is not about numbers or terms or dates but personal relationships. It is about developing relationships of trust and mutual respect. The negotiator must become relationship oriented rather than deal oriented. The problem with deal orientation is that the difficulty of creating and enforcing any legal agreement across multiple legal and government jurisdictions can be insurmountable. A deal orientation is essentially static in nature while the world is dynamic. Negotiators who have an effective ongoing relationship will be able to agree to disagree and not have the disagreement negatively affect their relationship. Therefore, working on developing solid mutually beneficial relationships is the first step to traveling the road to success.

The effective international negotiator knows how to probe, how to ask questions, and how to listen. He or she seeks areas where needs are mutual and hence, easiest to satisfy, as well as being the first step toward establishing trust and relationships. Once mutual needs are established, meeting individual needs can be begin to be accomplished. Sharing of information is crucial toward success. Effective international negotiators have staying power. They recognize things take longer to communicate across cultures, that relationship building can be a time-consuming process, that the long-term perspective must be pursued. They must remain calm, not lose sight of the ultimate objectives of the negotiation, be flexible and willing to accept new conditions, remain on the creative lookout for needs, and communicate a commitment to the negotiation and the satisfaction of mutual needs. Experienced international negotiators create agendas in advance and try to get buy-in from the other side on the agenda before the actual start of the negotiation.

3

Why 2: Cross-Cultural Negotiating Behavior

WESTERN CULTURE

English negotiators reflect their cultural characteristics; they are very formal and polite and place great importance on proper protocol. They are also concerned with proper etiquette. British negotiation behavior is characterized by the soft sell. British negotiators are reserved and mannered. The status and the role of the negotiators are extremely important. The British culture is relatively high context compared to the American culture: that is, nuances of communication are important. In general, most Westerners expect a prompt answer when they make a statement or ask a question.

The French expect everyone to behave as they do when doing business. This includes speaking their language. Negotiations are likely to be in French unless they occur outside France. The French enjoy conversation for the sake of conversation, but they are also very pragmatic about details of the proposed agreement during negotiations. They are very much individualists and have a sense of pride that is sometimes interpreted as supremacy. The French follow their own logic, referred to as "Cartesian" logic, when negotiating. Their logic is based on principles previously established; it proceeds from what is known, in point-by-point fashion, until agreement is reached. Protocol, manners, status, education, family, and individual accomplishments are keys to success when dealing with the French (Moran and Stripp, 1991). The French prefer detailed, firm contracts. They enjoy conflict and debate and will interrupt even the opening presentations with arguments of little or no relevance.

The French are philosophically analytical, believing that cold logic leads to the right conclusions. In negotiation behavior, the French favor the formal, confrontational approach. The negotiation is considered a debate between the buyer and the seller. The similarity of characteristics of the negotiator to the buyer is also important. The French pride themselves on reasoned discussion. They dislike being rushed into decisions, preferring instead to examine various options in decisions. Punctuality is expected. They tend to be formal in their negotiations and do not move quickly to expressions of goodwill until relationships have endurred. The French dislike formal face-to-face discussions, especially on national security matters.

This French tendency developed not because the French want to avoid social conflict, but because they want to avoid situations where concessions might have to be made to stronger states or coalitions of states and wish to preserve their independence in a situation of declining national power. Protecting their own status and prestige is sometimes best achieved, the French feel, by rejecting discussions or concessions, or taking a conflictual stand on grounds of principle.

Their style can change dramatically depending upon with whom they are negotiating. Traditionally, they rely on highly rational abstract logic and general principles, and their positions are often rigid and legalistic. Like the Japanese, they may not have fall-back positions. Like the Soviets of yesteryear (and the Russians of today), they can be abrupt and confrontational. The French are friendly, humorous, and sardonic; they are more likely to be interested in a person who disagrees with them than with one who agrees. The French are very hard to impress and are impatient with those who try too hard to do so. They are inner oriented and base their behavior on feelings, preferences, and expectations.

Decision making is more centralized in France than in the United States; it tends to take longer for decisions to be reached and applied. French expectations are similar to those found with Americans. To the French, negotiation is an established art with a long. long tradition in international diplomatic and business relations, with French negotiators and the French language at center stage. They do not see the negotiating table quite so much as a place for bargaining as one for searching out the reasoned solutions for which they have so carefully prepared. The negotiating setting becomes more of a debating forum with flexibility and accommodation simply for the sake of agreement less than expectation. Negotiation in France has careful preparation, research on possible precedents, and logically stated arguments leading to a solution.

They love discussion and will even negotiate minor details. They are concerned with a concise, rational presentation of ideas in verbal and written form. They appreciate a rational, factual, and logical presentation of issues in a direct and confrontational style. The French are extremely formal and attentive to manners; courtesy and respect is mandatory for success in France.

Protocol is important and formal in Germany. Dress is conservative; correct posture and manners are required. Seriousness of purpose goes hand in hand with serious dress. Germans tend to use a handshake at the beginning and end of meetings. One must remember to use titles when addressing members of the negotiating team and to use please and thank you freely. Since Germans believe friendships and personal relationships can complicate negotiations, they prefer to keep a distance between themselves and the other team of negotiators. Since Germans tend to be detail oriented, having technical people as part of the negotiation team is important. Being punctual is expected. German negotiations are planned and well organized, and direct in their approach. German protocol is formal. Germans tend to be very conservative. Correct posture is a sign of inner discipline. Manners are of utmost importance to Germans. The society is quite paternalistic. Corporate decisions are made at the top but with a great deal of detail from workers. Quality is important, and decisions are pondered and carefully scrutinized to be sure that such quality exists in any projects they should undertake.

To an American, Germans may seem pessimistic due to their ability to entertain every perceivable negative point possible. Once they accept a project, however, they give 100 percent to its successful implementation. Negotiators are distant and impersonal. German culture is low context, therefore specific terms and concepts are very important. They balance between their own profit and the satisfaction of their client. The Germans are men of their word; a handshake is as good as a written contract. However, they are very concerned with the precision of the written word. Although the German negotiator always has a goal in mind, he may be obtuse in letting the American know what the goal is. But once the objective has been related, negotiations proceed quickly. The Germans do accommodate logic and thoroughness. They are very "face conscious." Care should be exercised in avoiding open disagreements when staff people are present. Germans are prompt, prepared, and have done their homework thoroughly. Germans view potential partners on German values of qualifications, power, and authority. German is the official language of Germany; most Germans, however, speak several languages.

The Swedes tend to be formal in their relationships, dislike haggling over price, expect thorough, professional proposals without flaws, and are attracted to quality. Italians tend to be extremely hospitable but are often volatile in temperament. When they make a point, they do so with considerable gesticulation and emotional expression. Impressed by style, they tend to dress well themselves. Italians often exhibit a calculated nonchalance. A common tactic is to close a negotiating session unexpectedly, pretending the whole thing is of minor importance. Urgency on your part might send a signal that you are desperate to do the deal.

The objective of American negotiators is usually to arrive at legalistic contracts. Therefore, the dominant concern is with getting the details right and using all relationships to facilitate the achievement of unambiguous understandings. American negotiations focus on a short term, results-oriented relationship with the potential for a variety of partners. In other words, American negotiators prefer a competitive environment. Americans concentrate on a mutual problem solving approach with an expected reciprocity. They expect results decided by events at the negotiation table. Americans tend to be bound by law, not by relationships, tradition, religion, or culture. Americans will honor a contract to the letter, whatever circumstances later arise. In the United States, negotiators approach the negotiation session and the decisions that result from it by essentially saying, "anything is OK unless it has been restricted." Conversely, Russian (formerly Soviet) counterparts approach the same situation with, "nothing is permitted unless it is initiated by the state." American negotiators usually operate as if today is the last day of their lives: negotiating with conviction and interpreting delays and hesitation as signs of stalling or ineptitude. They often exhibit words and behaviors perceived as tough or insensitive. This tendency to get to the point is responsible for many negotiation failures: in most places in the world, the one who asks questions controls the process of negotiation and thereby accomplishes more in bargaining situations.

ASIAN

In certain Asian countries such as India, Nepal or Sri Lanka or in the Middle Eastern countries such as Egypt or Saudi Arabia, the social relationship developed between the parties is more significant than the technical specifications and price. In cultures like China and Japan, pride and honor are of great importance. Because of the influence of

Confucianism, honesty, integrity, and sincerity in dealmaking are greatly appreciated in these countries. Many cultures are holistic, especially in the Far East, where all issues are to be discussed at once and no decisions made until the end. Especially in the Far East, the negotiating session is less a forum for working out issues than it is a formal and public expression of what has already been worked out beforehand. Asians may use cooperative styles when negotiating among themselves but can be ruthless with outsiders.

The Asian negotiation process is as much a ceremony and courtship as it is a form of business communication. The negotiation style in the Asian context is often described as relationship-oriented, and concentrates on a long-term, single-source arrangement. The implication of this style is that it is collaborative and will lead to some mutual satisfaction. The form is often more important than the functional. In contrast the American style of negotiation is to concentrate on the results (the ends) as an outcome. This focus on results is very characteristic of Western cultures.

Throughout Asia, war strategy has became commercial strategy. Asians may open a negotiation by dwelling on their company's vulnerabilities, such as small size and other feigned weaknesses, to swell Westerners' confidence and induce them to ask for fewer concessions than the Westerners are prepared to request. Some Westerners might think the orphan strategy is an expression of Asian humility. Instead, it often conceals a hidden agenda. For example, a claim of weakness is soon followed by a request that the foreign side ease its credit terms to lighten the financial burden on the Asian side. Or the Asians demand conciliatory "favors" outside the contract. The Koreans tend to believe their initial position is always right and will do everything possible to avoid yielding that position.

Asians valud details in formulating their business decisions; they consider information gathering to be the heart of a negotiation. However, what they call a "know-how exchange" often becomes "information rape," with the Asian side planning to reverse-engineer a Western product from the outset of collaboration with the firm. The Asians' objective of sharing in a company's know-how without paying for it may be partially cultural in origin. In Asia, no notion of proprietary know-how took root; new technology was shared by all. Knowledge was kept public, and to imitate or adopt someone else's methodology was considered virtuous, and a great compliment to the person who created it. Borrowing another person's know-how was considered to be neither thievery nor unethical. Knowledge is to be transmitted to the country as a whole, not hidden away.

As the Chinese saying goes, negotiations can be like "grinding a rod down to a needle," when the Taoist concept of *wu wei* (nonassertion) is applied to business negotiation and the strategy is to seek long-term success through minimal short-term effort: state a position and wait, hoping that opponents will yield on concessions in order to close, the deal. Time is not money for Asian negotiators; it's a weapon. Asian negotiators often open a negotiation, extend an invitation to visit their country, supply some technical information, and dedicate time and resources to forging an agreement. Unfortunately, the final contract often remains elusive.

When negotiating with the Japanese, you need a completely different beginning game. They often want to spend days or even weeks creating a friendly, trusting atmosphere before discussing business. Positions are expressed indirectly to obscure conflicts, even though you are negotiating to resolve these conflicts. Direct questions are regarded as rude, and the meaning of answers may depend upon extremely subtle signals. Certain ways of saying yes actually mean no. Japanese are data collectors and hypothetical reasoning does not convince them. For the Japanese, the role of seller is more important than for other cultures. They give greater deference to the needs of their buyers. Viewing negotiation as a process of exchange involving several proposal-counterproposal iterations, Americans inflate their demands in initial proposals and expect later to give and receive concessions. Their Japanese counterparts often do not promptly reciprocate with a counterproposal. Thus the Americans offer concessions, hoping that they will kick the exchange model—the negotiations—into gear. The Japanese, however, ask many questions. By the end of the talks, the Americans feel frustrated with the extent of their concessions and conclude that the Japanese do not negotiate. Although the Americans may believe that the Japanese are shrewdly trying to determine how much their American counterparts will concede, it is quite likely that these Japanese are operating from a different model of negotiation: negotiation as a process of fathering information, which when consistent and complete, will reveal a "correct, proper, and reasonable" solution. In Japan business often goes to the party respected the most. Recognizing who is deserving of such respect takes more time than most Westerners are inclined to give. Moreover, the Japanese consult with all parties involved before they make decisions. If a delivery date is specified, they are likely to check with the managers responsible for ensuring that it can be met before they will agree to it. The entire organization is involved and a consensus of that organization is necessary before they can continue.

They spend considerable amounts of time asking detailed questions about financial, market, manufacturing, and structural issues relevant to the negotiation, as well as questions that some outsiders would perceive as irrelevant. The Japanese also tend to spend time becoming acquainted with the potential partner before developing the framework for a partnership. The Japanese prefer to avoid formal negotiations because negotiations are a form of social conflict, and "every Japanese has been taught at his mother's knee to avoid social conflict." For the Japanese negotiator, the development of personal relations with his counterpart is critical, but the relationship is not established primarily for the purpose of manipulation. Rather, personal relationships are of value to the Japanese negotiator for informal, frank discussions, where social conflict is minimal and progress can be made on a pragmatic basis. The Japanese negotiator has neither the aggressively blunt style of the Russians nor the subtle manipulative style of the Chinese, but he can be extremely rigid because the complex Japanese consensus-building, decision-making process that sets the limits for the negotiation is itself rigid and inflexible. Japanese positions are offered as final solutions, fair to all, which cannot be bargained away. The Japanese should never be placed in a position in which they must admit failure or impotency. They resist pressure for deadlines and delivery dates. They go to considerable length to conceal their emotions; they are uncomfortable when others lose control and show anger or impatience.

For a Japanese, personal relations are established not for manipulative purposes but because through them social conflict can be minimized. Most Japanese negotiators are very careful not to offend or use strong words and expect their opponents to do likewise.The Japanese proclivity toward shunning confrontation and avoiding hurting other people's feelings has led them to the development of sixteen ways of how to politely avoid saying "no." A *Hai* from a Japanese means "I understand," not necessarily a "yes" commitment. Knowing when an answer is in fact a "yes" or a "no" is a case in expert judgment and gut feeling or intuition. (in this regard, the Japanese are not alone: Mexicans also usually avoid saying "no"; it is necessary to read gestures, not the words, to get an accurate response from them.) In order not to hurt the feelings of another person, many Asians are inclined to tell people what they want to hear, rather than the facts, so as not to lose face. They are not consciously lying or concealing, just attempting not to inflict hurt to the other party. Rather than verbally argue when challenged, a Japanese will remain quiet. This does not symbolize stubbornness but instead is a defensive technique to encourage harmony.

The Japanese are not very argumentative, extroverted, or persuasive in the American sense. They prefer to be quiet when right, respectful, and patient. Modesty and self-restraints are highly valued in their culture. They do not criticize in public but seek harmony among all. The Japanese prefer to avoid formal negotiations, since to them negotiations are a form of social conflict and avoiding social conflict is penultimate in that society. The Japanese, in their pursuit of harmony and avoidance of conflict, often do not seek eye contact; this is not a virtue to Americans. On the other side of the table, the Japanese view the American stare as rude, aggressive, and improper behavior. Americans, in foreign eyes, are seen as being extremely argumentative, whether right or wrong, impersonal when arguing, and accommodating when presenting arguments.

The Japanese see negotiation as a fluid irrational process calling for diligent preparation. Instead of addressing issues directly, and openly stating positions and counterproposals, they prefer to infer the other party's assessment of the situation. The Japanese often repeat previously stated positions, using ambiguous language, and appear to be inconsistent. The goal is a just, fair, and proper deal with a long-term harmonious relationship with the other side. The idea of persuasion is foreign to the Japanese culture; they avoid confrontation and debate that is the norm in American negotiations. They would prefer to work behind the scenes to eliminate the possibility of losing face. Emphasis is placed on exchanging extensive detailed information. Risk avoidance (*kiken kaihi*) is a key principle in Japanese negotiating.

Japanese value emotions but hide them. The Japanese are truly as emotional as the Italians, but their emotions are directed toward or against others. The Japanese also go out of their way to conceal their sentiments; showing emotion is considered in bad taste and poor conduct for any Japanese, let alone a businessman. Formal display of emotion means loss of respect/face. The American is therefore advised not to lose his temper when dealing with Japanese or others in Asia. Calm is respected by the Chinese and shows sincerity, seriousness, and competence. To them aggressive or assertive behavior is rude.

In China, protocol that should be followed during the negotiation process would include giving small, inexpensive presents. As the Chinese do not like to be touched, a short bow and brief handshake will be used during the introductions. Last names are used in conversation and printed first when written. Business cards may or may not be used by the Chinese. Alcoholic beverages are not consumed during meals until the host proposes a toast; the guest should toast the other people at the table throughout the meal.

In China, it is proper for the guest of honor to leave first; this should be shortly after the meal is finished. The Chinese consider mutual relationships and trust very important. Therefore, in the beginning time will be spent enjoying tea and social talk. However, the Chinese are some of the toughest negotiators in the world. Technical competence of the negotiators is necessary, and a noncondescending attitude is important because the Chinese research their opponents thoroughly to gain a competitive advantage during negotiation. Nothing is final until it is signed. The Chinese delegation will be large. They rarely use lawyers, and interpreters may have inadequate language skills and experience. The Chinese focus on practicality, they deal in the concrete and particular. The Chinese approach is to use the negotiating process to establish a human relationship, often one of an essentially dependent nature, and therefore, the bonding of "friendship." Consequently, they tend to seek out members of the other side who they feel would be more empathetic to their view and thus, more malleable. They attempt to identify foreign officials who are sympathetic to their cause, to cultivate a sense of friendship and obligation in their official counterparts.

The Chinese are quick to probe for and then exploit, in jujitsu fashion, any compelling interests of the other party. In particular they feel they have the advantage whenever the other party exudes enthusiasm and seems to be single-mindedly pursuing a particular objective. For the Chinese, working to a common goal is the most important feature of the negotiations. This means the development of a long-term relationship. The Chinese prefer an instrumental and competitive approach to bargaining. Chinese conduct negotiations in a linear manner of discrete stages and in a distinctive (but not unique) style. They pursue their objectives through a variety of stratagems designed to manipulate feelings of friendship, obligation, and guilt, the games of *guanxi*. The Chinese tend to stress at the outset their commitment to abstract principles and will make concessions only at the eleventh hour after they have fully assessed the limits of the other side's flexibility. After protracted exchanges, when a deadlock seems to have been reached, concessions may be made to consummate an agreement. And while the end-game phase may produce a signed agreement, the Chinese negotiator will continue to press for his objective in the post-agreement phase (implementation stage), giving negotiations with the Chinese the quality of continuous bargaining in which closure is never fully reached. To the Chinese (and most East Asian cultures), a contract is relative to the conditions, if the conditions change the contract should likewise be altered.

Business is conducted in a formal yet relaxed manner in India. Bribery is common and having connections is important. One must remember to avoid using the left hand in greetings and eating; one should request permission before smoking, entering, or sitting. Building relationships is important, and introduction is necessary. Use titles to convey respect. Intermediaries are commonly used. Since people of India place importance on building relationships, the negotiation process can be rather long by American standards. Indian management is paternalistic toward subordinates. Due to status differences, group orientations are generally not used by the Indians. Indians do not approve of displays of emotion, and negotiators must use patience and allow the Indians to take the lead in the negotiations. Indians view negotiations as a truthful way of solving problems mutually with a focus on finding a solution that will please everyone involved. It is not uncommon for an Indian negotiator to answer a question according to what he thinks the other party would like to hear as a means of accommodating the foreign team to maintain harmony and a good working atmosphere.

LATIN AMERICA

Latin Americans emphasize general principals more than problem solving. An American businessman was invited by a Guatemalan to supply equipment for a cereal factory that the Guatemalan was planning to open in his country. The American supplier focused on the financing of the purchases and the Guatemalan's credit rating. The contractor, who eventually got the production line order, concentrated on how the production line was going to operate and how it would meet the Guatemalan's needs. The winner even sent a representative of the company to live on site for the duration of the contract. Social competence is paramount in Latin business. Handshaking and asking about the health and well-being of business contacts and their families are expected. In business, people are addressed by their titles and maternal and paternal surnames. Business cards are exchanged and should include the negotiator's academic degrees.

Emotion and drama carry more weight than logic for Mexicans. Mexican negotiators are often selected for their skill at rhetoric and making distinguished performances. Negotiation is perceived from their perspective as a time to test Mexican honor and to determine the attitude of the other party toward Mexicans. Mexican culture is dominated by courtesy, dignity, tact, diplomacy, protocol, and social competence. In formal settings they often respond with the rhetoric and lofty principles befitting a country that many Mexican leaders consider to be a repository of moral values. They also respond frequently with manufactured delays. Latin Americans place a high value on verbal agility and have a tendency to respond quickly; they may even answer a point once they have understood it even though the other side has not finished. While North Americans find it perfectly appropriate to conduct business discussions at lunch, Mexicans and Brazilians may consider serious business negotiations out of place in such a setting.

In Latin America, a *macho* is confident, charismatic, eloquent, and witty. A *macho* shows his dislike for plans, schedules, and legal details and a preference for ad hoc and free-wheeling decisions. If one is important, one should expect to be interrupted frequently. This is not seen in Latin America as being impolite so much as a display of eagerness to share points of view. Personal relationships take priority over institutions, laws, and regulations in Latin America. This need for a personal relationship is critical and must be created before anything else can be accomplished. The only way to get anything done in Latin America is through a "friend"or a "friend of a friend." If a Latin American asks you for a favor, he is showing you that he feels a personal relationship has been started. At the very least one should indicate "I will see what I can do" to show you will try and that you care about his or her problem.

Many Latins tend to get passionate and emotional when arguing; they enjoy a warm interaction as well as a lively debate. In Latin America, sensitivity is valued. Interactions between Latins can be highly emotional and even passionate. In fact, many tasks in negotiating a business operation cannot be effectively communicated and accomplished unless the person displays his emotion and thereby demonstrates how close this issue is to his heart. Emotions shown by Latins may only reflect their feelings at that moment in time. Emotion, drama, and feeling play a much larger part in negotiations compared to the American considerations of efficiency.

For Brazilians, the negotiating process is often valued more than the end result. Discussions tend to be lively, heated, inviting, eloquent, and witty. Brazilians enjoy lavish hospitality to establish a comfortable social climate. They tend to spend much time ensuring that the proper tone is set for negotiating. Compatibility and mutual trust are primary concerns. What is beyond the present hardly exists. Brazilian motivators are power, prestige, and recognition; monetary gains are secondary. They would rather play safe and retain what they have rather than lose in an attempt to gain more.

ARAB CULTURE

The Arab will start with outlandish position, then retreat with generosity. In many Arab countries the opening bid is ritualistically extreme because the negotiator expects to back down. In the Arab world, a person's word may be more binding than many written agreements and insistence on a contract may be insulting. Arabs prefer more normative relationships and value systems are important. An Arab speaking English is often thought by Westerners to be shouting, as Arabs tend to speak more loudly than most Westerners. The tone of voice interpreted as sincere by Egyptians sounds belligerent to Americans; Americans, though, speak louder than Europeans and give impressions of assertiveness not necessarily intended.

The Egyptians are motivated by pride in their country's past, an acceptance of the need for a strong ruler in the pharaonic mold, and the traditions of a highly developed bureaucracy. The Egyptians are suspicious of negotiations. It is common for negotiations in business or government offices in Egypt or Saudi Arabia to be interrupted frequently by telephone calls, secretaries wanting signatures, and even visitors seeking an important word with the person. While Western executives would interpret these interruptions as a sign of discourtesy or lack of interest, the Arab feels that it would be extremely rude to refuse a telephone call or a visit from an associate.

RUSSIA (AND THE FORMER SOVIET UNION)

During the Cold War era, Soviet negotiators had certain advantages over their Western adversaries because they were backed by an authoritarian government. Western capitals, and Washington in particular, cannot develop a negotiating position on a major issue without letting the public in on some of the internal controversies. This gave Soviet delegates valuable intelligence about the strength with which Western positions were held. Soviet negotiators enjoyed a further advantage in that they could support their long-term strategy and day-to-day tactics with fully coordinated propaganda machinery, whereas Western countries spoke with many voices. In short, Soviet negotiators seemed to command all that was required for carrying out the most cunning strategies: complete secrecy in planning, freedom from domestic interference in execution, and the coordinated support of a powerful authoritarian regime. The Soviets appeared to have all the advantages with none of the disadvantages.

The Soviets saw negotiations as part of a larger struggle for increased power and influence that could have been won if the negotiators were tough enough. Rather than cultivating friendly relationships, the typical Soviet strategy then (and Russian strategy today) has been to put the Western counterparts on the immediate defensive with confrontational, blunt, and combative tactics. The Soviet negotiator traditionally took rigid and extreme positions at the outset; he made concessions "slice by slice" in Salami-slicing tactics. A quid pro quo was expected for each concession. He sought generally worded agreements that gave the Kremlin maximum flexibility in implementation. A widely applied tactic was to wear down the Western team with the help of long drawn-out sessions, all-night meetings, stern lectures at the conference table, and avoidance of the slightest compromise until the opponent was exhausted and gave in to the Soviet terms. As the Russian culture dominated the Soviet Union then, the negotiating tactics used by today's Russian negotiator are similar to those used by the Soviet Union during the Cold War.

The Russians think from the general idea to the particular; they deduce implications from axioms rather than the other way around. The traditional Russian negotiating style is less subtle and more aggressive than that of the Chinese. While Chinese hosts structure the negotiating environment to enhance a sense of obligation on the part of their guests, the Russians often try to wear down their counterparts with tactics such as all-night negotiating sessions. Status is paramount to Russians; every Russian upon meeting another for the first time must first establish an hierarchy and the superior/subordinate position of each party involved.

4

How 1:
Verbal

Language is highly important. When people from different cultures communicate, culture-specific factors affect how they encode and decode their messages. Negotiators should check understanding periodically, move slowly, use questions liberally, and avoid slang and idioms. Even the discussion of negotiation, compromise, and agreement has different meanings to different cultures. Both the American and Korean meanings for the word "corruption" are negative; however in the United States, the word connotes being morally wrong while for the Koreans it implies being socially unfortunate. The Mexican will not compromise as a matter of honor, dignity, and integrity. The Arab fears loss of manliness if he compromises. In Russia, compromise has a negative connotation; principles are supposed to be inviolable and compromise is a matter of integrity. For Russians, a negotiation is treated as a whole without concessions.

In the American culture, those who refuse to bargain are viewed as cold, secretive, and not really serious about conducting business. The Dutch are not hagglers; you should make your offer fairly close to your true asking price; if you start making large concessions you will lose their confidence. The Swedes are methodical, detailed individuals who are slow to change positions. Bargaining is not highly valued in Swedish culture; those who bargain, who attempt to negotiate by offering a higher price in order to concede to a lower price, can be viewed as untrustworthy, inefficient, or perhaps out for personal gain at the expense of others.

The English (and American) notion of "fair play" seems to have no exact equivalent in any other language. In French, word and concept were adopted together as *le fer pl'e*. In Spanish, *juego limpio* has been tried for application in sports, but it fails to transmit most of the basic thought. Generally, this is a culture-bound idea, as is often the case. The Chinese language does not have a word for "privacy." The closest word the Japanese have for "individualism" is one that denotes selfishness. So it is for practically every language and culture: words exist in one language that do not have meaning or existence in another language.

The linguistic framework can be based on three factors: topic allocation, verbal immediacy of speaker and listener references, and topic progression. Topic allocation refers to the individual's need for personal autonomy concerning such aspects as independence, self-determination, and privacy; speakers can refer explicitly to the speaker, the listener, to both, or to neither. Often, if the message is delivered explicitly (the first three situations), it will be interpreted as assertive and confrontational. If delivered implicitly (to neither party), it will tend to put the listener more at ease and is usually interpreted as less threatening. Choice of an implicit method may soften or minimize negative effects or avoid specification, thus allowing for the possibility of later modifications. Nonetheless, if delivered explicitly, this can lead to perceived immediacy and a sign of involvement. Some cultures tend to be more implicit while others tend to be more explicit. For example, Spanish negotiators are more person-oriented while Danish negotiators are more task-oriented. The Danish negotiators prefer to use strategies in which the topic of conversation does not explicitly concern persons, and in which topics and persons are separated from each other; when they want to address topics within the opposite party's domain, they proceed by asking implicit questions, seldom commenting on each other's behavior (Grindsted, 1994).

Verbal immediacy refers to how closely speakers associate themselves verbally with the interaction, with the topics they communicate about, and with their listener's or own utterances; this can range from remote to intimate. Spanish negotiators prefer to establish a high degree of immediacy to the here-and-now of conversation; they are not inclined to separate the task from the person but prefer to bring their persons into the center of the interaction and allow the other party to penetrate much further into their own personal territory. Danish negotiators prefer a low degree of immediacy, proceeding in a tentative, coordinated, linear, compromise-seeking fashion.

Topic progression refers to the sequencing and structure inherent in a dialogue. For example, in Grindsted's (1994) study, the Spanish negotiators explicitly made an opening move while implicitly making the closing move; the Danish negotiators took the opposite sequence. Their opening move was tentative and nonconfrontational while the closing move was expressed explicitly when an agreement was reached. As a result of differences between the two groups, the Spanish negotiators would interpret Danish negotiators as emotionally uninvolved and impersonal, afraid of intimacy, and too concerned with doing business. Danish negotiators would interpret Spanish negotiators as self-assertive, confrontational, and uncooperative, consuming more time and energy in the negotiations than necessary. Both view the events from their own perspective, which is entirely logical but entirely incorrect when viewed cross-culturally.

Argumentation in global negotiations involves a blend of logic, emotion, and dogma. Negotiators who use logic try to persuade their counterparts with substantive proof, that is, empirical (statistics, analyses, financial statements) or factual evidence. Negotiators who use emotional proof try to persuade their counterparts with motivational proofs by providing evidence from historical and cultural tradition. Negotiators who use dogma try to persuade the other side with authoritative proofs by providing a statement of opinion from an expert. Dogmatic bargainers make fewer concessions, achieve fewer agreements, take longer to reach an agreement, and are more prone to view compromise as a defeat. Emotion and drama carry more weight than logic for Mexicans. Latin Americans place a high value on verbal agility and have a tendency to respond quickly; they may even answer a point once they have understood it even though the other side has not finished. For the French, argument is an admirable skill and mastery of logic an intellectual accomplishment worthy of great respect. The French are proud of their verbal mastery.

The tendency of many American. business negotiatosr to get straight to the point has been responsible for many failed cross-cultural negotiations: in most places in the world, the one who asks questions controls the process of negotiation and thereby accomplishes more in bargaining situations. Americans are, as a rule, good at arguing but terrible at listening. Dean Rusk said, "One of the best ways to persuade others is with your ears—by listening." An old Farmer's adage is, "God gave you two ears but only one mouth so you can listen twice as much as you talk." An Arabic proverb says, "If I listen, I have the advantage; if I speak, others have it." It is never appropriate to speak unless you can improve the silence.

RATIONALE IN NATIONAL NEGOTIATING STYLES

The line of reasoning method most persuasive to most Americans may not work at all in other cultures. Americans are usually swayed by expert opinion and hard evidence and usually want to concentrate on the facts available; other cultures prefer to spend what to the Americans are inordinate amounts of time on principles. Mexican and Russian negotiators habitually start with the most general aspects and purpose of a negotiation session by defining major and minor issues, categorizing them, and then deciding on the main points to be solved. The Chinese seek agreement on general principles; they expect the other party to reveal their interests first while the Chinese mask their own interests and priorities.

The concept of discussing problems in a systematic, sequential, orderly manner is promoted by Americans while the Japanese prefer *haragei*, to talk around a subject in order to get a holistic view. Only after this is accomplished will the Japanese go into details. They prefer avoiding any area in which an agreement cannot be easily reached. Instead they tend to move to another topic in its place. To Americans, this often appears as if the Japanese are trying to elude the issue. To an American, an unsolved issue is a point of contention. This, not any general principle, must be dealt with first before the agreement as a whole can be considered. Americans are attracted to problems like fish to water; by way of contrast, Japanese are attracted to similarities and points of commonalities. Many cultures are holistic, especially in the Far East; all issues are discussed at once and no decisions made until the end. Especially in the Orient, the negotiating session is less a forum for working out issues than it is a formal and public expression of what has already been worked out beforehand.

Many who come from a non-Western tradition have to learn the value of give and take as well as the confrontational aspects of Western-style negotiation. In many cultures, especially those from East Asia, people depend more upon feelings and personal relationships than intellectual confrontations. In numerous other cultures, conflict avoidance is central and paramount in any negotiations. In these cultures, mediators, go-betweens, facilitators, brokers, and middlemen are used to assist in smoothing the negotiation process. In the Middle East, the Bedouin model is often used: intermediaries enjoy trust of both sides; the honor of both is uppermost; face saving is important; and gestures of generosity and reciprocation must be adhered to. On the other hand, the authoritarian traditions of the Latins often spurn use of mediators or third parties.

A primary bargaining strategy of the Chinese and Japanese is to ask questions to put the opponent on the defensive. Many times the initial meeting is merely used to gather information, which is then fed back to their superiors and peers for deliberation and a carefully prepared response. The Japanese strongly believe it is folly to make an offer until one knows what the other side wants. This explains the slow start, lack of initial proposal, the emphasis on information gathering, and the long, drawn out preliminary ground work that is usually encountered when negotiating in Japan. The Japanese need detailed information to build the foundation for whatever decision they intend to put forward. Should the venture fail, no one can be rebuked or blamed. On the other hand, in Latin America questions are not valued as in the Orient; in fact, there they are often interpreted as prying and inappropriately nosy.

Latins expect their manager to tell them what they can and cannot do, to provide authority, to give detailed instructions. Latins would not think of contradicting a superior and making a suggestion that the superior had not already, in some fashion, suggested. Americans, thus, often view Latins as lazy, slow, and not motivated, while Latins see the Americans as irresponsible, immature, informal, disrespectful, and insensitive to the needs of the people they are depending on. The proficient international negotiator understands the national negotiating style of those on the other side of the table, accepts and respects their cultural beliefs, and is conscious of his or her own mannerisms and how they may be viewed by the other side.

DIFFERENCES IN DECISION MAKING

In international negotiations one must also take into account the nuances in other cultures' decision processes—that is, the way officials and executives reach decisions and instruct their negotiators, as well as personal styles of decision-making behavior. In most of the non-Western world, decision making does not rest with an individual. Many cultures go to extraordinary lengths to avoid individual action on any problem; group responsibility replaces individual decision making. Americans view the Japanese inability to deviate from their position as indicating stubbornness and thus perceive the Japanese as unwilling to compromise or as uninterested in keeping the negotiation process alive. To the Japanese the Western concept of "decision making" is alien and not applicable to the Japanese process (*ringi* —consensus building from lowest levels to the upper level), which can be thought of as more of a direction-indicating process. The Japanese come to a negotiation with a hard-gained time-consuming intra-organizational consensus already established, which can not be easily changed at the bargaining table, no matter how small or seemingly irrelevant. To the Japanese, the Americans in their give and take appear insincere and unprepared as they do not appear to have a prepared position. To the Latins decisions are typically made by those individuals who are in charge of decision making in this area. In Korea, middle managers have major veto powers but no authority to commit their organization to a long-term agreement.

Newtom Minow, former chairman of the U.S. FCC quipped that: In Germany, under the law, everything is prohibited, except that which is permitted. In France, everything is permitted except that which is prohibited. In the Soviet Union, everything is prohibited, including that which is permitted. In Italy, everything is permitted, especially that which is prohibited. To Americans anything is permitted unless it has been restricted by the state or by company policy. For the Russians, nothing is permitted unless it is initiated by the state. Politics has an all-pervasive influence on Chinese and Russian behavior while the Americans tend to separate and compartmentalize business from politics. The former Soviets had an authoritarian government with a basically oligarchical decision-making network controlled from the Politburo. Not just major decisions but many details of negotiations were set at the top, almost to the point of complete subservience to instructions from Moscow. In such a decision-making framework, the Soviets had an advantage in that they could develop negotiation position and tactics without other domestic considerations. But they were typically so much at the mercy of instructions from superiors that at times it seemed to foreign observers that they needed permission from the Kremlin before they could even speak at the negotiating table.

Unlike that found in the American democracy, other cultures have strong authoritarian elements. The Mexicans have a president with immense authority, but any presidential direction is slowed or frustrated by a formidable and powerful bureaucracy. The Mexican president is the principle decision maker; governmental negotiators therefore have limited discretion in actions and decision-making capabilities by American standards. Likewise, the Egyptian president has politically a very strong position but the actual implementation of a negotiated agreement eventually requires the acceptance of the powerful Egyptian bureaucracy. For long-term commitments in Brazil, decisions are made at the top of organizations; implementation of such decisions by the bureaucracy tend to be cumbersome and time consuming.

The entire purpose of the bureaucracy in China is to diffuse decision making so that responsibility is difficult to locate; no one wants to be absolutely in charge.

The classic North American hierarchical model of Responsibility-Accountability-Power does not hold universally; the "top man's word" may not be enough. In the Chinese political culture, there is no assumption that decision power must be tied to accountability. On the contrary, in the eyes of the powerful, proof of authority and responsibility lies in being shielded from accountability. Those below them will protect them from criticism and their mistakes. The Chinese blur lines of responsibility and provide vague and conflicting signals as to the limits of their negotiating authority. As a government official, most Russian negotiators, until recently, could only discuss what they were told by their superiors. They could go no further and had to get approval for further moves, actions, and responses from their superiors. Fear of disciplinary action forced them to carefully follow orders. The Soviets took virtually no step in their public or private lives that did not depend on the state.

Americans love to compare negotiating to playing a poker game; they are quick to take advantage of a better power position or strength. The Latins are also great power players; to be stronger than the others is particularly cherished. The Japanese relish subtle power plays in their goal of achieving conciliation. The French typically have an elaborate, well-prepared opening position but few if any intermediate fallbacks before their minimum position is reached. In Eastern Europe, it was common occurrence for one team to negotiate one day, followed by a fresh team the next; it thus became very difficult for Western negotiators to ascertain which team was most important or which had the final authority.

The accomplished international negotiator prepares for his negotiation by understanding the decision-making pattern of the specific culture, learning the limitations of the delegate's authority and who within the nation or company will make the final decision. He readies himself for traditional culturally based power plays that may occur within the negotiation.

PERSONAL RELATIONSHIPS

To most Orientals and Latins, good personal relationships and feelings are all that really matter in a long-term agreement. After all, the written word is of much lesser importance than personal ties. Once personal trust has been established, cooperation increases. The social contacts developed between the parties are often far more significant than the technical specifications and the price. The Chinese word *guanxi'* signifies that personal connection requires significant personal obligations. In many countries the heart of the matter, the major point of the negotiations is in getting to know the people involved. Brazilians and many Latin Americans can not depend on their own legal system to iron out conflicts so they must depend on personal relationships. Relations are important because of the need to have contacts. Contacts can help you determine who to approach in order to get the business moving; government is very much involved in business in many countries. Social competence is paramount. Relationships are important for Latin Americans; in many cases, the people they do business with is more important than the company; the quality of the personal relationship plays a vital role in the business relationship. Personal affinity is also immensely important to Mexicans and other Latins. No one rushes into business but rather spends time in pleasantries that assist in the creation of a suitable climate for interaction. The goal is to nurture a mutual confidence, engage in informal discussions, and seek solutions to problems. Therefore personal rapport, preliminary meetings, telephone conversations, and social activities are necessary when dealing with businesspeople "south of the border." Brazilian negotiators like relationships to be continuing, and dislike opposers who are overly task-oriented.

Americans negotiate a contract, the Japanese a relationship. In many cultures, the written word is primarily used to satisfy legalities. In their eyes, emotion and personal relations are more important than cold facts in business relations. The key issue is: "Can I get along with these men and their company and do I want to sell (or buy) their products?" rather than "Can I make money on this deal?" They are particularly interested in the sincerity of those they are negotiating with. The Japanese are especially unwilling to do business with someone they think may prove to be arrogant or unpleasant: "I do not do business with a man who does not like us!" Japanese do not separate personal feelings from business relationships. The effective American negotiator should therefore display cultural empathy, be polite and honest, go out of his way to be good natured, practical, social, frank, responsible, and efficient—traits Japanese and most other Orientals value.

To the Malays trust is fundamental to a successful relationship: a person's capability for loyalty, commitment, and companionship is uppermost to the decision to do business. Arab buyers often base their buying decisions on the personality of the salesman, rather than on the quality of the product. The Koreans love to lavish attention and intimacies on their friends in contrast to the hostile and blunt treatment they give out to those they don't know. Building relationships there is necessary to good business. Indians place importance on building relationships and the negotiating process can be rather long by Western standards. West Africans see friendship as an element of the business relationship. They tend to treat a foreigner's motive as suspect if they feel they are being hurried through negotiations without regard to local custom.

The development of a personal friendship is an important prerequisite to building long-term business contacts with foreigners. It can also, however, be used to the disadvantage of the foreign negotiator.

The French

Negotiable issues are more important than relationships for the French. French negotiators are primarily interested in identifying and analyzing key issues of any negotiation. A clear distinction is made between business acquaintances and personal friends.The French are surprised by the direct and objective style Germans use to attack a problem; Germans must adjust to the French penchant for placing a problem on an intellectual plane. The French say *"necessite fait loi"* (necessity makes law). Trust has to be earned, they are impressed only by results. The French prefer detailed firm contracts. The French pride themselves on reasoned discussion. They dislike being rushed into decisions, preferring instead to examine various options in decisions. Negotiations are likely to be in French unless they occur outside France.

The Chinese

The Chinese believe they are the center of human civilization and as such should be revered. It is useful for a foreigner to try to understand Chinese cultural traits but a Chinese never believes that a foreigner can practice them better than the Chinese.The Chinese consider mutual relationships and trust very important. Chinese reserve a special place in their negotiations for "old friends"—foreigners they have dealt with before or who are introduced to them by someone they trust. Chinese like to use the "old friends" ploy as a means to ask for special treatment in the name of their friendship; They may feign hurt feelings if the other side refuses.

The Chinese attempt to establish an emotional bond with the other side. An effective strategy by the Chinese is to attempt to identify members of the opposite team who are sympathetic to the Chinese cause, to subsequently cultivate a sense of friendship and obligation in their counterparts and then to pursue their objectives through a variety of stratagems designed to take advantage of feelings of friendship, obligation, or even of guilt. Deeply rooted in Chinese traditions is the belief of reciprocity of actions; favors are to be considered investments with return expected, if not for oneself then for passing them on to subsequent generations. To the Chinese, a friend is one who will work to resolve problems that an unsympathetic person would not. The American negotiator should be cognizant of these assumptions and consequences. He should, therefore, not promise more than he can deliver.

The heavy use of shame as a social control mechanism from the time of early childhood tends to cause feeling of dependency and anxieties about self-esteem and produces self-consciousness about most social relationships. A great deal can be gained by helping the Chinese to win face and a great deal will be lost by any affront or slight, no matter how unintended. The Chinese concept of sincerity is the opposite of the American concept. The Chinese believe that they can manifest sincerity only by adhering carefully to prescribed etiquette. Chinese view negotiations as partly information gathering operations and frequently play off competitors against each other to get the maximum technical intelligence out of the presentations. The Chinese often have no intention of reaching an agreement but use the negotiations process to gather information that is unavailable in their own country. In relationships, Chinese want a sense of reliability and permanence.

Frequently the Chinese will begin negotiations as though they were empowered to make all decisions. When snags arise, however, they will suddenly claim that they must defer all issues to higher authorities, which can block further progress for unpredictable lengths of time. This delaying phenomenon is widely known to those who have dealt with the Mainland Chinese. Although it can be conscribed to the communist bureaucracy and the desired of those on top to remain in control of all facets of Chinese life, similar delays have been present for as long as the Chinese civilization has endured. These delays are more directly tied to the Chinese cultural desire for bureaucracy and centralized control then to the communist party beliefs; Fifty years can not overcome five thousand years of history.

Chinese and American negotiations are often characterized by very little success. Three significant factors that limit success are:

1. The attitude of the Ameican firm (items such as patience, sincerity, and personal relationships were important to the Chinese but were ignored by the American side).
2. Product characteristics (uniqueness, Chinese needs, and American technical expertise, which often did not fit the circumstances).
3. Lack of familiarity with Chinese culture (business practices, customs, politics, and language).

Therefore, rules for negotiating with the Chinese are:

Practice Patience
Accept as normal prolonged periods of no movement
Control against exaggerated expectations
Discount Chinese rhetoric about future prospects
Expect that the Chinese will try to influence by shaming
Resist the temptation to believe that difficulties may have
    been caused by one's own mistakes

Russians

For the Russian, the instinctive question is "who is stronger, who weaker?" and any relationship becomes a test of strength. Russians frequently test one another in the early stages of a relationship. It is not uncommon for two Russians to get into an argument shortly after they have gotten to know one another. If both argue long and hard for their respective points of view, however the argument comes out, their friendship has the possibility of deepening. If, however, one gives in too easily, they are not likely ever to become friends. The winner will not respect the loser for having given in so readily; he will not trust him. How can a man's word be good if his mind can be changed that easily?

The Russians tend to regard negotiations as debates. They are so ideologically oriented that giving and taking are seen as immoral, a compromise of their principles. Instead of trading concessions, they restate their original position, with all of the arguments supporting it. This process can continue indefinitely; they keep repeating themselves until the other side sees the error of its position and accepts the Russian position. The Russians think from the general idea to the particular, they deduce implications from axioms rather than the other way around. The Russian political culture is dominated by authoritarianism and risk avoidance and the necessity for control. The concept of individual autonomy is not natural. Russian society prefers the safety, the known, however unsatisfactory, to the perils of change, which promise progress but might as likely deliver disaster. Characteristics of the Russian negotiating style include passivity, fear of responsibility, adherence to formalities, standard formulations, avoidance of spontaneity, or taking unauthorized initiatives. The American and Russian ethical attitudes do not coincide: both sides evaluate behavior differently. What an American may consider normative positive behavior (negotiating and reaching a compromise with an enemy), a Russian perceives such behavior as showing cowardice, weakness, unworthy; the word 'deal' has a strong negative connotation in contemporary Russian.Russian negotiators have these negotiating traits: extreme initial positions (then withdraw some, expecting concessions in return); limited authority; emotional tactics; perceiving adversarial concessions as weakness that should be followed by the Russians taking a harder line; being stingy in their concessions; ignoring deadlines; having great suspicion of the other side and expectation that the other side will be hostile to them; having a reluctance to compromise; extensively using publicity and propaganda as a means of negotiation; having a willingness to suddenly abandon their position or commitment without particular concern for continuity or credibility; being reluctant to use informal meetings as a negotiating tool; and seeking agreements in principle.

Japanese

The Japanese seek signs of sincerity and are much more sensitive to relationships than Western businessmen. They often judge visitors by the way they can strike emotional chords in them. The Americans typically view negotiation as a process of exchange involving several proposal-counterproposal iterations, Americans inflate their demands in initial proposals and expect later to give and receive concessions. The Japanese concentrate on relationship-based issues. Sincerity and good intentions are necessary for a harmonious relationship. The emphasis in Japan is on understanding where the other person is coming from.

STATUS AND PROTOCOL

American egalitarianism can also present a problem in cross-cultural negotiations. Friendliness for Americans is merely an expression of egalitarianism, a way to emphasize similarities, to clear the decks to enable Americans to get the to the business at hand. While Americans want relationships built on equality and similarity, Europeans expect to build relationships based on the acknowledgment of differences, on respect for status, on deference to title. In less egalitarian cultures, ascribed criteria are more important than achieved ones, with some being more critical than others.

Negotiations between equals is basically a Western concept; it is not found in such status-oriented societies as the Japanese, Korean or Russian. For an American, calling someone by his first name is an act of friendship and goodwill. In other cultures—French, Japanese, Egyptian—the use of a first name at a first meeting is an act of disrespect and therefore a bad thing. The Japanese and Koreans rate others as either junior or senior to them but rarely as an equal; the Russians view others as either inferior or superior to themselves. All of them, the Koreans, the Russians, and the Japanese, tend to look at negotiations as war, a macho challenge. They believe in the rightness of their initial position. The Japanese when pressed explain their position fully and explain their underlying intentions in order to persuade the other side of the rightness of the Japanese position, but they will hesitate to yield their own position. The Chinese have a reverence for age and authority; unless one sports a beard be prepared for an uphill battle.

American informality in down playing status, in using first names, in attire, and other ways of showing casualness, is not universal. The Japanese dress conservatively—they always prefer dark business suits. To be dressed casually during negotiations with the Japanese would therefore be inappropriate. The Japanese do not believe in using first names unless it is between the very best of personal relationships. In Asia, honorifics, title, and status are extremely important; address your counterparts by their proper title. Frankness and directness, virtues for Americans, are not desirous to Mexicans in formal encounters nor to Japanese at any time. Americans and Germans are more likely to start out expecting to trust the other party until proven untrustworthy, while in Latin America and some parts of Asia people would be inclined to mistrust until good faith is proven. American humor is sometimes seen as inappropriate; the Japanese art of being overly humble and apologetic seems condescending and artificial to the West.

Most Westerners expect a prompt answer when they make a statement or ask a question. In a culture that values directness (German) you can expect to receive clear and definite responses to questions and proposals. Western cultures tend to believe that human relations cannot stand still and that they must be continuously reinforced to progress toward greater intimacy. The Chinese accept that relations can remain on the same level for an indefinite period of time. What they want is a sense of reliability, not warmth.

Some cultures have developed strong traditions governing daily life and social interactions. The Mexicans in formal settings respond with rhetoric and lofty principles. They are proud of their country and traditions but frequently exhibit a fear and suspicion of the gringos from the north and their possible motives. Little tradition exists in solving business problems by holding public meetings; the Mexican appreciation of form and ceremony goes back to their Spanish roots. Protocol and status are important to Koreans; they feel slighted if one does not recognize their proper status and position in life. The Arabs are highly ritualistic in their social interaction; an intimate knowledge of their customary formality and protocol is required to succeed with members of their society. The Russians are highly conscious of protocol and not inclined to accept any surprise changes in the negotiating agenda or venue. In Japan, tradition extends even to the proper way one must present a business card or drink tea and sake.

The valued American handshake is often out of place in Japan, where bowing is customary and the exact angle and number of bows are important according to whom you are meeting. Even use of the hands can violate unspoken rules of proper conduct. The American thumbs up and forefinger-thumb "OK" is considered an obscene gesture in many cultures. When meeting a devout Moslem, never shake with the left hand or utilize the left hand for any purpose—in Islam, the left hand is associated with the human excretion function. Any use of it in an interaction with a Moslem is therefore considered rude and a personal affront.

Women in business have a complete set of different protocol rules. Men may shake hands with women, but not in Arab countries. Women may kiss women but not men in Latin America. At the end of business in Latin America, men may embrace other men but not women. In the Arab cultures, men embrace each other in public, not women.

An appreciation, understanding, and respect of national protocols, rituals, or special status symbols is in the best interest of the successful foreign negotiator. The competent global negotiator subordinates his or her own preferences to that of his hosts or guests.

SOCIAL ASPECTS OF NEGOTIATION

The function of entertainment and other social activity related to negotiation varies markedly from culture to culture. The unbelievably high level of entertainment expenses incurred by the Japanese are seen to be part of the preliminary stage of establishing interpersonal relationships; eating has long been established as a rapport-building activity. Americans feel comfortable in a relaxed social setting to conduct business; negotiators in other cultures may feel awkward in such settings and may even see this as a breach of etiquette toward one's guests. Americans eat in public and bathe in private, the Japanese vice-versa. Japanese rarely bring wives or family members to a business gathering. The French, likewise, believe the home is for more intimate relationships and not for conducting business. The bazaar model of bargaining through a series of formal sequential steps is found in Egypt and in many parts of the Middle East. It starts with a preliminary period of discussing issues that go well beyond the transaction that is contemplated; subsequently focuses on establishing a personal relationship often with endless rounds coffee and tea; finally the actual bargaining aimed at a compromise position commences. The parties engage in the fine art of haggling, sometimes simply for the fun of it. No step must be passed over. Patience is the key to success.

In social interaction, face saving is crucial to the Japanese. Decisions are often made on the basis of saving someone from embarrassment. To the Americans decisions are typically made on a cost-benefit basis with little or no consideration for saving face. For the Latins face saving is critical to preserve honor and dignity. Different values and different priorities are clearly given to the social aspects and business considerations by different cultures. The French do not see negotiating as a place for bargaining but as one for searching out the reasoned solutions for which they have so carefully prepared. They start with a long-range view of their purposes and place lower priority on accommodation in short-range decisions.

Gift giving is a custom in many parts of the world. In India, South Korea, and Japan, gift giving plays a far more prominent role than in the United States. However, in Germany, Switzerland, or Belgium, business entertainment and the exchange of gifts is not commonplace. In the United States, the primary purpose of gifts is to create goodwill. Gift giving is usually not to create a close personal relationship but to smooth the business association. Americans gift gifts at holiday times, to commemorate important occasions, to repay hospitality or in appreciation for special service. Each culture has gifts that are taboo.

Each society also has its own gift-giving protocol that should be followed. In most cultures, gift giving involves an element of reciprocity.

Do give a gift in Japan, never give one in China. It is not so much the cost but the source or nature of the gift that impresses. In many cultures, especially the Orient, giving a gift creates an obligation between parties, a reciprocal gift is required if you have received a gift. This can quickly spiral out of control as the reciprocal gift must be more expensive than the gift received. Be sure to offer a gift on the first meeting with a Japanese company; but if a gift is tendered to you, open it only when you get home or back to the hotel. Expect to be invited home in Australia, do not expect to be invited home in Japan or France. If invited to a host's home in Asia or Africa, do not compliment an item too much, your host might feel compelled to give you the item you are admiring. Always ask about the spouse and family in Latin America; never ask about the spouse in East Asia.

To an American, ceremonies as part of the negotiating process are time-consuming, useless, and an unnecessary expense. However, ceremonies can provide each party to the negotiation with tangible representations of the effort expended. The ceremony focuses the participants on the new relationship. Some form of ceremony should be held to memorialize the negotiation. The most common ceremony is the banquet or party that accompanies the execution of the agreement and the beginning of the relationship. Americans have a fondness for calling the signing of a contract the "closing." It should be remembered that negotiation is a process not an event. The ceremony should mark a transition not the end.

The deft multinational negotiator recognizes ethnic differences in the display of personal feelings and relationships. He or she is primed for them and has prepared the proper response.

INTERPRETERS, TRANSLATORS, AND BICULTURAL BROKERS

To augment this or her own capabilities, a business negotiator can employ cultural experts, translators, outside attorneys, financial advisors, or technical experts who have at least moderate and preferably high familiarity with both the counterpart's and the negotiator's cultures. These experts serve two distinguishable roles, as "agents" who replace the negotiator at the negotiating table or as "advisers" who provide information and recommend sources of action to the negotiator. The use of go-betweens, middlemen, brokers, and other intermediaries is not an uncommon practice within many cultures and represents a particularly effective approach to most any cross-cultural negotiation.

Translators turn the words of one language into the words of another while interpreters make the thoughts of a person speaking in one language intelligible to a person who speaks in another language. Interpreting is a difficult, exhausting job. Interpreters are forever mentally alert, translating, evaluating. They must make the thoughts of one language clear in another while taking into account the context of the discussion. Interpreters need to be treated well and should be, if at all possible, included as a member of the negotiating team, to be briefed, and to brief on the negotiating scenario.

Using the other party's language greatly improves communication and trust. For example when their satellites met in space, the Americans spoke Russian and the Russians spoke English. Both sides knew that speaking the other's language reduced communications problems and increased trust. The same principles apply to many business negotiations.

As a general rule, you should not negotiate in a foreign language unless you know it extremely well. Otherwise you will be focusing your attention on the language rather than on the substance of the deal. Having an interpreter, even if you know the language, gives you additional time to consider your response to the other side's statements. Each party should haveits own interpreter or interpreters. You should bring your own interpreter whose interests are the same as yours. One should not rely on the other side for interpretation. Before negotiations actually begin, briefings should be held with the interpreter to explain the nature of the deal and what exactly you are expecting in the way of translation.

One must understand that the need for an interpreter significantly increases the time required to conduct the negotiation. Abilities and competencies of interpreters drastically vary. Having a mediocre interpreter can do more harm than good. An interpreter also acts as a filter. Instead of coming to know each other, the parties have to rely on the interpreter for communications. Thus, an interpreter could actually impede the development of a close working relationship between the two sides.

Being an interpreter, no matter how proficient, may not be enough. To be truly efficient, one should not only know both languages but both cultures and how to do business in both cultures. These individuals are called bicultural brokers, and although rare and usually expensive, they are often worth every penny paid to them. Studies have indicated that the likelihood of success increases when one uses one's own interpreter and then increases again upon the use of a bicultural broker (Gulbro and Herbig, 1996). These talented people should be utilized to the fullest, even to the extent of welcoming them onto the negotiating team as a full-fledged member. They should provide the members of the negotiating team with regular briefings and counseling sessions on how to more effectively do business with the other side and how to more effectively carry on negotiations.

Interpreters are most efficient when you speak slowly and carefully; repeat yourself often; do not use jargon, slang or idioms; explain complex ideas more than once; speak only a few sentences at a time; do not interrupt; and provide ample opportunity for breaks for interpreters. It is often advisable to have another bilingual person available to serve as a back-up listener who can provide additional insight to the conversation. One should speak not to the interpreter but towards one's opposite number. Loss of face and status could result otherwise.

A tactical advantage exists to having an interpreter (even though one may speak the foreign language perfectly). By waiting for the translations, the time to contemplate one's response doubles. Working through an interpreter can provide a manager with time to think and to observe the listeners' reactions to one's words. The French are reluctant to negotiate in English and use this tactic because of pride in their language and the fact that at one time the French language was the accepted medium of expression in diplomacy. The Soviets used this tactic because it gave them twice the usual time to prepare a response or to formulate a question. They were also able to move many a negotiations to their benefit by claiming not to understand arguments favorable to the other side or by clarifying their own comments when they did not elicit the desired response from the other side.

Do not feel intimidated or insulted if the other side momentarily begins to talk amidst themselves in their own language and no interpretation is made. Most people break into their native language at a negotiation because it is easier and more efficient to discuss things among themselves and not necessarily because they have something to hide.

5

How 2: Nonverbal Communications in Cross-Cultural Negotiations

Nonverbal behavior may be defined as any behavior, intentional or unintentional, beyond the words themselves that can be interpreted by a receiver as having meaning. Nonverbal behaviors could include facial expressions, eye contact, gestures, body movements, posture, physical appearance, space, touch, and time usage. They are all different from culture to culture. Nonverbal behaviors either accompany verbal messages or are used independently of verbal messages. They may affirm and emphasize or negate and even contradict spoken messages. Nonverbal behaviors are more likely to be used unconsciously and spontaneously because they are habitual and routine behaviors.

The wide range of behaviors called nonverbal behavior can be divided into seven categories. Gestures, body movement, facial movement, and eye contact are combined in the kinesic code commonly called body language. Vocalics refers to call vocal activity other than the verbal context itself. Also called paralanguage, vocalics includes tone, volume, and sounds that are not words. Behaviors that involve touching are placed in the haptics code. The use of space is called proxemics, and the use of time is chronemics. Physical appearance includes body shape and size, as well as clothing and jewelry. Finally, artifacts refers to objects that are associated with a person, such as one's desk, car, or books. It should be emphasized that these codes do not usually function independently or sequentially; rather, they work simultaneously. In addition, nonverbal behavior is always sending messages; we cannot not communicate without using them, although, at times, the messages may be ambiguous. This wide range of nonverbal behaviors serves various functions in all face-to-face encounters. Most important, emotional messages at the negotiating table are expressed nonverbally by gestures, tone of voice, or facial expressions. The other side's interpretation of your statement depends on the nonverbal more than what was actually said. Nonverbal communications is significant. What cannot be conveyed through words is sent through gestures and body movements.

The meaning of any nonverbal communication act depends upon the individual involved, the context in which the act is performed, and the cultural backgrounds of the interacting people: the tremendous impact of the "silent language" on the negotiation process. Everything counts during the negotiation: the time of the negotiation (morning, lunch time, late in the evening), the table (round, square), the lights (white, in the middle of the room), the use of microphones, the breaks, the phone calls, the space between the chairs, the way the negotiators dress, and so on. Everything is important. Effective negotiators are fully aware of the existence of all these factors and of the fact that they are able to use them to their advantage. One word of caution: an individual gesture must be approached cautiously. It is clusters of behavior that provide the most accurate of and greatest amount of nonverbal meanings.

Most of the time we send and receive nonverbal cues without being conscious of them. Between sixty and seventy percent of the meaning in social interactions is derived from nonverbal cues. Former United Nations Secretary-General Dag Hammarskjold summarized the importance of nonverbal behavior in the negotiation process: "The unspoken dialog between two people can never be put right by anything they say." In negotiation, what is not said is in many cases more important than what is openly expressed by the parties involved. Effective negotiators are particularly good at controlling (consciously or unconsciously) their body language and at the same time adjusting to the many nonverbal signals they will receive from the opposite negotiator(s). It is important to be aware of nonverbal cues since the negotiator may unintentionally transmit false or confusing messages to the other party, the negotiator may not pick up on or may misinterpret the nonverbal cues being transmitted by the other side, or effective communications may require the usage of nonverbal messages. Most important, emotional messages at the negotiating table are expressed nonverbally by gestures, tone of voice, or facial expressions. The other side's interpretation of your statement depends on the nonverbal more than what was actually said. Nonverbal messages tend to have more credibility. When a conflict exists between verbal and nonverbal messages, the latter should be given greater weight.

Only ten to fifteen percent of a region's culture is visible. Nonverbal communication can be telling as it can help one determine the exact meaning of what the other side is saying and also can help the negotiator get his own message across. Liking and disliking, tensions, and appraisal of an argument are shown by numerous signs such as blushing, contraction of facial muscles, giggling, strained laughter, or just silence. Whenever a party is to negotiate, the negotiator must see and observe the other party. While seated, people lean forward when they like what you are saying or are interested in listening, or they sit back on their seat with crossed arms if they do not like the message. Nervousness can manifest itself through nonverbal behavior, and blinking can be related to feelings of guilt and fear. It is difficult to evaluate nonverbal communication, as all elements are connected to the subconscious and emotions. The more simple and direct the language, the more precisely a position is defined, the stronger the commitment is likely to be.

NOISE

Cross-cultural "noise" (noise consists of the background distractions that have nothing to do with the substance of the negotiators message) can derive from gestures, space (proximity), or behavior that seems overly or insufficiently courteous. It can also stem from clothing or office surroundings that do not feel right for the occasion. The confusion comes, of course, because such surprises conflict with expectations and lead to misinterpretation of the situation or the intent of one's respondent or the meaning of the message itself. Or they simply make it more difficult to pay attention to the main subject. Noise occurs more often in cross-cultural negotiations than in domestic settings, for a whole new range of noise reflecting cultural differences may be introduced. Gestures and body postures that have a meaning in a certain culture can have a completely different significance in a different cultural environment. Sometimes the noise can be so great that little if any of the communications gets through.

The most irritating "noise" to Americans when negotiating with the Japanese is the use of silence or long pauses before responding. The Japanese often use little verbal activity, nod frequently, use silence, even close eyes while others are speaking (this helps them concentrate in Zen Buddhist fashion). Silence to a Japanese means one is projecting a favorable impression and is thinking deeply about the problem. The Japanese proverb on silence: he who knows does not speak, and he who speaks does not know. When in an impasse in negotiation, the typical Japanese response is silence, withdrawal, or change of subject. Japanese politeness can at times come across as artificial and excessive to many Americans. The adept negotiator recognizes potential sources of noise and consciously attempts to minimize its production while at the same time has prepared himself for likely noise elements from the other side of the table so as to minimize their effects on his performance.

While Americans feel comfortable with a space distance of three feet (and very little touching), Mexicans and Italians typically get extremely close to their counterparts. Some cultures believe in virtually eyeball to eyeball contact; the Japanese and English prefer greater distances. Mexicans use some physical contact to signal confidence, such as a hand on the upper arm. Americans who are standoffish from the *abrazo* (Latin American embrace) signal a certain coolness to their Latin hosts. Americans may have difficulty playing the high social status role that goes with important positions in societies such as Mexico. There is an art to being waited on and deferred to while at the same time being protective of the personal dignity of people in a lower social position. American expressions of impatience and irritation when things in Mexico do not work or delays are encountered create considerable noise—both figuratively and actually. Mexican practices relating to the role of women create their share of noise, too. Mexicans communicate with hand movements, physical contact, and emotional expressions. Space is close, people stand close to each other, sit close to each other, and regularly touch and embrace each other.

An American attributes an unwillingness to engage in a frank conversation to an Indian who does not look the American directly in the eye; the Indian attributes to the American an attempt to control and dictate by means of direct physical confrontation. To look away is a sign of showing respect to Indians while in the United States, respect is shown by looking directly at the speaker. In contrast, the French have direct and intense eye contact which the Americans will attribute to aggressiveness and stubbornness. The French person meanwhile is likely to attribute weakness, casualness, and insincerity to the American when the intense gaze is not returned or is avoided. Americans also unknowingly create noise for negotiators from other cultures: slouching, chewing gum, using first names, forgetting titles, joking, wearing overly casual clothing, being overtly friendly toward the opposite sex, speaking too loudly, being too egalitarian with the wrong people (usually the lower class), working with one's hands, carrying bundles, tipping too much. American egalitarianism is not the norm in many other cultures.

An American's directness and overbearing manner may signal to the Japanese a lack of self-control and implicit untrustworthiness; at the very least it signals a lack of sincerity. Such noise in one's conduct, although perfectly natural in communication with another of one's own culture, may have the unintended effect of derailing the message when in a cross-cultural setting.

LOW CONTEXT VERSUS HIGH CONTEXT

Nonverbal communications is a key element in all negotiations. It is especially vital that its ramifications are fully understood in cross-cultural settings. What words fail to convey is told through gestures and body movements. Humans will often disregard the spoken word when physical expressions indicate otherwise. People in non-Western cultures are more prone to understand nonverbal implications than those in the West. Seemingly harmless and even mundane behavior such as crossing one's leg and exposing the soles of one's shoes or putting hands in one's pockets are, in some cultures, considered in poor taste, offensive, and insulting to the host. The Japanese believe in intuitive mutual understanding and are adept at the analysis of nonverbal behavior. They do not understand why Westerners talk so much and often appear to contradict each other while at the bargaining table. The Japanese can relate large amounts of information to one another with merely a glance, a movement, or even silence. Nonverbal communications can be highly efficient.

Cultures can be predominantly verbal or nonverbal. In verbal communications, information is transmitted through a code that makes meanings both explicit and specific. In nonverbal communications, the nonverbal aspects become the major channel for transmitting meaning. This ability is called context. Context includes both the vocal and nonvocal aspects of communication that surround a word or passage and clarify its meaning—the situational and cultural factors affecting communications. High context or low context refers to the amount of information that is in a given communication. These aspects include: the rate at which one talks, the pitch or tone of the voice, the intensity or loudness of the voice, the flexibility or adaptability of the voice to the situation, the variations of rate, pitch, and intensity, the quality of the voice, the fluency, expressional patterns, or nuances of delivery. Nonverbal aspects include eye contact, pupil contraction and dilation, facial expression, odor, color, hand gestures, body movement, proximity, and use of space.

The greater the contextual portion of communication in any given culture, the more difficult it is for one to convey or receive a message. Conversely, it is easier to communicate with a person from a culture in which context contributes relatively little to a message. In high-context cultures, information about an individual (and consequently about individual and group behavior in that culture) is provided through mostly nonverbal means. It is also conveyed through status, friends, and associates. Information flows freely within the culture although outsiders who are not members of the culture may have difficulty reading the information.

In a low-context communication, information is transmitted through an explicit code to make up for a lack of shared meanings—words. In low-context cultures, the environment, situation, and nonverbal behavior are relatively less important and more explicit information has to be given. A direct style of communications is valued and ambiguity is not well regarded. Relationships between individuals are relatively shorter in duration and personal involvement tends to be valued less. Low-context countries tend to be more heterogeneous and prone to greater social and job mobility.   Authority is diffused through a bureaucratic system that makes personal responsibility difficult. Agreements tend to be written rather than spoken and treated as final and legally binding. Insiders and outsiders are less closely distinguished; foreigners find it relatively easier to adjust and immigration is more acceptable. Cultural patterns tend to change faster in low-context societies. In low-context cultures, initial relationship creation may be passed over fairly rapidly, while in high-context cultures, this is a very important function throughout the process; the decision whether or not to sign may depend on the relationships established. The Germans do not appreciate emotional gestures; hands should never be used to emphasize points. They believe in calm under pressure. The United States, with its European background, assumes that the only natural and effective way to present ideas is by logic. Low-context countries include the Anglo-American countries and the Germanic and Scandinavian countries.

A high-context communication is one in which most of the information is either in the physical context or internalized in the person, while little is in the explicit transmitted part of the message. In high-context cultures, the external environment, situation, and nonverbal behavior are crucial in creating and interpreting communications. Members of these cultures are programmed from birth to depend heavily upon covert clues given within the context of the message delivered verbally. In languages spoken in those high-context cultures (such as Arabic, Japanese, Chinese), subtlety is valued and much meaning is conveyed by inference. High-context communications is faster, more economical, more efficient, and more satisfying, but if common programming does not exist between sender and receiver, communications is incomplete. High-context individuals are seeking information on many levels in addition to the spoken word but when dealing with low-context cultures, the spoken word is primarily all they get. On the other hand, low-context individuals are quite confused by the ambiguity contained in the spoken or written answers of high-context individuals. By reading inaccurately, misinformation and miscommunications results.

In high-context cultures, relationships between individuals are relatively long lasting and individuals feel deep personal involvement with each other. These cultures place great importance on personal relationships. Members from such cultures will focus energies and time on developing an understanding and trust of the other person and less attention to the specifics of the deal. Only when convinced of the other's integrity, reliability, and sincerity and only when comfortable doing business with the other party, will a member of a high-context culture negotiate in earnest. The need for confidence and trust in the other party is particularly strong in countries where the businessperson is unable to depend upon a strong and independent legal system to settle their conflicts and hence they are forced to depend heavily on personal relationships.

In high-context societies, those in authority are personally responsible for the actions of subordinates, which in turn creates super loyalty by subordinates to their superiors. Agreements tend to be spoken rather than written. The Japanese believe that if the situation changes, the contract should be renegotiated. Insiders and outsiders are clannish. The Japanese talk around a point, believing that the point should be discovered from the context. *Haragei* (belly language) is the Japanese expression that implies being able to communicate without words. Actual cases exist of entire communities (Sicilian) able to carry on whole conversations by gestures alone. High-context cultures can be found in East Asia (Japan, China, Korea, Vietnam), Mediterranean countries (Greece, Italy, Arabia, Spain, to lesser extent France), the Middle East, and to a lesser extent Latin America and South America.

In high-context countries negotiators require sufficient knowledge of the culture to communicate understandably and acceptably. It is only if they are in a position to share the assumptions of the people with whom they are dealing that they can build up relationships and have a highly satisfactory interaction. These assumptions will embrace the cognitive structures of the people concerned and the world view that they hold, which are derived from culture. In high-context cultures, the external environment, situation, and nonverbal behavior are crucial in understanding communications. In a low-context culture, a much greater portion of the meaning in a given communication comes from the spoken word, which is more literal and detailed oriented. High-context cultures such as Mexico look at their North American counterparts as more structured, rigid, and direct. Often Mexicans are unable to speak frankly about some matter due to the desire to save face. To the low-context culture, the written word is binding, regardless of what evolves later; to the high-context culture, the contract is a sign of good faith and the relationship between the two parties, not the contract, is what matters; the contract is a symbol of the bond between its drafters. For high-context cultures, the human side of the negotiation process is more important than the technical aspects.

Americans tend to be low-context, focus on substantive issues, on what is being said: "Just the facts, madam." The Russians are considerably higher context. Issues involving authority, risk, and control and how they affect the relationship among the negotiating parties are so important to them that it may be difficult for a Russian negotiating team to get to the subjects on the agenda until those issues are resolved. Form and substance are inextricably linked. For Russians, silence should not be taken as consent but rather as disapproval. Silence leaves them with their options completely open. They can either say nothing, implying acquiescence and approval, or later express disapproval and state that they had never agreed to any such thing. Or they can do both at different times depending on their interests at the moment.

ADAPTIVE BEHAVIOR IN CROSS-CULTURAL ENCOUNTERS

In some areas of the world, it is customary to overstate a case, in others to understate it. There are many situations and countries in which it is necessary to use interpreters because neither party has an adequate command of the language of the other. This is particularly so in countries such as the Arab states and East Asia. Some of these languages are so flexible in their translatability that it would be unwise to accept agreement in them. Arabic is one such language. Arabic manifests itself in a general vagueness of thought and in an over-emphasis on the psychological significance of linguistic symbols at the expense of their exact meaning by fitting the thought to the word rather than the word to the thought. Words become substitutes for thought rather than their representation. Over-exaggeration and over-assertion become natural means of expression, with the result that a simple statement in English cannot be translated into Arabic literally without losing part of its meaning. Within their own counties, Arabs are compelled to assert and over-exaggerate, otherwise there is a good chance other Arabs would misunderstand them. If an Arab says what he means without exaggeration, others might think he means the opposite. This can lead to misunderstandings in negotiation by non-Arabs who do not realize that the Arab speaker is merely following traditions inherent to his language. Arabs often fail to realize that non-Arabs mean exactly what they say if it is put in a simple, unelaborated manner. To many Arabs, a simple "no" may be perceived as a sign to continue rather than a direct negative. Communications is made more complex by the need to interpret Arab behavior in a way in which his interpretation reflects the intended meaning.

Americans tend to be considerably uncomfortable with silence. They tend to fill up the spaces between the words. Other cultures turn American willingness to talk against them by consciously making Americans uncomfortable with silence to make them talk and eventually open up. While the spoken word remains one of the most powerful and flexible tools of communication in negotiation, translation of meaning is not confined to it. Some sensory data cannot be paraphrased or even identified by speech. The spoken language is only one, although the most important in the majority of circumstances, of a multitude of graphic, olfactory, tactile, spatial, temporal, and symbolic means of communication. The ambiguity of spoken language can be reduced when read in conjunction with these nonverbal sign systems. Understanding within a language can therefore be assisted by the interpretation of the nonverbal. These are in relation to expressions of emotion and the communicating of attitudes of a negotiator.

When a negotiator takes the view that his opposer is being unjustly demanding, unreasonably resistant to proposals, or punitive in the exercise of a greater power in relation to what he considers his share of available outcomes, it is likely that intangible issues related to the anticipated or actual loss of public face or self-esteem will emerge. The negotiator is likely to react in a way that will protect him from injury, for example, in terms of the expectations of his peers or those in authority in his organization—and this can manifest itself in a stream of nonverbal signals about his inner status. These will take the form of facial expressions and other gestures, sometimes supplemented by vocalizations such as grunts and groans.

The negotiator has to be sensitive to the emotions being displayed by his opposer, when the emotion arises from a state such as anxiety or from milder states or moods, feelings of displeasure or shame. Emotions are often difficult enough to handle without compounding the difficulty with misperception. It is up to the negotiator to ensure that he does not, through insensitivity to such emotions, drive his opposer away from the relationship while settling within his own objectives remains a possibility.

Emotions have been used as a tactic. Stalin alternated friendly and cordial discussions with hostile and adversarial outbursts. His emotional tactics threw the other negotiators off balance and helped strengthen a weak negotiating position. Other Soviet leaders also used this tactic (e.g., Khrushchev's shoe-banging in the United Nations). However, such tactics should be used gingerly and can often result in much greater loss than any foreseeable gain.

Emotions affect the ability to negotiate because every emotion brings with it an impetus to take action related to the shown emotion. Emotions can effect your ability to communicate as well as your behavior and can be used to manipulate your actions. Emotions, attitudes, and feelings of one party toward the other are not always what they seem. The Japanese are not emotional but consider themselves passionate. To Latin Americans, the *Norte Americano* is a "dead corpse" with no color, no life; it is too cold, too serious in business, and unable to loosen up and enjoy itself. In the Latin business world, the range of emotional expression is considerably greater. On the other hand, Asians consider Americans too free in business settings with emotions such as anger, frustration, disappointment, and friendliness. Asians consider it immature to display emotion; one keeps one's thoughts and feelings to oneself. A display of anger is particularly destructive in Asia and one should not display it in any form. Anger disturbs harmony.

Differences in body language between cultures are many. In many cultures, beckoning to someone with the forefinger is considered ill-mannered. Never touch an Arab on the top of the head, for that is where the soul resides. Never show the sole of one's shoe to an Arab, for it is dirty and represents the bottom of the body. Similarly, never use your left hand to a Moslem, for it is the hand reserved for toilet functions. Americans, Germans, and Russians shake hands forcefully; in some parts of Europe a handshake is usually quick and to the point; in Asia, it is often limp. An Asian might view an American as too abrupt and heavy-handed after a typical American handshake, while an American might view those with less firm handshakes as unassertive.

Laughter and giggling in the West indicates humor; in Asia it more likely indicates embarrassment and humility. Latins embrace one another at the end of a successful negotiation; central and eastern Europeans not only embrace but kiss each other on the cheek.

For strategic reasons, signals are often sent that are not genuine. A buyer does not always wish to convey how keen he is to have a particular product or service nor a salesman how much his company needs a particular sale, in case his opposer revises his objective upward. Personal inclinations and interests of one or both the negotiating parties may be at odds with the interests of the organizations they represent. Opening moves and concessions allow each party to gauge the other's preferences and intentions and give each the opportunity to present or misrepresent information.

NONVERBAL COMMUNICATIONS EXAMPLES

The Arabs want direct, face-to-face discussions, but do not to bring open disagreements into a formal session. In fact, rather than say that they disagree, many Arabs will say they agree, but then take actions that gently that hint they do not agree at all. They hope that the other party will get the message. Arabs will seldom provide a direct "no," even if they disagree. Hesitation signals that disagreement exists. A person of status is not expected to hesitate over an answer. If you don't know, stall but don't say you don't know. Arab men don't hesitate to walk hand in hand, arm in arm in public. Saudi Arabians look closely into another's eyes in the belief that they can tell if that person is telling the truth or lying by movements of the pupil. Americans think that keeping direct eye contact is a sign of openness, honesty, and assertiveness; other cultures view it as confrontational, aggressive, hostile, and rude. Italians, Arabs, and Latin Americans use their hands a great deal to emphasize or support what they are saying. The French shake hands without particular conviction and without even a verbal greeting—which a German may misread as indifference.

In Japan and the Arab countries, the direct negotiations are combined with social activities. One purpose of these activities is to demonstrate hospitality. Another, more serious purpose is to determine whether you are the sort of person with whom they want to do business. An easy way to create a bad impression is to discuss business at the wrong time. That is, the social process can be as important as the negotiations process. The Portuguese prefer that no business be discussed at a meal until the conversation is complete and coffee is served.

The Japanese are willing to meet face-to-face, but they also use third parties much more frequently than we do. They are also so uncomfortable with open conflict that they hardly ever express it directly. They talk around it, or do not react at all, or give indirect hints that they disagree. In fact, they hardly ever say no directly; one must infer it from the way they say yes. When a Japanese says "yes" he may mean "no" and often "maybe" but rarely an unconditional "yes."*Hai* indicates understanding rather than agreement. If he draws breath between his teeth and says something like "*sah*" or "it is very difficult," he means "no." Japanese are more influenced by what is not said. The Japanese interpersonal communication style includes less eye contract, fewer negative facial expressions, and more periods of silence.

Flat, level tones in English regularly connote boredom or sarcasm. In Russian, on the other hand, the level tone is much more widely used with a natural matter-of-fact interpretation. A Russian will therefore tend to speak English with many level tone endings. To his own ears the sentence sounds intentionally neutral, but to the English listener he sounds uninterested and rude. By the same token the English speaker negotiating in a foreign language has to be cognizant of the correct pitch, loudness, speed and rhythm associated with the meaning he intends to convey. An Arab speaking English is often thought by Westerners to be shouting, as Arabs tend to speak more loudly than most Westerners.The tone of voice interpreted as sincere by Egyptian sounds belligerent to Americans. Americans tend to give the impression of assertiveness, even when not intended.

The range and use of emotions drastically differ across the globe. Some cultures, for example Orientals, inhibit emotional expressions while others, such as Latin American and Mediterranean cultures, are most more demonstrative. Yet within each culture there is a perfectly clear range of visual expression from mild to intense, and it is a question of being attuned to the particular culture to read the existence of emotional intensity. Italians tend to be extremely hospitable but are often volatile in temperament. When they make a point, they do so with considerable gesticulation and emotional expression. Impressed by style, they tend to dress well themselves. Moreover, they enjoy haggling over prices. Indians do not approve of displays of emotion. Chinese negotiators rarely telegraph their next move through a show of emotions. The level of friendliness or impersonality remains the same whether negotiations are approaching agreement or failure. A Thai's laughter in meetings may not indicate amusement. Often it is an embarrassed response when the Thai does not understand the point of the counterpart or simply does not wish to reply.

In Bulgaria, nodding one's head means "no" while shaking one's head means "yes." A "thumbs up" gesture is considered vulgar in Iran but friendly in Brazil. Folding your arms may be considered disrespectful by a Fijian. Pointing at something with a finger is considered rude in many places in Africa. In Greece, waving may be taken as an insult. The "A-OK" gesture considered perfectly appropriate by an American is likely to be viewed as obscene by a Brazilian.

Stress is the abnormal response by the body to unusual demands placed upon it. Stress can be created in many ways. Stress can be utilized to produce concessions by the other side. For example during the 1972 Nixon-Brezhnev Moscow summit, the Soviet negotiators frequently changed the setting and agenda of the meetings and refused to provide the Americans with access to telecommunications equipment and administrative support. In addition, the American negotiators feared justifiably that the Soviets were electronically monitoring their conversations.

MISREPRESENTATION AND NONVERBAL SIGNALS

Deception is frequently practiced in all social interaction, and negotiation is no exception. Negotiators who feel it necessary to practice deception should be able to do it well. This they can learn by becoming adept at detecting its practice in others.

When an individual practices deception, his behavior tends to fragment. Verbal and nonverbal components of a message conflict and it is possible to detect the deception as a result. Nonverbal leakage of deception has been widely studied and the results are important for all executives involved in face-to-face activities in various kinds of exchange relationships. Experiments in the United States suggest that lying is characterized by a number of nonverbal behaviors:

1. Hand actions normally used to emphasize verbal statements are significantly reduced.

2. Touching the face with the hand increases dramatically, particularly covering mouth and touching the nose. This does not mean that a person covering his mouthmust be lying. It does mean that he is more likely to be lying at times when he covers his mouth than at times when his hand does not cover

it. The same applies to touching the nose. Variations include stroking the chin, scratching the eyebrow, and pulling the earlobe.

3.   There is an increase in the number of body shifts in the person concerned. They are slight changes in the resting posture of the trunk as the speaker moves from one sitting position to another.

4.   The hand shrug becomes more common as other gesticulations decrease in frequency.

5.   What distinguishes facial expressions when lying from when telling the truth, are micro-expressions so small and so quick that only trained observers can detect them.

When contradictory signals are received it is the nonverbal signal that should be trusted. In the face of contradictory signals it is useful to refer to the believability of the gesture. Here is a seven-point scale in terms of decreasing believability:

1.   Body stress signals: These are signals resulting from stress to which the nervous system automatically reacts and produces involuntary changes in the body of the individual. Sweating or licking of dry lips or heightened pitch of the voice are signs indicating this stress, which may stem from lying, or fear, or excitement. These are the surest signals because they cannot be controlled even when the individual is aware of them.

2.   Lower body signals: It is the lower parts of the body that are least easily labeled. Foot-tapping can indicate impatience when verbal behavior indicates interest.

3.   Body posture signals: General body posture is often a giveaway, as when one nods, murmurs accord, and even leans forward in an attentive position, while sags or slumps show boredom.

4.   Unidentified gestures: Many hand actions are indefinite movements to which no names have become attached.

The negotiator who makes aggressive gestures with his hands while talking of the need for cooperation is contradicting his verbal claim.

5. Identified hand gestures: Many hand gestures are deliberate and definite. Such actions are not to be trusted if they appear as part of a contradictory signal.

6. Facial expressions: People are so aware of their faces that they can exercise considerable control over them to reinforce spoken deceptive behavior.

7. Verbalizations: When oral messages are given these can only be trusted when there is no contradictory behavior.

If one must lie, the best way to deceive is to restrict all signals to words and facial expressions. The most efficient means of doing this is either to conceal the rest of the body or keep it so busy with a complicated mechanical procedure that all its visual deception clues are stifled by the demand for physical dexterity. That is, if you have to lie, do it over the phone or when peering over a wall, when threading a needle, or when maneuvering a car into a parking space. If much of you is visible and you have no mechanical task to perform, then to succeed with your lie you must try to involve the whole of your body in the act of deception, not just your voice and face.

Nonverbal behaviors are often performed too weakly or too strongly for their particular context. The reason for this is that a person's true mood is interfering with the behavior he is trying to project. Gestures and expressions embody subtle complexities. When the performer's mood is inappropriate he fails to convey these complexities to the degree required to convince.

With under- and overreaction there is a danger when negotiators from different cultures meet that they will misunderstand each other. The man who holds the eye too long as Westerners may believe of Arabs, or is overfamiliar or personal as Englishmen may believe of Americans or Indians, may well be looked on as overreacting. In fact, they can be behaving in accordance with the norms of their own cultures where rules in relation to public display have not dampened their actions to the degree that they have in the other party's culture. On the other hand the opposer who underplays the intensity of gaze, as a Japanese might do by the standards of American or West European negotiators, may well be regarded as deceitful. As trust is an essential component in effective negotiation, negotiators are required to familiarize themselves with the culture with which they are interacting. People often deliberately manipulate clues. The idea that the sender has about himself is converted into body signals that others have to decode. By creating a favorable impression on others, a negotiator can gain material advantages and sustain at the same time a positive and satisfying self-image.

When contradictory signals suggest that the self being presented is not the true one, a negotiator has to refrain from making and emphasizing points that make it clear that he knows of this. If a negotiator wishes to be seen as strong and competent in the eyes of his own organization as well as in the eyes of the other side by easing the demands, this may indicate a view of his opposer as a worthy adversary to whom concession must gradually be made. A failure to make any concessions that are perceived as real by the opposer may interpreted as a reflection on the latter's own competence, particularly if he can return to his constituents with some evidence of concessions won. A negotiator who believes he is seen to be capable and effective will most likely behave in an cooperative manner. If we destroy his face, we have destroyed the relationship.

Negotiating across cultures carries the risk of misperception arising from differences in the manipulation of clues. Misinterpretation can introduce antagonisms in the relationship. In many Western countries there is something of a taboo on verbal presentation. While Australians have an achievement orientation they also have "tall poppy syndrome"—one must not take too much credit for one's accomplishment or be seen to stand out above the crowd. Observers have noted a similar attitude in Sweden to setting oneself apart from others in terms of what is said and what is. In India and the Arab countries, on the other hand, this is acceptable social behavior. People are not forced back into nonverbal signals as in the Western and Australian cultures. An understanding and acceptance of these differences in direct verbal and nonverbal behavior can smooth the bargaining process.

6

When:
Before and After—
Time, Planning, Debriefing

TIME

Time, how we define it in our lives, how it affects our work, and the role it plays in our worldview, is a universal aspect of all cultures. A culture's attitude toward time determines the importance placed on the development of personal relationships in business. In a culture where everyone is busy, where there never seems to be enough time to get everything done, little chance is given or importance given to building long- term solid personal relationships. In those cultures where time is less of a constraint, a certain valuing of personal relationships exists, if for no other reason than that there is time for them. While Americans might expect a meeting to begin and end at a certain time, with a series of important points discussed in between, Latins typically arrive later than the time stated, expect to discuss a great many items not on the Americans' agenda, and keep the meeting going long beyond its stated end-time. Latins set schedules not based on points on a clock but rather on a series of events: first, do this; then when it is finished they move on to the next task. They give each task the time needed to complete it. They are not deadline oriented.

Americans schedule; the clock "runs" for them; everything must be organized, compartmentalized, and have a beginning and an end. Their whole life often appears to be dominated by time and they are in a constant hurry to make use of it. Time is a commodity that must not be wasted; it must be maximized. In other cultures, time does not rule the day. The more important determinants of any activity might be the weather or the needs of friends or family. Therefore, time is defined in terms of seasons, days, and stages of personal life. They are controlled by, not attempting to control, time. The Chinese with over 5000 years of cultural heritage, have a different perspective on time. When Mao Tse-Tung was asked what he thought of the French Revolution, he replied (only halfjoking), "It is too soon to tell." Producing a satisfactory agreement in as short a time as possible may be one of the least concerns of the Chinese. The Chinese generally believe that a considerable amount of time should be invested in establishing a general climate of understanding, trust, and willingness to help, in matters quite apart from the issues brought to the bargaining table. They do not view time as a constraint or as a set of limits in which a particular task must be completed.

Many in the West, especially Americans, are constantly in a rush throughout their entire life. No wonder most of them cannot change their behavior when entering a negotiation. Seen through foreign eyes, Westerners always seem to be in a hurry, under pressure for results, and suffering from a "do it yesterday" syndrome. With time running out on self-imposed and frequently arbitrary deadlines, Americans tend to give away more than planned in order to finish "on time" and move on to the next deal. In this scenario, experienced Asian negotiators know that all they have to do is stall, be patient, and they will eventually be handed a favorable contract by an American just so the American can have one signed. Whereas most businesspeople in the West try to be punctual, the Japanese are even more conscientious and precise in keeping appointments. With Arabs one should plan longer, less formal negotiating sessions. The international negotiator should clearly understand how people in each culture view time and value punctuality. Equally important is that he gives himself enough time for completing a negotiation and that he will not be pressed by self-imposed deadlines.

International deals take longer to conclude than purely domestic transactions. The business tempo is slower in most countries: government approval may be required and top people in the company or bureaucracy may not be able to keep their appointments. McDonald's negotiated for nearly ten years to open its first hamburger restaurant in Moscow. IBM needed almost two years to secure an agreement to build a computer plant in Mexico. Negotiating a joint venture in China takes an average of two years. It takes much longer to negotiate with Europeans and the Japanese than with Americans. This is especially true if the foreign firm has not had extensive exposure to American. business practices and specifications.

The organization of most European and Japanese businesses and their mode of operation usually require considerably more time to negotiate than is the case in American firms. In the case of European firms, it usually takes at least twice as much time, and up to six times as long is often required for Japanese firms. The extent to which American expectations of the duration of a negotiation can differ from those of a foreign foe was demonstrated at the Paris peace talks to end the Vietnam War: the American negotiators checked into the Ritz Hotel while the North Vietnamese leased a villa for two years.

Global deal makers need patience and must be prepared to commit time to the process. A good negotiator should be patient—though not primarily in order to sit in Geneva for months at a time hearing the opponent repeat speeches and repeating his own. He should be patient in working for seemingly lost causes, because by doing so he may slowly change the opponent's views and objectives. He should be patient to live with conflict and uncertainty and know that he may have succeeded even if (or precisely because) his negotiations failed. Above all, he must maintain the will to win.

DIFFERENCES IN CULTURAL VIEWS OF TIME

Cultures can differ in time conception, time perspective, and time experiencing. A preferred temporal perspective (toward the past, the present, or the future) exists in each culture and provides the foundation for certain forms of negotiational behavior. An orientation toward the future implies an expectation of an advancement or a progressive development; negotiators are able to predict, plan for, and change forthcoming events and conditions. An orientation toward the present implies a predominance of the state of the moment; the negotiator's only concerns are those that are happening now. An orientation toward the past implies a belief that everything that is or will be has also existed or taken place in a period before the present. Temporal perspective influences overall strategy, especially issue formulation and decision making.

Americans typically arrive five minutes early for a business appointment and begin their business at the appointed time or shortly thereafter. Japanese negotiators expect your team to be ready and present precisely at the appointed time. Failure to arrive on time is viewed negatively. For Germans, punctuality is next to godliness, the appointment begins as the clock chimes the hour. In Nigeria, the starting time is only approximated and tardiness is not negative. The attitude towards time is less rigid for Latin Americans than North Americans; delays of thirty minutes or more are not surprising. When setting times for appoints one should ask "*la hora inglesa, o la hora espanola?*" or "the English hour" (promptly at the time specified?) or "the Latin hour" (thirty minutes or more late). Much business in Spain is conducted over the evening meal, which seldom begins until late in the evening, often closer to midnight. No business is conducted in the afternoon during siesta (2:00 to 4:00) when lunch is commonly held. This is not at all uncommon with many Latin American countries.

Cultures also have different ways of organizing and using time. Monochronic time (linear) emphasizes schedules, segmentation, and promptness; these cultures compartmentalize events and concentrate on one thing at a time. In these cultures, only a limited number of events are permitted within a given period and scheduling provides for priority setting. The future can be altered, an implication of expectation of advancement or progressive development; negotiators are able to predict, plan for, and change forthcoming events and conditions. Monochronic cultures are concerned with causality. In such cultures, communication and argument are based on the need for logic. Monochronic cultures are "doing oriented" as they concentrate on the future.

Polychronic time (circular) stresses involvement of people and completion of transactions rather than adherence to a preset schedule. Time is not limited; it is endless with no beginning or end. Time exists beyond humanity, external to the control of human beings. The future is not solid or firm and cannot be planned. Appointments are frequently broken and important plans may be changed right up to the minute planned. A predominance of the mental state of the moment exists. The negotiator's only concerns are those that are happening now. Because it is nonlinear, many things happen at once, a simultaneous use of time. Traditional societies, non-industrial cultures, are typically polychronic. Polychronic societies are concerned with equilibrium; communication and argument are based on the need for balance. Polychronic cultures are "being oriented," viewing the here and now as the focus.

The monochrome nature of Germans and Americans (ranking activities by priority and impact and doing one thing at a time) frustrates French polychronic tendencies (do more than one thing at a time and be open to inevitable disruptions). The Japanese, because of their circular polychronic sense of time, stress end results and are less concerned about how long the process takes to get there, and are thus less concerned about adhering to time schedules, instead preferring to focus on the end result. Time is not as important to a Japanese as it is to one from the West. Not being hasty is a sign of wisdom and sincerity. Japanese value high quality over immediate gain and they wait patiently for the best possible result. Americans are most comfortable discussing items in an orderly (linear) fashion while Latin Americans wish to discuss many points at the same time, talking over and louder than another when attempting to emphasize a point. Since life is unpredictable, punctuality is not emphasized and delays occur frequently, especially when other, more important concerns take priority. Polychronic cultures do not necessarily place their faith in tomorrow as tomorrow is suspect, unknown. Monochronic cultures are future- embracing while polychronic tend to be future-suspicious and present-embracing. If we cannot control tomorrow, let us make the best of today.

Monochronic cultures' preference for linearity and logic appears to polychronic cultures as one-dimensional and sterile. Monochronic cultures, on the other hand, tend to find polychronic cultures illogical and unproductive. Polychronic cultures, by way of contrast, view monochronic cultures as being without concern for human reality and applicability. The monochronistic approach of planning for the goal implies limits and inflexibility. The polychronistic commitment to the goal implies openendedness and fluidity. For monochronic cultures, the mighty oak is the strongest tree while for polychronic cultures, the flexible willow is the symbol of strength.

Different cultures value differently the amount of time devoted to the goal pursued. Americans want to make a deal quickly, reduce formalities to a minimum, and get down to business. For relationship-oriented cultures, a need exists to invest time in the process so that the parties can get to know one another well and determine whether they wish to embark on a long-term relationship. The Japanese view time as a continuum and are long-term oriented; they are conservative and patient. In the West time is a commodity in limited supply; it can be saved, wasted, controlled or organized. In the Near East time is not scarce. In Arabic cultures, it can be foolish to plan for "only Allah can know the future." *Ansh'Allah* it is said, "God Willing." In Ireland, time is less important as "God made so much of it."

For the French, traditionally, concern is not on time but on precision and quality. While Americans typically opt for the deadline, the French will opt for taking what they consider a reasonable amount of extra time to get the product or project to the level of quality they believe necessary. Americans see the deadline, the schedule as more important, while the French view the quality as their primary concern.

WHEN TO NEGOTIATE?

Climatic conditions may influence timing if negotiations are expected to be lengthy. Both good times and bad times to negotiate exist and vary from country to country, from region to region. Stay away from traveling and conducting negotiations during holidays and vacation periods. German and French businesspeople take far more vacation days than do Americans, and do not expect to conduct business on weekends or holidays. In France, August, the traditional month for vacations, is an extremely difficult time to contact a businessperson let alone bargain with him or her; almost everyone is on holiday during that time frame. In China and Korea, little business is transacted on the lunar new year, which falls in late January or February. Many Japanese businesses are closed from April 29 to May 5 for spring vacation. Australians and Chileans take their summer vacation in January and February.

Religious and national holidays should be checked (i.e., it is advised not to engage in negotiations in the Middle East during Ramadan [March] when Moslem true believers fast from dawn to dusk). In the United States, the time frame between Thanksgiving and New Years can be considered lost time and unproductive for negotiations. Passport and visa requirements and health certifications may require time before leaving and may limit one's stay within a country.

NONTASK AND RELATIONSHIPS

Different cultures value differently the amount of time devoted to the goal pursued. Often negotiations will not be allowed to progress until the foreign negotiators are able to understand their counterparts as people. The more consequential and long-term the deal under discussion, the more time and effort will need to be spent developing a relationship before beginning substantive discussions. In certain countries such as India, Nepal, or Sri Lanka or in the Middle Eastern countries such as Egypt or Saudi Arabia, the social contacts developed between parties are more significant than the technical specifications and price.

The first stage of a negotiation, nontask sounding, includes all those activities that might be described as establishing a rapport or getting to know one another, but does not include information related to the "business" of the meeting. A fundamental difference between American culture and those who rely more heavily on personal relationships in business is one of attitude. An American is more apt to size up the other side within the context that is, "getting down to business." In some cultures, such an approach is considered brash or too aggressive, and may create a sense of uncertainty. The Japanese, for example, feel uncomfortable with the American urgency to get down to business. Establishing rapport or nontask sounding in cultures like the Japanese is not achieved through the exchange of information related to the business of the meeting as would probably be the case among American negotiators, but rather through a focus on getting to know the parties as individuals. Nontask sounding is general discussion between the parties of negotiation, learning about one another, learning to feel comfortable with one another, and getting an impression of what kind of person the other is.

The Japanese negotiation process usually starts with an introduction from a reference, a go-between, a *shokai-sha* (third-party introducer), who has arranged the initial meeting. It is preferred that the *shokai-sha* has a strong relationship with the buyer and thus is influential; the buyer does not want to damage the harmony and the relationship with *shokai-sha* by rejecting the proposal. He usually attends the first meeting as well as the last meeting, the signing ceremony. Before the first meeting he is a prime source of information for both parties. In case of an impasse in the talks between the two sides (either during the negotiations or afterward, during normal conduct of business), he is often asked to become involved to settle their dispute, to become a *chukai-sha* (mediator). At the first business meeting, the highest level of protocol is used for important strangers or those who must be shown a high degree of respect.

Japanese executives spend substantial time and effort in nontask sounding so problems do not develop later. The Japanese believe that once the relationship has been established, further negotiations will proceed more smoothly and quickly. Three levels of executives are typically involved—top-level, middle managers, and operational staff. The top executives are brought into the negotiations to sign the agreement only after all the issues have been settled and agreed upon by lower-level executives. The use of top executives communicates commitment and importance. The executive meetings are held in relaxed and comfortable accommodations, such as restaurants and hotels. The Japanese executives are making judgments about the others' integrity, reliability, commitment, and humility. Middle managers are there to bless intermediate agreements; operational staff executives are there to negotiate. During this stage of business introduction, the Japanese attempt to discover the other's position and the mission.

Every member of the Japanese negotiating team must meet and feel comfortable with every member of the other side's negotiating team. Information specific to the issue under negotiation is not considered in the beginning; rather, the parties seek to get to know each other. This stage may include entertainment and gift giving. The Japanese believe that if a harmonious relationship can be established at the beginning of the negotiating process, the conflicts can be avoided later on. Considerable time and expense are thus devoted to getting to know each other. Americans negotiate a contract, the Japanese a relationship. In Japan, as in many other cultures, the written word is primarily used to satisfy legalities.

In the view of the Japanese, emotion and personal relations are more important than cold facts in business relations. The key issue is: "Can I get along with these men and their company and do I want to sell (or buy) their products?" rather than "Can I make money on this deal?" The Japanese are particularly interested in the sincerity of those they are negotiating with. The Japanese are typically unwilling to do business with someone they think may prove to be arrogant, unpleasant, or does not like them as individuals, a company, or a nation as a whole: "I do not do business with a man who does not like us!" Japanese do not separate personal feelings from business relationships. The Japanese feel that if their relationship is not yet anchored and may drift, they will stall and hesitate to do business until they are comfortable with the other party. When two Japanese companies are creating a new relationship, they are accepting each other inside their respective groups.

Japanese are cautious in their interpersonal communication styles. In the Japanese culture, cautiousness signifies patience, dependability, and sincerity. Too much logical reasoning to the Japanese is often considered threatening, confrontational, and argumentative. The Japanese tend to base their understanding of people on intuition and a considerable amount of emotion. They have a tendency to avoid logical argument to achieve a sense of understanding. The United States is an objective society versus Japan's polyocular society: the Japanese take the view that all phenomena can be seen from multiple points of view, and the more angles, the more whole and comprehensive understanding will occur.

It is important for American businesspersons to understand about nontask sounding since the American businessman/women traditionally does not engage in "small talk" before an agreement. While the American businessperson is interested in learning more about the person with whom he/she is negotiating, generally that impression is gained while discussing business issues. The American businessperson must appreciate that in some cultures such behavior will appear to be rude. The time spent in establishing rapport or nontask sounding determines the ultimate success of the negotiation. If the negotiator is not comfortable with the individual as a person, the negotiation may continue but it will seldom end successfully since that first step is not achieved. In those cultures where a personal friendship is required, future disputes or problems can not be adequately resolved unless the relationship has been established. As a rule, the more consequential and long term the deal under discussion, the more time and effort will need to be spent developing a relationship before substantive discussions can begin.

TIME AS USED IN NEGOTIATING

The Japanese prefer relatively brief sessions, but they need many sessions with a great deal of time between them. The group must thoroughly discuss all issues and reach consensus on their next position before they meet again with the other side. Therefore, a negotiation that might require a few days for two American companies can take months in Japan. The Japanese should never be placed in a position in which they must admit failure or impotency. They resist pressure for deadlines and delivery dates. When negotiating with the Japanese, you need a completely different beginning game. They often want to spend days or even weeks creating a friendly, trusting atmosphere before discussing business. Positions are expressed indirectly to obscure conflicts, even though you are negotiating to resolve these conflicts. Direct questions are regarded as rude, and the meaning of answers may depend upon extremely subtle signals. They spend considerable amounts of time asking detailed questions about financial, market, manufacturing, and structural issues relevant to the negotiation, as well as questions that some outsiders would perceive as irrelevant. The Japanese also tend to spend time becoming acquainted with the potential partner before developing the framework for a partnership.

Arabs tend to have long negotiating sessions with extensive and perhaps repetitious philosophical discussions, but there are relatively few sessions. Therefore, the total negotiating time may not be particularly long. Russian negotiators tend to be stonewallers. They will spend an extraordinary amount of time, and repeat positions again and again, slowly wearing you down. The Russians are often unpredictable, arriving late for appointments or simply canceling them without notice. Social competence is paramount in Latin business. Handshaking and asking about the health and well-being of business contacts and their families are expected. In business, people are addressed by their titles and maternal and paternal surnames. Business cards are exchanged an should include he negotiator's academic degrees. In India, building relationships is important, and as such, a longer period of introduction is necessary. One should use titles to convey respect.

The objective of typical American negotiators is usually to arrive at legalistic contracts, and therefore the dominant concern is with getting the details right, and to using all relationships to facilitate the achievement of unambiguous understandings. Consequently, they tend to minimize time spent in nontask related activities at the beginning of negotiations. American negotiators usually operate as if today is the last day of their lives: negotiating with conviction and interpreting delays and hesitation as signs of stalling or ineptitude. They often exhibit words and behaviors perceived as tough or insensitive. The English and Americans deal with issues concurrently but separately, they like all subjects brought to the table but dealt with only one at a time. Germans spend a lot of time on procedural aspects. They want well-planned, well-organized negotiations that are efficient and effective and they use agenda-setting and organizing as a means of achieving these goals.

For the Chinese, since time is cyclical, deadlines are not understood and not therefore restrictive. Chinese see the negotiating process as an opportunity to elicit as much information as possible, particularly that of a technical nature. This tendency may be associated with the issue of face and their reluctance to display ignorance. They tend to understand in terms of wholes and total systems and their appreciation of technology may be limited until they have grasped how the diverse elements fit into the system. The Chinese approach to the negotiating process is to establish a human relationship, often in an essentially dependent nature. Therefore, their prime goal is to create the bonding of "friendship."

The Chinese consider mutual relationships and trust very important. Therefore, in the beginning time will be spent enjoying tea and social talk. However, they are some of the toughest negotiators in the world. Technical competence of the negotiators is necessary, and a noncondescending attitude is important because the Chinese research their opponents thoroughly to gain a competitive advantage during negotiation. Nothing is final until it is signed. The Chinese tend to stress at the outset their commitment to abstract principles and will make concessions only at the eleventh hour after they have fully assessed the limits of their interlocutor's flexibility. After protracted exchanges, when a deadlock seems to have been reached, concessions may be made to consummate an agreement.

Patience in negotiating with the Chinese is based on the following assumptions: The Chinese must have time to receive and digest any information they need; The Chinese bureaucracy is sluggish and slow; The Chinese have a long-range perspective and are not in a hurry; The Chinese want to avoid mistakes and want to be sure of everything; The Chinese have a great need to build relationships; Chinese subordinates have great fear of criticism from above; and the Chinese do not trust fast talkers who want to make quick deals. Patience is the negotiator's most important asset. The Chinese take it very easy and check all possible implications of the issues under discussion. They do not want to make mistakes. They fear that they may be criticized later on and be blamed for possible future problems. The Chinese often seem to feel no pressure to respond promptly to the other party's initiatives but when they make a proposal they expect immediate responses. They complain about foot dragging and suggest that delays violate the spirit of the relations. Chinese view life as a flowing stream, simultaneously blending into each other, before and after, nothing ever ends.

Asian negotiation is as much a ceremony as it is a form of business communication. The negotiation style in the Asian context is often described as relationship-oriented, and concentrates on a long-term single-source arrangement. The implication of this style is that it is collaborative and will lead to some mutual satisfaction. The form is very important. In contrast, the American style of negotiation is to concentrate on the instrumental and results as an outcome. Focus on the instrumental is very characteristic of Western cultures. When the Taoist concept of *wu wei* (nonassertion) is applied to business negotiation, the strategy is to seek long-term success through minimal short-term effort: state a position and wait, hoping that opponents will yield on concessions in order to close the deal. Time is not money for Asian negotiators; it's a weapon. Asian negotiators often open a negotiation, extend an invitation to visit their country, supply some technical information, and dedicate time and resources to forgiving an agreement. Unfortunately, the final contract remains elusive.

Brazilians are more concerned about the involvement of people and the completion of a transaction rather than adherence to preset schedules. Brazilians like to take time in developing a long-lasting business relationship; getting down to business is viewed as inefficient and rude. Lunch is a time to develop rapport rather than to discuss pure business. One should not cut corners in establishing a trust relationship and less emphasis is placed on time.

Although most Thais are highly punctual and consider it discourteous not to be, a negotiation will last for as long as it takes to establish a long-term relationship; artificial constraints such as time and schedules will not be placed on their negotiating and decision-making processes. In Mexico, time commitments are desirable objectives, not firm promises. Mexicans are people oriented rather than task oriented; they do not allow schedules or business to interfere with family or friends.

Spanish negotiators require establishing personal rapport as a first step to building loyalty and trust, centering on family and mutual friends. The Spanish believe time is plentiful and take their time. The Spanish view negotiating as an enjoyable process, where the results are almost by-products. While Chinese hosts structure the negotiating environment to enhance a sense of obligation on the part of their guests.

TIME AS A NEGOTIATING TACTIC

Time moves at a different pace for the Chinese and most Orientals. Chinese are more sedate, and they move at a rate that will please them and at a pace that is in their own self and national interests. This slowdown is sometimes used as a conscious bargaining ploy to exploit natural American tendencies for impatience. One could call this technique the "Chinese Great Wall Syndrome" or, when used by the Japanese, the "Japanese Ginza Tactic": the foreign hosts take the visitors touring and entertaining (Great Wall, Ming Tombs, Forbidden City, Temple of Heaven or in the case of the Japanese, Mount Fuji, Tokyo Harbor, the Ginza) until the end of his deadline and then negotiate a very favorable agreement. To the Westerner, particularly Americans, they would rather spend time leisurely sightseeing and chatting than negotiating the agreeemnt. It could also be partly host, partly friendship/relationship oriented. Chinese use time in raising key issues at awkward moments—at late night banquets. Locals proceed to throw elaborate dinners, whisking them from one cultural site to another. The talks then begin a day before they are scheduled to depart. The hosts remain steadfast and refuse to make the slightest compromise. As departure time nears, the Americans become anxious and make large concessions in order to reach an agreement, even in one classic case, making final concessions or signing the agreement in the limousine speeding to the airport. Stall tactics are especially effective when dealing with Americans due to their impatience and seriousness given to deadlines. Two methods to handle delaying tactics are to hold up the possibility of competition, or adhere steadfastly to the schedule.

The Chinese are masters of the creative use of fatigue. If your hosts fill nearly every minute of your stay with social events, they are controlling your time. You have less chance to discover alternatives, make other contacts, or to review the discussions thoroughly. By controlling your activities, they have reduced your negotiating leverage. Lavish hospitality is often generated to create obligation on a personal level, which it is hoped will then cause you to make decisions favorable to your generous hosts (which may or may not be in the best interests of you or your organization). Do not reject the hospitality but reciprocate so as to eliminate any obligations you may have incurred. To be honest though, in the case of the Chinese, delays are frequently caused by the fact that the Chinese negotiators want to be certain of all details and provisions of the contract and not be held liable by their superiors for any mistakes. The Chinese play off rivals for their business. Often rivals will be invited for discussions at the same time in different rooms of the same building (or even the same room at adjacent tables). The rival has the opportunity to match or better your offer, and you his, and so on.

Delays could also mean, as in the case of the Japanese, an intense studying of the proposal as a consequence of soliciting approval from all company departments that will be affected by the outcome of the negotiation. With the Japanese, one would want to schedule many sessions with a great deal of time between each (weeks or even a month) in order to allow the *ringi* (the Japanese consensus decision-making process) to operate. Delays from Mexicans are indicative of the different view of time most Latins have; they are more relaxed and in less of a hurry than most North Americans. While a Latin or Asian might be concerned about hosting you properly, an American might see endless hosting behavior as evasive, an attempt to avoid substantive issues. However, any delays due to hosting behavior is strictly relationship building.

Asians use delays for several reasons. Delay could be used to test the will and patience of foreigners and to attempt to intimidate them. Another possible reason for delay is that an Asian wants to kill a deal without losing face and hopes the Westerner will take the hint and walk away as a friend, not a frustrated foe. When Asian negotiators use delay tactics that push foreigners to the brink of anger, they many be seeking more than concessions. They may be testing the Westerners' commitment to a deal or their accountability. They may want to clarify the unequal status between buyer and seller. By delaying, they send a message that their interest may be waning; the Westerners may weaken in their resolve to hold out for a stated price.

Koreans tend to be especially keen to take advantage of negotiation deadlines by inflicting numerous delays with the help of flimsy excuses. The Soviets often tried to wear down their counterparts with tactics such as all-night negotiating sessions. The Soviets wished to conduct long sessions at times and places convenient only to themselves or unpleasant to the opposition. In the initial stages of a negotiation, Russians tend to show little interest in order to exhaust the opposition and gain concessions. Negotiations can often be long, arduous, and demanding due to the bureaucracy..

Delays can be intentional—sometimes not because the opposing negotiators are being extra careful in evaluating your arguments, but because they do not like them. They are waiting for you to change your position. Some foreign negotiators do not perceive or catch these hints and become irritated by the delay.

An explicit threat with a time limit can be a potent weapon; however, prudent negotiators use it only when they are fully prepared to carry it out or are certain that they will not be challenged. A time limit makes it all too apparent if they are caught bluffing, and this damages the credibility of their threats in the future.

Other commonly used tactics include (1) intimidation by creating physical or emotional discomfort (providing insufficient heat or air conditioning, light, ventilation, seating you facing blinding sunlight, permitting constant interruptions, setting aside no time for lunch, ongoing discussions with insufficient time for rest; and (2) putting last-minute time constraints on the table to extract last-minute concessions. The Chinese have the reputation of waiting until the negotiator is practically on the plane to provide definite answers.

PLANNING AND BRIEFING

Preparation is of great importance. Skillful negotiators prepare more intensely than do others. Planning is the largest single factor in determining success or failure of negotiations. Meetings tend to fail in inverse proportion to the time spent in preparation and in direct proportion to the time spent preparing. During the preparation stage, as much information relevant to the negotiation should be assembled as practically as is possible. The preparation includes research, selecting negotiators, choosing a negotiating strategy, and making various tactical choices. Being prepared means being physical and mentally rested, in top condition both physically and mentally. International negotiations can be mentally demanding due to time zone changes, and different cultures, languages, foods, and lodging. The likelihood for serious health problems also increases due to stress and culture shock. A negotiator should probably refuse to begin until ready, both physically and technically.

The team should adequately prepare for negotiation before it leaves home. It should conduct extensive preparatory meetings during which members share what they know about the other side, determine the information they need to get, anticipate the other side's proposals and positions, identify their own and the other side's underlying interests, and decide on a bottom line—the point at which they will walk away from the discussions. Frequent caucuses are helpful during negotiations with foreigners, since the caucuses help relieve the tensions introduced by different cultural and business practices.

In addition, the team should plan on arriving at least one to two days before the start of the actual negotiations. This time will allow for acclimatization, discussions with the interpreter/bicultural broker, survey of the meeting site, and for last-minute checks on all material necessary for the negotiations. Additional time may be necessary depending on the level of the talks and the time planned for the discussions.

7

Who: More or Less— the Composition of the Negotiating Team

Teams that include women could provide advantages in areas such as Scandinavia where female participation is taken for granted but disadvantages in more masculine societies such as Japan and Arab countries. Some cultures provide great status to seniority—Japanese and Chinese—and expect the other side to do likewise. An Asian team is likely to be led by a senior older person who may lose face if forced to deal with a younger person as an equal. In many countries and in many cultures throughout the world, it is customary for the general principles of an agreement to be worked out by high-level officials and the details by more junior staff.

Due to the long-term nature of many international negotiations, often members of the teams will change. Discussions may be started with one manager only to have a different manager for the next session. The people who will be dealing with the other side on a continuing basis should be part of the team that negotiates the initial agreement. A stable negotiating team can facilitate negotiations. In addition, being aware of the history of the negotiations helps to clarify what the parties had in mind when they drafted specific provisions of the contract. Also in many countries, particularly Asian, promises made are viewed as having been made to individuals, not company representatives. If the person implementing the agreement were not involved in the initial negotiation, the other side may feel less bound to comply with its contractual requirements. Lack of continuity among members of the negotiating team also often conveys a message of unreliability and disorganization. The will of the group in Japan, the decision taken, the path to be followed is often revealed by the senior negotiator. Each member of the team has a specific role to play in the negotiation and the spokesman for the group is often the one senior individual present, often the one sitting in the center of the group.

STATUS AND SELECTION

Gender, competence, experience, status, age, even personal attributes can all be used as criteria in choosing individuals to send to the negotiating table. If two cultures that use different sets of negotiator selection criteria meet at the negotiation table, a tremendous clash of expectations will definitely occur. For the typical American team, who usually chooses its negotiators on the basis of substantive knowledge of the issues at the table, gender or age of the negotiator is often incidental to the composition of the team. Gender and age, though, often play key roles in the selection of the negotiator in other countries. For status-conscious societies, young American businesspersons are not well received: it is difficult for them to believe that someone so young has decision-making authority.

Hierarchy is important to many East Asian cultures and one will not make much progress with East Asians until they know where they stand vis-a-vis status with you. For the Japanese, the most senior official should be greeted first. The angle and duration of the bow is dependent upon the relative status of the two: the younger, less senior bows lower and longer as a way of establishing the proper relationship between the two individuals. Sending lower-level executives to negotiating sessions will convey insincerity and lack of respect and interest in the discussions; everything will move more slowly as a result. In these situations, matching team leaders becomes not a luxury but a requirement. Many societies are status conscious and demand an opposite number with equivalent rank. The Korean negotiating team is selected on the basis of status, knowledge, and expertise. Traditionally, the elders were regarded as decision makers. Today, many younger individuals are involved in that role as well. Respect for elders, the family, education, and power is paramount to the Korean culture. Korea is a formal society and protocol is important.

In most Arab counrties one's family is the primary determinant of one's position. People get their jobs, status, and social position because of their family connections, almost without regard for their abilities. The same is true in most of Latin America and the developing nations in general. Despite their egalitarian rhetoric, the Soviets followed the same basic pattern, with one important exception: The children of high- ranking party officials went to the best schools and got the best jobs almost regardless of their ability, but their privileges were much less secure than those of the wealthy people in other countries. If the father is purged or demoted, the entire family suffered.

In Japan the picture is more complex. The Japanese measure individual achievement much less frequently and closely than we do, and promotions are based upon seniority except at the highest levels. For example, some companies do not formally evaluate an employee's performance for the first ten years of service, and every person hired at a certain time might get similar raises and promotions. However, Japanese companies do have an enormous commitment to the group's achievement.

Mexican negotiators are often selected for their skill at rhetoric and making distinguished performances. Negotiation is perceived from their perspective as a time to test Mexican honor and to determine the attitude of the opposing negotiators towards Mexico. In Latin America, it is not unusual to have key figures at the bargaining table who have little or no knowledge of the issues but are there because of their relationships with key industrial or political figures. French negotiators are often selected according to their schooling. Schooling and social class in France and in other parts of Europe, especially the United Kingdom, quite often determine who conducts business.

Germans are also extremely status conscious. One should always refer to one as "Herr" or "Doktor." Formality means wearing a suit at almost all times. Germans are hard bargainers because they are so well prepared and serious about their work. They are likely to ask you for business references, for demonstrations, and for testimonials. They want to talk to your technical people and your customers.

AUTHORITY AND DECISION MAKING

You clearly need to know people's negotiation authority. If you underestimate it, you may lose the deal. If you overestimate it, you may weaken your bargaining position. It can be difficult or impossible to learn it during the negotiations. People often lie to inflate their egos or to gain a negotiating advantage. Confirming the authority and responsibility of the other side's negotiator ahead of time can preempt use of lack of authority excuse. You should therefore try to determine their authority before the negotiations begin and confirm your judgment during the negotiations. In negotiating any deal, you do not engage the other side's entire organization but only its negotiation team, which acts as the link to the other organization. They act as agents for their companies and organizations. It is necessary to determine how much authority they actually have. A negotiator may have less decision-making ability than claimed; this permits the negotiator to save face if authority is revoked.

If someone does not have enough authority to negotiate a binding deal, try to avoid negotiating with that person. Otherwise, you may make concessions to reach a deal only to find that the other side rejects its negotiator's concessions and insists on additional negotiations (i.e., more concessions from you). The Soviets repeatedly used this technique. A Westerners reached an agreement with an apparently important person, and then was told, "Commissar Smirnov has been sent to Siberia for crimes against the people. We repudiate any agreements he has made, but will negotiate in good faith with all sincere parties." This approach is a variation on the salami technique. You have a salami, If someone tries to take it all at once, you would fight or leave. But you will not fight that hard for just one slice of salami. So the first negotiators take a slice. Then their bosses take a slice. Then their bosses take a slice, and so on, until they have your entire salami!

Restrictions on authority, such as the buyer who has approval limits, is more difficult to deal with than someone who has complete authority. Restrictions on authority, on the other hand, gives users negotiation strength. Authority limits provide the negotiator with a face-saving way of testing the firmness of an opposer's stance and provide him with a face-saving way of giving in. The Chinese, because of their bureaucratic need to diffuse responsibility and their social need to avoid loss of face, use such behaviors widely. The Russians often use it deliberately to exert pressure for price concessions.

Greek and Latin American top managers prefer to maintain personal control of all aspects of the process and may head the team rather than delegate this role to a subordinate. Sometimes, delays in the final decision arise because even members of the team are unsure as to who has the authority to agree. Chinese negotiators do not hesitate to stop a session in order to get instructions from their superiors. Chinese negotiating teams can have as many as ten or more members with vague responsibilities and no easily recognizable leader. It becomes necessary to determine who is actually in charge of the negotiating team and why that person was chosen to be the leader of the team. In Korea, the chairman has ultimate approval and only he can grant final agreement. Often it becomes necessary to hold out the final decision maker from the detailed negotiations to counter such tactics.

One must necessarily understand what is the negotiator's flexibility. For example, Japanese negotiators may have almost none. In many negotiations all they can do is report their team's position and listen as you report yours. Their decision-making pattern requires them to develop a consensus among many people after thoroughly discussing the alternatives. Any change in a position must therefore be referred back to those who participated in the original decisions.

Often the team on the other side of the table is not composed of the final decision makers. The Japanese often use the tactic of concealing their top man by positioning him on the fringe of his team, inconspicuously and initially making no contribution while a junior member acts as spokesman. The Japanese team leader might only be marginally technically competent in the specific subject matter under negotiation but still be the undisputed head: his credentials for leadership include seniority and frequently a degree from the right school. He may have been chosen because he represents the company consensus that was achieved before the negotiations started. His symbolic authority is high and his team gives him great deference. So one can't assume that the makeup of the other side's negotiating team is identical to your own team.

Internal decision-making systems can be consensus or authoritative. In the latter, leaders or powerful individuals make decisions without concern for consensus. Decision making is not delegated to the entire team. In consensus decision making, negotiators do not have the authority to make decisions without consulting superiors. The team leader must obtain support and listen to advice from team members.

SIZE OF NEGOTIATING TEAMS

The size and expertise of the negotiating team depends on the nature of the deal and the parties' cultural background. The number of negotiators considered appropriate for a negotiations vary by culture. Chinese teams tend to be large, following Mao's dictum of concentrating a superior force in numbers against the opposition. Chinese interpreters often have inadequate language skills. China typically sends a large team that includes not only functional experts and administrators but also representatives of local, provincial, and national authorities. The Chinese large negotiating teams are usually very well coordinated and operated as a cohesive unit. It, therefore becomes extremely difficult to impossible in playing off the interests of different Chinese. The Japanese negotiating teams will also usually consist of large groups.

Americans typically prefer to use small negotiating teams or even go it alone—the "John Wayne" syndrome of international negotiations, the lone gunslinger. Negotiating teams usually assembled by American companies are generally far too small, numbering one to two people. The rationale for doing so is typically cost. Advantages and disadvantages of this approach exist. A single negotiator has difficulty if faced with an entire team. Bringing a team to the negotiating table allows you to bring expertise to bear in each area under negotiation, allows you to benefit from instant input in areas of consideration, and provides the emotional support necessary to prevail. Tasks can be divided among team members. As some of these tasks must be preformed concurrently during negotiations, it becomes difficult, if not impossible, for the solo negotiator to do an adequate job. To avoid being intimidated by sheer numbers, the Western negotiator is well advised to be prepared to bring sufficient staff to provide numerical balance (including sufficient technical experts). Nonetheless, limits do exist; as the numbers rise, performance decreases and structure eventually becomes unworkable.

Americans tend to be regularly outnumbered by their foreign counterparts. Japanese and Chinese are noted for their massive delegations. American companies find it expensive to field a large team overseas. Managers may often decline the offer of additional help because they want all the credit for themselves (a fact nurtured by the accomplishment-oriented reward system). The typical American go-it-alone mentality puts American companies at a serious disadvantage when engaging in the international negotiating process. Effective negotiating requires a team effort. When a delegation is small, its members must perform many tasks concurrently, whereas a large team can divide responsibilities. One person can not do everything a team is capable of doing: One person does the speaking, another takes notes, the third analyzes the other side's replies, the fourth formulates strategies and tactics, the fifth develops questions, the sixth (bilingual) member watches over the interpretation and the other side's nonverbal messages, while the seventh takes the day off and returns refreshed the next day. The psychological benefits can not be underestimated. Having people on either side nodding in approval will confirm the correctness of your position. A large team in certain societies may also bestow prestige on the leader, suggesting that he or she is a powerful person. Nonetheless, large teams have their disadvantages as well: often when an American company does send over a large delegation, its members do not work well together, they do not have agreed upon positions, and have not spent sufficient time ironing out their differences. Coordination and consensus must be present.

Japanese typically negotiate in teams made up of experts in relevant fields. The negotiating team usually consists of five males with one member serving as the symbolic head. The first individual introduces the parties initially and facilitates the signing ceremony. The other four slots are typically filled by operational staff, middle managers, a CEO, and a mediator. The qualities admired and sought in Japanese negotiators include commitment, persistence, ability to gain respect, credibility, good listening skills, pragmatism, and a broad perspective. A successful negotiation reflects the efforts of the entire Japanese team. The senior negotiator sits in the middle of his team on one side rather than at the head of the table. The top Japanese executive is seated furthest from the door. Those with authority to make a deal sit to the leader's immediate side with those with lesser roles at the two ends. Japanese negotiations have an air of formal politeness, conservative conduct, and good manners. Proper business etiquette must be observed at all times.

Both advantages and disadvantages exist in negotiating by team. The advantages are having more complete preparation, several viewpoints, faster decision making, mental support, and strength in numbers. Having team negotiations are the norm in most nations. Disadvantages to team negotiating are that it is very expensive, it requires the careful management of many egos, and the roles and expectations of individual team members must be resolved before negotiations begin. In addition, the team must form a consensus before negotiating with the other side, as the opportunity for internal disagreement is substantial (differences regarding priorities, roles, and negotiating skills). Decision making can also be more cumbersome with more members, and the efficiency of decision making may suffer.

INTERMEDIARIES

To augment his or her own capabilities, a business negotiator can employ cultural experts, translators, outside attorneys, financial advisor, or technical experts who have at least moderate and preferably high familiarity with both the counterpart's and the negotiator's cultures. These experts serve two distinguishable roles: as "agents" who replace the negotiator at the negotiating table or as "advisers" who provide information and recommend sources of action to the negotiator. The Japanese prefer to follow an indirect, harmonious style when dealing with others. Go-betweens help move the process along and interpersonal harmony is considered more important than confrontation. The use of go-betweens, middlemen, brokers, and other intermediaries is a common practice within many cultures and represents a truly potentially effective approach to cross-cultural negotiation as well.

In Latin American countries, black Africa and parts of Asia and most Arab countries, the use of family and friendship ties is widespread and is a necessary and important means of doing business. To these, using personal ties and connections, because of their reciprocal nature, means using up old credits or accumulating new liabilities. There is usually a value attached to the use of personal connections.

LAWYERS

American teams often include a legal representative, which could have an adverse effect when dealing with cultures (particularly Asian) that stress conciliation and compromise rather than conflict. Lawyers do not enjoy as much prestige in most cultures as they do in America. Lawyers are not always well liked. "May your life be filled with lawyers," says an old Mexican curse. Lawyers in these countries (Mexico, Japan) rarely participate in the actual negotiations and are used only to review the terms. From the American perspective, bringing in a lawyer early may indicate that the talks have gone smoothly and that only loose ends have to be tied up. However, the foreign negotiators may conclude that the Americans do not trust them.

In some cultures, lawyers are considered to be more of a problem, a hindrance to an agreement, than an advantage. In Japan, rarely is an attorney present during the initial part of the negotiation or thereafter. Lawyers do not enjoy as much prestige in Japan as they do in America. The Japanese view lawyers as people who complicate the personal relationships, get in the way of basic understanding and of allowing the parties to get to know each other better, and in general obstruct the development of necessary cooperative business relationships. A long-term business relationship between two parties in Japan is expected to be built on the principles of mutual trust, friendship, and cooperation rather than on the legalistic grounds that a lawyer would tend to emphasize. The Japanese regard the introduction of an attorney into a business negotiation as an unfriendly act, a sign of distrust, or an implied threat of litigation since lawyers are traditionally used for that specific purpose in Japan. This naturally bodes ill for the negotiation. Bringing a lawyer to one's first meeting with a Japanese company is often the kiss of death to an agreement. Any contract is secondary in business transactions to the harmonious relationships; Japanese negotiators prefer conciliation and mediation over litigation. The Chinese also shun legal considerations and instead stress ethical principles. In some cultures, the use of lawyers as negotiators raises concerns on the other side about possible future lawsuits. In these situations, they should be introduced as advisers or counselors rather than lawyers.

The Japanese prefer conciliation and mediation over litigation in business matters for several reasons: reduced costs, the limited number of attorneys in Japan (some cases drag on for as long as ten years before a final decision is reached; and the Japanese emphasis on harmony or reconciliation (*chotei*). The prewar Japanese Constitution stated that "Japan must strive to resolve interpersonal cases by harmony and compromise." Arbitration is viewed as a negative action which damages the business relationship. Legal approaches and confrontation are rarely used. Those approaches would destroy the harmony and trust required for continued business dealing and it is almost impossible to regain once it is lost. The Japanese wish to maintain the relationship for mutual benefit rather than seek a one-time gain.

RISK AND REWARDS

The attitude of a culture towards taking of risk certainly can affect the negotiating style and behaviors of that culture in international business negotiations. The low risk-taking propensity of many Latin cultures is partly based on a fatalistic attitude toward the world: since bad things will always happen, one should be extremely careful in one's actions in order to avoid running an even greater risk of bringing on negative situations. In Japan, low risk-taking comes about from the fact that the unexpected can easily destroy the harmony so carefully and longingly established.

Risk is omnipresent in the world, and especially so in the conduct of international business negotiations. Negotiators are subject to several kinds of risk, including image loss (in the eyes of other negotiators), position loss, and information loss. Power in a negotiation is created by the perceptions of the negotiators about their ability to influence each other. It is not necessary to create an incentive to negotiate. Power may be exercised without mention or use or it may be diminished by its exercise or threatened exercise. The degree of one's power is measured by the ability to achieve a given result with the least effort or expenditure.

TRUST

Cultures also divide on trust, some basing trust on law while others base it on friendship. The French are more inclined to mistrust until faith and trust is proven by their counterparts. Trust has to be earned; the French are only truly impressed by results. Trust based upon written laws establishes codes of conduct. If an agreement is broken, negotiators from such cultures expect some higher authority to impose sanctions or force performance. Trust based upon friendship and esteem relies upon the harmonious nature of the relationship to ensure that expectations will be fulfilled. You trust the other side when you believe in the truthfulness of what the other party says. When there is high trust, negotiators are more more likely to take a mutual problem solving approach and to share information. When trust is low, they tend instead to depend heavily upon persuasive arguments, threats, and other forms of confrontational behavior. In Arabic cultures, the need to become family is critical for trust and agreement to occur.

It is in their interests to do business with you. They will not resort to unethical behavior during the negotiation process. They will respect information and opinions made in confidence and not leak these to outsiders. They will do their best to convince their constituents to accept any agreements that they make with you. They will do their best to implement the agreement. In cultures like China and Japan, pride and honor are of great importance. Because of the influence of Confuciansm, honesty, integrity, and sincerity in dealmaking are greatly appreciated in these countries. Negotiators from the PRC tend to play up notions of friendship, mutual interest, and the importance of shared trust, then appeal to these principles at later meetings in order to shame their counterparts into giving them the best possible terms.

High power distance cultures correlate with low degrees of trust. Russians respond to unknown outsiders with fear and suspicion but have strong loyalty to those outsiders with whom they are able to develop personal relationships. High trust cultures tend to be the Anglo-American and East Asian. Low trust cultures include those of Japan, Greece and other Mediterranean countries, and Latin American countries. Trust becomes crucial when building personal relationships. Issues of trust are the most difficult relationship problems to repair. American negotiators often try to resolve issues of trust by formalizing the intent of the parties in an ironclad contract; they then try to hold the other side to the contract, regardless. In many cultures, it is the person or the relationship that your counterpart trusts, not a piece of paper. Building trust is a long process but worth every effort.

JAPANESE NEGOTIATIONS

In negotiations with the Japanese, the word "negotiate" and its usual translation *kosho* have different meanings. *Kosho* has nuances of fighting, conflict, strategy (*senryaku*), and verbal debate (*iiau*), whereas Western-style negotiations lacks these overtones and usually suggests discussion, concession, and conference (March, 1985). Negotiations between Japanese is like that between father and son. The status relationship is explicit and important. The son (seller) carefully explains his situation and asks for as much as possible because he will have no chance to bicker once the father (buyer) decides. The son (seller) accepts the decision because it would hurt the relationship to argue and because he trusts the father (buyer) to care for his needs.

The Japanese negotiation process is based on the importance of maintaining harmony in relationships. Norms are established concerning obligations to others, benevolence, and the importance of others' attitudes. The Japanese see negotiation as a fluid irrational process, calling for diligent preparation. Instead of addressing issues directly and openly stating positions and counterproposals, they prefer to infer the other party's assessment of the situation. The Japanese often repeat previously stated positions, using highly ambiguous language and appear to be inconsistent. The goal of this process is a just, fair, and proper deal and a long-term harmonious relationship. To a Japanese businessman, a business negotiation is a time to develop a business relationship with the goal of long-term mutual benefit. The economic issues are the context, not the content of the talks. Once the relationship is established, the other details can be settled quickly. In Japan, personal relationships are always subsumed within the context of a business relationship—friendship first and business second.

The Japanese tend to look at negotiations as war, a macho challenge. This behavior goes back to the high level of masculinity within the culture. The Japanese concept of masculinity includes achievement, heroism, assertiveness, and material success. They believe in the rightness of their initial position. The Japanese when pressed explain their position fully and explain their underlying intentions in order to persuade the other side of the rightness of the Japanese position, but they will hesitate to yield their own position. In Japan, the negotiator comes to the table having already discussed with other departments the terms under which to settle and cannot accept substantial modifications without checking back. Thus the consensus, once made, can not be changed unless the entire process is undergone again.

American informality in downplaying status, in using first names, in attire, and in other ways of showing casualness is not universal, and in particular does not apply at all in Japan. The Japanese dress conservatively—they always prefer dark business suits. To be dressed casually during negotiations with the Japanese would therefore be inappropriate. The Japanese do not believe in using first names unless it is between the very best of personal relationships. In Japan honorifics, title, and status are extremely important; one addresses his or her counterparts by their proper title.

Japanese bargainers bring with them a carefully considered agenda. The Japanese are more flexible toward setting the order of topics but much less flexible about the choice of topics. Before action is taken, much time is spent with relevant department heads defining the question, seeking their approval, and gathering sufficient information for a plan. The Japanese come to a negotiation with a hard-gained time-consuming intra-organizational consensus already established, which can not be easily changed at the bargaining table, no matter how small or seemingly irrelevant. To the Japanese, the Americans in their give and take appear insincere and unprepared as they do not appear to have a prepared position.

Japanese are as emotional as any other peoples but they direct that emotion toward or against others and tend not to display it on a personal basis. Japanese value emotions but hide them. The Japanese also go out of their way to conceal their sentiments; showing emotion is considered in bad taste and poor conduct for any Japanese, let alone a businessman. The Japanese proverbs *No aru taka wa tsume wo kakusu* ("an able hawk hides his talons") and *Tanki wa sonki* ("a short temper means a lost spirit") illustrate their feelings on showing emotion. Arguments and overt expressions of frustration or anger are considered detrimental to the spirit of friendship that should surround any interpersonal interaction; these are considered major character flaws and not appropriate behavior.

A formal display of emotion means loss of respect/face. Winning at the bargaining table is unacceptable if it involves loss of face (*kao*) for either party. The need to save face and not be a failure in the negotiating process are paramount considerations. Risk avoidance (*kiken kaihi*) is a key principle in Japanese negotiations. Confrontational negotiating techniques are seen as impolite and disrespectful and will not lead into a relationship of trust. The Japanese are deliberately vague on specific issues in the early stages of a negotiation, so that any later reversal will not result in loss of face. An outright rejection of a proposal would result in the loss of face.

The most important stage to a Japanese is the information gathering stage. In this stage, the information exchanged regarding both parties' needs and preferences or both parties' subjective expected utilities of the various alternatives are open to the participants (Graham, 1986). Only after the buying side feels that they have established a trustworthy relationship will business be brought up. Japanese negotiators are concerned with understanding the other side's point of view. Exchanging information and asking for more information is a constant with the Japanese. A complete understanding is imperative to them; they ask endless questions to identify the needs and preferences of both parties while offering little information and ambiguous responses so as to attempt to understand the situation and associated details of the other's bargaining position. The reasons for needs and preferences are critical data for Japanese, who seek to place information within an interpretive context. The Japanese tend to provide relatively little information; they are polite and seek to avoid offending the other side. It is important for the Japanese to be polite and to communicate the *tatemae* (face or facade)without giving offense, while holding back the possibly offensive but informative *honne* (real self). They present their needs and preferences in a tactful manner. Japanese firms operate through the consensus and group decision-making process. Each phase of the discussion process may generate more questions that must be answered. The emphasis is on exchanging extensive detailed information. A primary bargaining strategy of the Japanese is to ask questions to put the opponent on the defensive. Many times the initial meeting is merely used to gather information, which is then fed back to superiors and peers for deliberation and a carefully prepared response. The Japanese strongly believe it is folly to make an offer until one knows what the other side wants. This explains the emphasis on information gathering, and the long, drawn out preliminary ground work that is usually encountered when negotiating in Japan. The Japanese need detailed information to build the foundation for whatever decision they intend to put forward. No one is blamed or rebuked for shortcomings in the deal or the failure of the venture or negotiations, as all concerned managers participated in the negotiating and final decision making.

Sellers present in detail all of the background, and only toward the end is the actual request/proposal made. The information flows mainly from seller to buyer. Several people on the same side may ask for the same information or explanation; everyone must be convinced, not just the key decision maker. No Japanese, especially the boss, feels qualified to speak for the group before a consensus has been reached.

The concept of discussing problems in a systematic, sequential, and orderly manner is promoted by Americans while the Japanese prefer *haragei*, to talk around a subject in order to get a holistic view. Only after this is accomplished will they go into details. Japanese like to talk about practical solutions, resolving matters case by case. They allow the solution to precede the principle. The Japanese prefer avoiding any area in which an agreement cannot be easily reached. Instead they tend to move to another topic in its place. To Americans, this often appears like the Japanese are trying to elude the issue. To an American an unsolved issue is a point of contention. This, not any general principle, must be first dealt with before the agreement as a whole can be considered. To the Japanese, those very same traits indicate lack of confidence in one's convictions and insincerity. Instead, terms such as thoughtful, cooperative, considerate, and respectful instill positives in the Japanese culture. The Japanese stress areas of agreement and try to avoid contention.

8

Where:
Place

The negotiators' decision on the site for the talks is important. The environment has an impact upon the outcome. Negotiation parties often negotiate long and hard about where they will meet before they sit down to discuss what they will negotiate. Parties almost always assume that the location they choose will have consequences for the ensuring process and ultimately the result. Site selection is an important aspect of protocol because it affects psychological climate, availability and use of communications channels, and the presence of time limits. When negotiations take place in a foreign land, the host assumes responsibility for arranging the physical space; these may have strategic implications such as status and power. Rules of protocol govern location, welcoming, transportation, presentation of credentials, business cards, dress codes, entertainment, ceremonies, receptions, seating arrangements, documentation, and departure.

The location of negotiations can favor one side or another. The agreement of the Western allies to meet the Soviets in Soviet-controlled Potsdam in 1945 allowed Stalin to manipulate the negotiating environment to his advantage. As a result, negotiators tend to prefer neutral settings: Malta for the 1989 meeting between Presidents Bush and Gorbachev; Paris for the Vietnam peace talks; a raft in the middle of the Neman River when Napoleon Bonaparte and Czar Alexander I met in 1807.

In theory you hold territorial advantage when you negotiate on home turf; the home field advantage can be significant. One tends to be more comfortable and to have more confidence in one's own backyard. One is more familiar with the negotiating environment. Negotiating at home obviates the need to travel and is far less expensive. You are near your information and support systems, home and family, and in a familiar environment. It is, however, hard to claim limited authority or to walk out if the negotiations take place in your company offices. It is easy to be distracted by other business. However, one advantage is that your team will not be distracted by the charms of a new, foreign environment.

Playing host provides you with an opportunity to treat the other side like royalty, thereby enhancing the relationship and potentially even incurring obligation on the part of the other side. Hospitality also confers a measure of control. You know where your guests are and what they are doing; you never know what you might learn. Making the other side feel like guests often means that they end up respecting you more and potentially end up providing you with more concessions. If the other side comes to visit you, it is highly likely that they will not be quick to walk out. The pressure will be on them to make extra concessions. However, one must be careful because in many foreign cultures the responsibilities of the host are much more substantial than in the United States. Foreign guests may likely expect more hospitality than Americans generally accord one another. For instance, hosting a Chinese delegation can become a twenty-four hour-a-day obligation.

The other side, not you, must run the risk of culture shock. You don't have jet lag and the consequences arising from it—the inability to concentrate and react well. You also have the possibility of controlling the environment, including the selection and arrangement of the room itself, seating, and the nature and timing of hospitality events. Playing host gives you an opportunity to impress the other side with your organization, its capabilities, its power. You have the access to local experts for needed advice and to superiors for quick authorization and consultation Negotiating at home is cheaper, especially now when the dollar is down. The visiting negotiator is away from his or her personal life and support system. The longer one is away, the stronger the drive to return home and hence to conclude the negotiations at whatever the costs. To add to these pressures, the host might deliberately cause delays or unexpected events can also prolong negotiations.

The Chinese are skilled at using their role as hosts to control the timing of meetings, the arrangement of agendas, and the pacing of the negotiations. They make it very clear that it is the foreign businessperson who is coming to China and is seeking favors from the Chinese. This has been true for centuries, the Chinese reminding visitors from afar that they were the guests and that as hosts, the

Chinese should dictate procedures, timing, and agendas of meetings. Because of detailed waits and problems in gaining visas, it becomes clear that the foreign businessperson is able to operate only at the tolerance of the Chinese. The Chinese gain advantages of surprise and uncertainty in agenda arrangements. Often visitors are not even given a definite schedule of whom to see or where to go. By playing the host's role, the Chinese are able to play competitors off against each other. The type of hotel reservations made reflect judgments about the relative status of competitors. The overall effect of Chinese hospitality can be overwhelming and most every visitor to China leaves with warm sentiments for the hosts.

When the Chinese play host, it allows them to use the tactic of surprise and uncertainty in their agenda. China can be an overwhelming experience for first-time visitors. Often living arrangements are not up to Western standards or expectations and can produce in visitors an impatience to get the deal over with and return home. The Chinese sometimes try to influence the other party by shaming them, by making them believe the difficulties and problems are of their own begetting, are their fault. Chinese hosts delight in structuring a negotiating environment that enhances a sense of obligation on the part of their guests. The Chinese seek a relationship with permanence, steadfastness, and faithfulness. To win them over it would be best if the Westerner could achieve some proficiency in Chinese, get to understand the intricacies of the culture, and live or at least visit the country as often as possible.

Often one has no choice but to go to the other's country. If you are the seller, usually you must initiate the relationship and call on the potential buyer. Numerous advantages exist in going there to learn about the other side and the environment. One may also wish to investigate the political or economic climate and consult with other people there.

Although there are many disadvantages to negotiating at the other side's location, it may well be necessary to view the other side, its facilities, its personnel, and its capabilities firsthand. The main advantage of going to the other country is that you have the opportunity to learn about the other side, its way of life. If you can get to visit the physical plant of the other side, so much the better; this can provide you with valuable data regarding the company's operations, its modernity, and professionalism. By going to the other side's territory, you show your seriousness of intent and desire to make a deal, signaling commitment. Sometimes, restrictions exist on the other side's personnel such that there really is no viable option except to travel to the other side's home base. However, negotiating at the other side's place could enable you to hide from your own constituents in cases about which you would prefer the negotiations to be secret. The visit may also provide insights into their capacities and how they manage their operations. Visiting the other side's turf may also save their expenses and thus express your concern and interest in their affairs.

Nonetheless, many disadvantages exist to negotiating in the host country. Culture shock and the physical and mental discomfort that results from it is always a potential liability. Physical fatigue, jet lag, is real and can hinder your negotiating efforts. Eat lightly and drink alcohol in moderation on the trip over. Give yourself a day or two before the negotiations to get acclimated. Being away from home can be expensive, frustrating, and time-consuming. One is away from one's support system. If you are the visitor, do not necessarily divulge the timing of your return trip. This may give the other side the edge on how to pace the negotiations, allowing them to wait until you are just ready to depart before discussing key issues. If you are the visitor, do not let the time, money, and investments in the trip dissuade you from the planning you have performed beforehand. Do not concede merely to close the deal; the best deal may be no deal at all.

An alternative often used is to alternate between their place and yours. Both parties share in the expense and time of traveling. Both parties have now made investments in the negotiations. Either is less likely to unfairly manipulate the environment for fear of retaliation by the other. The choice of a neutral location provides neither party with special advantages or disadvantages. It also is the proverbial worst of both worlds in that neither party has the opportunity to observe or learn about the other. If the learning is not necessary, time and convenience may mandate a neutral location. In times of conflict, it also may be a preferred option. One must also never assume that a neutral site, especially one suggested by the other side, is necessarily neutral.

A fourth alternative is to negotiate from both sites, linked by teleconferencing, videoconferenceing fax, and phone. However, personal meetings may still be necessary. High-context societies like to meet the other party and establish a physical, personal relationship. The Japanese attempt to conduct real negotiations away from the formal negotiating hall, using formal session to announce agreements reached elsewhere. Often the real negotiation is between the lowest-level bargainers who have established a rapport, a relationship of trust with the equivalent operational level manager on the other side. This is often done after hours, usually in one of the many bars and restaurants in Tokyo.

9

What:
Contract

Negotiations are entered into only for the purpose of reaching an agreement. An agreement is an exchange of conditional promises in which each party declares that it will act in a certain way on condition that the other parties act in accordance with their promises. Depending upon cultures involved, promise breaking is tolerated, expected, or even desired. Contracts are rarely easier to enforce in foreign countries than in the United States and achieving a remedy based on the legal merits may be impossible. In Korea, do not sign a contract in red ink, as it means you expect it will come to a bad end.

Two types of agreements exist: an explicit, detailed, written contract that covers all contingencies and requires no future cooperation and binds the parties through an outside enforcement mechanism. The explicit contract assumes that no relationship exists between the parties apart from the exchange (personal relationships are unnecessary and friendship may be a hindrance). Communication is limited, covering only substantive issues, is formal, and relies heavily on technical language. Obligations are limited to those specific, detailed actions provided in the contract. Although circumstances may change, obligations do not, and each is bound to his explicit commitment.

The other is an implicit, broad, oral agreement that, in accepting unforeseen change as normal, leaves room for the parties to deal with the problems and begins the formation of personal relationships. The implicit agreement assumes that the importance of the relationship overrides substantive concerns. Implicit agreements depend heavily on relationship. They tend to be more concerned with personal noneconomic satisfactions than the substantive exchange. Communications is extensive, covering subjects apart from the substantive concerns of the negotiations, formal and informal and verbal and nonverbal. Obligations are unlimited and unmeasurable. The future cannot be foreseen or included. Trouble is expected, maneuverability is left. The negotiations process is long and drawn out.

Arbitration is the most widely used method of settling international disputes. It is basically a process whereby two groups or persons agree to submit the dispute to a non-aligned third person and further agree that they will carry out that third person's decisions. Arbitration avoids going to court and the uncertainties of an unknown legal system. International arbitration has a time-tested set of rules and procedures to govern the arbitration, the organization to manage the proceedings, and an established group of experienced arbitrators.

In some cultures, the negotiations process effectively ends when the contract is signed, elsewhere it may not be so. From the American perspective, a contract represents the culmination of a series of negotiations, the end result of an arrangement, the development and delineation of procedures, rules, regulations, and standards, by which all parties agree to behave with each other from that point forward until the exact state stipulated as the termination date of the contract. Under the terms of the developed contract, there can be no variation, no modification unless so indicated and agreed within the contract. That is why American contracts are lengthy; every contingency must be carefully anticipated and thought through ahead of time. The contract becomes a contract of objectively verifiable and predictable action between two parties. An American would not hesitate to sign a contract with his or her own worst enemy, if it were sufficiently endowed in legal terms and offered him or her sufficient profit potential.

In Anglo-Saxon cultures, the action of signing a contract symbolizes an intention to fulfill the stated terms. A legal advisor is often included in the team to reduce the level of misunderstanding and conflict after signing. Elsewhere, for example with the Chinese, the contract may not represent finality but a starting point. The objective of American negotiators is usually to arrive at legalistic contracts, and therefore the dominant concern is with getting the details right, and to use all such ongoing relationships to facilitate the achievement of unambiguous understandings. The Chinese approach to the negotiating process is rather to establish a human relationship, often essentially dependent in nature. Therefore, their primary goal is to create the bonding of "friendship." Consequently, they negotiate to do business with each other, often leaving the specific terms to be determined in the future based on the circumstances that occur. When the Chinese suddenly find themselves in a situation where honoring a particular term in the contract will be difficult, they may turn to their partners, expecting not only understanding but support and help in getting them out of their dilemma by changing the terms in the agreement. Americans react with disbelief on this action. In response, the Chinese feel abandoned and deceived by a trusted business partner, who is unwilling to help them in their hour of need.

For many Americans, the purpose of a business negotiation is to arrive at a signed contract between the parties. The signed contract is a definite set of rights and obligations that strictly binds the two sides. Americans tend to be bound by law, not by relationships, tradition, religion, or culture. Being high-context and explicit, Americans will honor a contract to the letter, whatever circumstances later arise. For the Japanese, among other groups, the goal is not the contract but the relationship. An American company in a transaction with a Japanese firm may view the contract as the essence of the deal while the Japanese believe the partnership is subject to reasonable changes over time; one party ought not to take unfair advantage of fortuitous events. While for an American signing the contract closes the deal, for the Japanese signing the contract just begins the relationship. Generally, Americans prefer very detailed contracts that attempt to anticipate all possible circumstances, no matter how unlikely. Because the "deal" is the contract itself, one must refer to the contract to determine how to handle a new situation that may arise. German contracts tend to be more specific than in the United States. To Germans, contracts are firm guidelines to be followed exactly. They spell out what in the United States is left to standard trade practice. Germans have two levels of signing authority; p.p. indicates someone with restricted authority while i.V. indicates a manager with full authority.

In other cultures, such as that of China, managers prefer a contract in the form of general principles rather than detailed rules. The Chinese often issue "memorandums of understandings" which are statements about the "spirit" of the agreement. Because, it is claimed, the essence of the deal is the relationship of trust that exists between the parties. If unexpected circumstances arise, the parties should look to their relationship, not the contract, to solve the problem. Koreans generally prefer short, vague contracts. For them, a contract should not be unduly restrictive. The American drive at the negotiating table to foresee all contingencies may be viewed by persons from another culture as evidence of lack of confidence in the stability of the underlying relationship.

Compromise is not a native word to Russians and to Russians have more the flavor of "to be compromised" than to make reciprocal concessions to arrive at a mutually agreeable or beneficial agreement. To many Russians, an offer of compromise is a sign of weakness. The natural impulse of many Russians when provided an offer of compromise is to go on the offensive, seeking to exploit and to establish dominance. An unreciprocated concession reeks of weakness and invites attack. There is a belief in Russia that there is only one truth and that you are supposed to try and achieve it, not compromise it. Avoid general agreements, in down details, since the Russians will generally adhere to the strict letter of an agreement but interpret any vagueness to the utmost in their favor. The Russian tendency is to put extreme proposals on the table, to stick doggedly to them through extended negotiations, and ultimately to modify them quickly and substantially. The Russians expect that when this is done, the other side will reject them firmly, thus allowing negotiations to move on in a more realistic manner. You win by demonstrating your seriousness; your adversary will have contempt for you if you give in easily, respect you if you have fought forcefully. Lenin's adage was: "If you strike steel, pull back; if you strike mush, push forward." Russians are good at creating clever contracts that are wordy and ambiguous and omit important details that they can exploit at a later date.

The French prefer to begin with agreement on general principles while Americans tend to seek agreement first on specifics. For Americans, negotiating a deal is making a whole series of compromises and tradeoffs on a long list of particulars. For the French, the essence is to agree on basic general principles that will guide and determine the negotiation process afterward; these principles become the framework, the skeleton upon which the contract is built. The French will not regard a deal as valid unless it has been drawn up in meticulous legal detail. Having codified elaborate agreements, their attitude then is very ambivalent. They will continually refer to the written text but they also feel the need to question them, or reinterpret them, or find ways of getting round them. In France there are two sets of rules, the written ones and the real ones. By way of contrast, Germans are explicit, highly detailed in their contracts; no room is left for interpretation. The opening offer from an Australian or Swede is likely to be closer to the final settlement than from a Russian, Chinese, or Egyptian, where it would be wise to leave lots of room to haggle.

In the Arab world, a person's word may be more binding than many written agreements and insistence on a contract may be insulting. A Greek sees a contract as a formal statement announcing the intention to build a business for the future. The negotiation is complete only when the work is accomplished. Mexicans treat the contract as an artistic exercise of ideas and do not expect contracts to apply consistently in the real world. Mexicans appear to be more concerned with the general wording of the agreement while Americans appear to be more focused on the specific wording of the agreement.

The Chinese seek agreement on generalities, dwelling on overall considerations, avoiding specific details as much as possible, and leaving the concrete arrangements to later negotiations. The wording of general principles often makes it possible to extract concessions. They can also at times quickly turn an agreement on principles into an agreement on goals and then insist that all discussion on concrete arrangements must foster those agreed upon goals. The Chinese demand for agreement on principles first can be used later to attack the other party for bad faith and for violating the spirit of the principles. The Chinese do not treat the signing of a contract as signaling a completed agreement but just the start of a relationship.

The first objective of Chinese negotiators is usually to get an agreement on general principles about the character of the evolving relationship. The agreement is only an objective and establishes the general form of the relationship with little attention to details. The Chinese usually insist at the initial stage that the details can be worked out later as long as both sides take a positive attitude toward the spirit of the general principles. The Chinese tend to have little appreciation for proprietary rights. Among friends there should be no need for secrets; the Chinese believe that the bigger and more successful a company is, the more it should be willing to share its knowledge at no cost to the Chinese. They accept it as their rightful due. They may even become resentful if denied free access to any knowledge they feel they deserve. In China, there is a handbook of acceptable contract items and if a clause is not in it, it is unlikely the Chinese side will accept it. When the Chinese negotiate a contract, they argue when they implement it.

The Japanese have a fundamentally different concept of contracts. They regard them as directional rather than final. The Japanese perceive a written contract as an expression of the relationship. Signing the contract is seen as only opening the relationship. A contract is a statement of the agreement now, and it is assumed that it will be reinterpreted or renegotiated if conditions change. Therefore, if conditions change in ways that make the contract unfavorable, they expect to renegotiate it. For example, they have repeatedly canceled or insisted on renegotiating contracts for the purchase of commodities when world prices have fallen below the level in the contracts. The Japanese prefer brief, written agreements that set forth basic principles; the gentlemen's agreement (involving honor and obligation) reached has more force than a legal contract. After the contract, if disputes occur, the Japanese try to resolve it by mutual agreement. The agreement primarily contains comments on the principles that the parties have agreed to use to guide their relationship, enabling them to respond to any changes that may occur at a later date.

Group orientation ideally results in a solution that is good for everyone, since all points of view are supposedly considered. Negotiations with group-oriented negotiators would be detail oriented in order to determine the proper solution. Your identity belongs to the group of which you are a part. The group would have to reach a consensus on any and all decisions, and this probably would not be done during the negotiation sessions. The individuals in the group would avoid making an individual decision. Individuals who are not group-oriented may believe that group-oriented negotiators appear to stall, are not interested in the negotiations, and give ambiguous statements. Group-oriented cultures tend to view contracts as flexible (Hofstede, 1991).

If you are individually oriented, you will be concerned with the best contract for your company and may not be concerned about whether the agreement is good for the other company. f there is more than one negotiator on your team, one person will probably control the negotiations and make the final decision concerning the various issues being discussed. Usually much individual sparring has taken place with members of the other team before the negotiation meeting. The individually oriented person would tend to interpret the contract very rigidly.

The persuasion phase and compromise stage of negotiations focuses on efforts to modify the views of other parties and sway them to your way of thinking through the use of various persuasive tactics. Americans see persuasion as a kind of conquest, whereas the Japanese look on it as a meeting of the minds. The Japanese verb "to persuade" (*fukumeru*) also means "to include." Any persuasion will be conducted behind the scenes, not during a formal negotiating meeting. For Japanese managers, persuasion as victory is secondary to the process of matching interests. Persuasion is typically used to compromise on certain conditions so that the two sides can close a deal. In Japan, there is not a clear separation of information seeking and persuasion. The two stages tend to blend together as each side more clearly defines and refines its needs and preferences. The time is spent as this task-related exchange of information means that little is left to discuss during the persuasion stage. The importance of maintaining harmony, avoiding loss of face, and gaining the agreement of all involved is most important. For the Japanese, it is more important to maintain the relationship than to be frank and open. The Japanese believe that little persuasion should be necessary if the parties have taken the time to understand each other thoroughly. Since the Japanese have spent a high percentage of their time on the first two phases, Japanese negotiators often do not feel the need to allocate much time to persuasion.

Their first position is rarely overstated, though sometimes fuzzy. Japanese like to regard their position as reasonable for both sides. The first proposal is carefully drafted and what they feel to be reasonable, reflecting the Japanese predilection for well-informed, best solutions based on consensus building. The Japanese tend to offer a proposal that approximates their needs and resist adjusting it. They offer what they feel is correct, proper, and reasonable. Japanese tend not to ask for much more than they expect to get. If the initial trust building was carried out successfully, they may not bargain on cost at all. This has inherent within it numerous weaknesses. Japanese negotiators develop defensive arguments with no consideration of persuading, selling, or converting the other side. Nor do they usually consider what the other side might be thinking or offering, including anticipated strategies and any concession strategies. Japanese negotiators often find themselves with no contingency or fallback plans, few officially authorized concessions, and an absence of clear policies on some questions.

In Japan, only a few persuasive tactics are appropriate: questions, self-disclosures, positive influence tactics, silence, a change of subject, recesses and delays, concessions and commitments. The repertoire of persuasive tactics available to bargainers in Japan is prescribed by status/power relations. Buyers (superior) can say things to sellers that sellers would not even consider saying to buyers. Of the traditional social hierarchy in Japan, the merchant (seller) ranks below all others, including peasants or farmers. To be involved in a money-making opportunity was not a highly regarded position in traditional Japan. Aggressive influence tactics can only be used by negotiators in higher power status positions and are only communicated through the low-level informal communications channels. Ceremonies provide each party with tangible representations of complex and uncertain abstractions. It focuses the awareness of the participants on some form of transition to a new or different relationship. Many cultures enjoy ceremony and functions and formalities, including speeches and dinners.

CONCESSIONS AND AGREEMENT

The concessions and agreement stage of a negotiation is the culmination of the negotiating process at which an agreement is reached. Often it is the summation of a series of concessions or smaller agreements. To reach an agreement that is mutually acceptable, each side frequently must give up some things; therefore concessions by both sides are usually necessary to reach an agreement. The Japanese believe that nothing is settled until everything is settled, which is why they typically provide concessions only at the end. They expect that these will lead immediately to the conclusion of the agreement—a holistic approach to decision making. The Japanese do not make any concessions until all issues and interests have been exposed and fully discussed. Usually any concessions are not decided upon at the negotiation table because of the nature of consensus decision making; negotiators must check with the home office before making any concessions to be sure that everyone agrees on the concessions. The Japanese believe that at this stage they should understand the other side's position and how it relates to their own so that they are in a position to decide what concessions are needed to reach a final agreement. The Japanese favor written agreements that are brief and identify basic principles. Listen politely to everyone in their group before making a group decision. However, once a concession is made it is usually considered as immutable and unchangeable by the Japanese.

Japanese dislike formal Western-style contracts. The Japanese tend to prefer brief, written agreements that set forth basic principles. Japanese written contracts tend to be very short (two or three pages), are purposefully loosely written, and primarily contain comments on principles of the relationship. The gentlemen's agreement (a loosely worded statement expressing mutual cooperation and trust that has developed between negotiating parties: these agreements allow a great deal of flexibility in the solution of unforeseen problems) often has more force than a legal contract since it involves a sense of honor and obligation. If something goes wrong after signing the contract, the Japanese attempt to resolve it by mutual agreement. If disputes arise, the common interests of both parties generally determine the outcome. Instead of submitting disputes to a third party, such as a court, the Japanese prefer to settle their differences through discussions with people who are familiar with the respective problems and situations. To submit an issue to court would bring embarrassment to many Japanese.

The Japanese do not view the signing of a contract as the end of negotiations. In the Japanese view, a contract is a piece of paper and people are human beings. Japanese firms want long-term business relations based on *kan*, emotional attainment. The Japanese have a stricter social code concerning obligation. The penalty for failure to discharge the obligation is dishonor of oneself, one's name, and one's family. Another reason for their dislike of fixed, written contracts is the Japanese feeling of extreme uncertainty about the future. The Japanese prefer that contractual obligations be left as vague as possible, in order to provide for a maximum of flexibility. The traditional Japanese view is that a contract is secondary in a business transaction, which should be premised on an ongoing, harmonious relationship between two parties who are committed to the pursuit of similar objectives; relationships, not contracts, are negotiated (Tung, 1982). Japanese contracts are always considered open for renegotiation. Japanese prefer disputes be worked out through mutual discussion. Generally, the Japanese view the use of legal documents as evidence of mistrust; if the partners have mutual trust, then it is unnecessary to cover all contingencies through formal legal contracts. The Japanese prefer flexibility in their business relationships. Any documents tend to be much shorter and are characterized by such phrases as "All items not found in this contract will be deliberated and decided on in a spirit of honesty and trust."

To the Japanese, a negotiated agreement is seen as an indication of the direction to be taken while adjustments and modifications can be made as conditions and circumstances warrant it. An agreement is seen only as the beginning of an adaptive process rather than the end. The American expectation of contractual finality is foreign to the Japanese way of thinking. The Japanese do not believe that a contract alone can ensure the success of a venture. According to Japanese thought, a truly wise man would not absolutely commit himself or herself since human interactions are so indeterminate. This flexibility means the Japanese will not lose face if future circumstances should change. The Japanese approach to contracts emphasizse the relationship. The contract is only a tangible acknowledgment of the existence of such a relationship, not a precise instrument that establishes and defines the relationship (Oikawa and Tanner, 1992). The Japanese feel that agreements require seasoning and maturity; as people work together, understandings become clearer and increasingly advantageous to both partners. As the relationship and conditions change, the assumption is that performance expectations ought to change. Flexibility, adjustment, and pragmatism, therefore, dominate the execution of long-term contracts.

Wise negotiators know that the best deal is one that is good for both sides. If the agreement is mutually beneficial, both sides have an incentive to maintain it. It is better to recognize the possibility of renegotiation at the outset and set down a clear framework within which to conduct the process. In short, recognize the possibility of redoing the deal, but control the process. Regardless of the other side's view on written contracts, it is still wise to document the agreement in simple, understandable terms so that the responsibilities and rights of both sides are clear. The language of the contract is often a disputable item. It is often desirable that two versions should be prepared—in your native tongue and in the other side's language. Care must be taken to ensure that both versions are equally accurate to the deal negotiated. Unless this is done, the parties may find differences in the two versions that will require further negotiations to settle.

10

Haggling

Many people have convinced themselves that haggling and negotiation are essentially the same process. Unfortunately, that misconception can lead to problems when either technique is used inappropriately. Haggling is a social style associated with bargaining, while negotiation is more of a formal process of reaching an agreement, with primary emphasis on end results. Haggling, by its very nature, is a time-consuming endeavor that requires a certain set of personal values, preconceived notions, attitudes, and motivations if it is to be pursued successfully. The process of haggling depends upon both verbal and nonverbal communication skills that require a working knowledge of human psychology (Herbig and Kramer, 1992). With its primary emphasis on the social aspect of the activity, haggling can often resemble a sporting encounter. This is especially true with the *suq* model of haggling, which is prevalent in Middle Eastern countries. To haggle successfully, regardless of the country involved, requires skill, practice, and experience.

"Haggling" means to bargain, to dicker, or to argue in an attempt to come to terms. As a highly structured behavioral system, haggling is marked with verbal threats, counter-threats, disclaimers of interest, and sign language. Its structural format is composed of several steps. These steps include a first offer by the merchant, followed by an initial rejection by the potential buye—made after objecting that the offer is ridiculous—followed closely by a counteroffer from the merchant, another counteroffer by the buyer—after an exchange of indignant words—another counter by the seller, a feign of interest in different items and a move to leave by the buyer, then finally, a completed transaction (Kassaye, 1990).

The art of haggling consists of skills that are often passed on within families as part of the traditional heritage of the culture. It is a set of interpersonal and cross-cultural skills improved by practice and experience. In haggling, time is not critical and not a major concern with the parties involved. In many cases, even when an inevitable conclusion is established beforehand, the haggling process must run its course. In a sense, Saddam Hussein haggled when he needlessly prolonged diplomatic negotiations. Through many tedious—almost verbatim—repetitions of the same demands, he succeeded in frustrating his opposition. His goal in this set of behaviors was not to reach an understanding nor was it intended merely to consume time, rather Saddam Hussein's method was classic haggling, used primarily as a stalling tactic to unmask the negotiating characteristics of the opposition. During the Gulf War, Saddam Hussein used the principles of haggling in many of his verbose, aggressive diatribes. The West, and especially President Bush, viewed these outbursts in Western terms instead of in the haggling ritual that Saddam was playing. In essence, although two were playing the game, only one knew the rules (Roberts, 1990). The result was miscommunications and missed opportunities on both sides' accounts.

In the modern world, haggling is most often found in the Middle East, Africa, and, to a lesser extent, in the developing countries of Pacific Asia and Latin America, including the Caribbean. This is not to say that haggling does not exist in the industrialized world. To witness haggling in the United States, one needs only to visit a local used car lot, flea market, or yard sale. In most cases, the process seen on used car lots resembles most closely the characteristics of a classic haggle. A strong economic incentive to haggle exists there, since wide variations in the actual purchase price are possible. The economic explanation for haggling does not seem to apply to flea markets, though. Generally, the merchandise found in flea markets or garage sales is of an inexpensive nature, making it most unlikely that the incentive to haggle would hinge upon the minuscule amount of money that could be saved. Rather, the social involvement with others provides adequate reason to haggle. The personal importance of social interaction in open market sales is quite evident, since for many people the social aspect of making their purchases is at least as important as any economic gains that may accrue. Outside of these several situations, haggling is not generally considered to be a legitimate part of typically American business dealings. This tends to be gender-specific; as a sex, women predominantly wish to avoid haggling; this distaste is not as prevalent among men.

In fact, to take advantage of the typical American's distaste for haggling, a current trend with automobile dealers is to resort to a "no-haggle" purchase and heavily advertise this policy. The object is to have one supposedly heavily discounted price—the final price—on the car and the consumer takes the price or not. The strategy is that those consumers who do not wish to deal with the traditional sales tactics and haggling with the dealer will be attracted to the dealer and be more comfortable when purchasing cars. Nonetheless, those people who enjoy negotiating (haggling with the dealers) and are well-informed usually end up saving more money than those who pay a no-haggle price (*Consumer Reports*, April 1993: 207–211).

CHARACTERISTICS OF HAGGLING

Since haggling is in most cases a social engagement between equals, it is most likely to be found in cultures that have a relatively low level of status consciousness within the society. As a time consuming activity, it is less likely to occur in highly time-conscious societies. In societies that discourage most forms of argument or confrontation, such as Japan, China, and most other Far Eastern cultures, haggling is not commonly encountered. Haggling takes place as a one-on-one activity. Any bargaining that involves large groups of people or takes place between firms will gravitate toward negotiation and away from haggling. Similarly, owners of small shops are more likely to haggle than proprietors of larger stores. Another distinguishing characteristic is context: Generally, one would be more likely to find haggling in high-context societies than in low-context.

In the Middle East and in other haggling environments, a major characteristic of haggling focuses upon the rights of the primary customer. Haggling, in the traditional sense, is an activity that attracts bystanders as well as customers. Some of the bystanders may be potential customers looking for some sort of advantage in the exchange occurring in front of them, while others may be trying to get price information that they can use themselves, or possibly even sell to others. In other cases, bystanders may simply be curious onlookers. Whatever the motives of the bystanders, they are expected to respect the right of the first customer to finish the deal or to retire voluntarily from the bargaining process (Uchendu, 1968). It is not considered proper behavior for a rival customer to make an offer until the first customer leaves or displays no further interest in bargaining with the salesperson.

In a traditional haggle, for both the buyer and the seller, the public bargaining session is a stage upon which neither wants to lose face. In some cases, a breach of protocol can lead to confrontations among rival customers. The personal relationship is quite important to hagglers. A great deal of bargaining time is spent simply building the relationship between parties.

Another salient characteristic of haggling is that there is a price range that is acceptable to both the buyer and the seller. A buyer with skill can narrow this price range and maximize his standing within the negotiating range. Of course, the seller is going to try to keep the price range at a higher level in order to retain as much profit as possible. For both parties to emerge as successful, each must be knowledgable as to the general worth of the product or service under consideration. If one party is not well informed as to the value of the product or is innocent of the processes of haggling, he may not only strike a poor bargain, but he may also lose status among his peers. As a result of this, Westerners tend to feel that they have been cheated when they conclude a deal while they are still not satisfied with the results. This tends to contribute to an unsavory reputation for bazaar merchants and others who haggle as unscrupulous merchants. In their own defense, they reason that all would-be hagglers should know the rules of the game beforehand.

The key to haggling in any country in which it is performed is establishing a personal relationship. In Middle Eastern countries the act of haggling is a practice of the "common man," therefore, men of honor and prestige in the Middle East do not haggle. Practically speaking, persons of high social rank may conclude a deal after an agent has haggled to a point of near conclusion, but almost never engage in the actual haggling process. In the classic *suq* (market) model of haggling, there is a preliminary period of discussion involving items of some general interest that go well beyond the scope of the initially intended transaction. The purpose of this seeming waste of time is to establish a personal connection between the bargainers. Once accomplished, the actual bargaining can begin. Possible loss of face is at stake for both participants, so to get over this hurdle a very strict collection of rules that form the basis of a tacit bargaining etiquette is followed. Both parties will begin the process far outside of the expected price range so as not to give away any advantage that the opponent might attain from being able to estimate the final position. Both parties have a reasonably well established idea as to how much they would be willing to compromise before the actual conversation begins.

Both parties will effect a series of moves and countermoves in an effort to determine what the other party is willing to do. The talks may go on almost indefinitely, because neither party wishes to take responsibility for breaking off the talks. One key element in finalizing a transaction is a mutual trust between the parties. Even an apparently trivial offense can bring on an end to the negotiations (Khuri, 1969).

Since haggling is also a process of price determination, the customer has the right to handle and examine the product closely before making an offer. Only when the customer is satisfied and has made up his mind is his bid for the item binding. Consultation with others is often a part of the process. Written contracts are quite uncommon. Haggling, in many cases, is an endurance test for both the seller and the buyer (Uchendu, 1968). Haggling over prices is considered a pleasure of doing business in Middle Eastern bazaars. Tips for effective haggling at such bazaars include dressing down, shopping around, being knowledgable concerning the merchandise you are haggling over, negotiating only with the proprietor, being patient, and offering to pay cash (Atcheson, 1992). By doing so you will secure the best deal as well as impress the proprietor with your respect and appreciation for the proper way of doing business in his homeland.

HAGGLING ENVIRONMENTS

Haggling primarily exists in the developing and undeveloped countries throughout the world, predominantly the Middle East, Africa, Latin America, the Caribbean, and Pacific Asia. It can even be found to a limited extent in the United States. The degree to which haggling is institutionalized varies from culture to culture. Several social and economic factors exist that determine the relative amount of haggling that is to be expected.

First, the degree of external control over individual transactions within an economy affects the presence, absence, and the prevalence of haggling that is permitted within a market. Haggling is generally associated with relatively open and more purely competitive markets, in which buyers and sellers conduct their business trade rationally. Where market prices are fixed by law or by some sort of price leadership arrangement, there is little likelihood of any sort of haggling process taking place. Tradition may also inhibit or limit haggling to a particular niche within the market. An example of this is provided by the customs of an East African society called the *Gikuyu (kikuyu)*.

Members of this culture see haggling as proper behavior in almost all transactions except the buying of custom-made knives, for which the smith has set his price based on the size of the knife. In other similarly oriented cultures, haggling is restricted to only a few particular items. Contrast this with the United States, where most markets are structured. Haggling in only a few specific purchase categories is acceptable. Haggling generally is seen, however, as an unacceptable route to final transactions in the United States and most other countries with highly developed economies (It is also not well recognized in Europe; the more economically developed and industrialized a country or society becomes, the further from its primitive roots it evolves, the more structured the market it tends to evolve toward).

A second influence involves ways in which a society's folk ethics and ideology may encourage or inhibit haggling. Some societies think of haggling as improper behavior. In the middle of the seventeenth century, Quaker merchants set their prices and refused to bargain on religious grounds. In fact, this refusal to bargain is the typical position taken by many merchants in industrialized Western nations. Although religious grounds are seldom invoked in the secular marketplace today, that basis may underlie many traditional ideas about the appropriateness of haggling as a technique for bargaining. In Christian dogma, one is suppose to set a "fair" price, fair to both the merchant and the customer. With this background, it is not difficult to see how resistance to haggling developed.

Thirdly, considerations of social prestige and personal honor may limit haggling to some degree. The behaviors of the Abyssinian Amhara provide us with a colorful example:

> Amhara trading practices are motivated not so much by the desire to derive a good monetary bargain as by the desire to carry out the transaction without being mocked, especially by Coptic peers. Unlike Arabs, the Amhara are too proud and not so intent on economic maximizing as to resort to badgering a customer. The seller may refuse to state a price and ask the buyer to make an offer. If the offer is reasonable and the purchaser is on the same socioeconomic level so that no problem of honor is involved, the transaction will be concluded promptly. (Messing, 1991)

A fourth set of factors involves the nature of the commodity being traded. Inherent quality and quantity of an item are characteristics that may determine the amount of haggling. In some cultures foodstuffs are not generally subject to haggling by the final consumers, but considerable haggling will be observed at wholesale levels.

Dreyfus and Roberts (1988) indicates clothing, tax audits, fur coats, broker's commissions, mortgage rates, houses, cars, and high-cost luxury items are among the itemsthat can be haggled, while subscriptions, airline tickets, mail-order merchandise, restaurant meals, and utility bills cannot.

The final factor considered here is the scale of the operation. Large firms do not lend themselves to haggling because a person-to-person interaction is generally absent. Since haggling involves a major investment of time, large firms cannot justify haggling on individual transactions because they must deal with large numbers of individual customers on a continuing basis. The time needed to haggle effectively increases as the value of each transaction increases, as well as when the number of customers handled by an organization grows. One can see this tendency in industrial markets, where most any transaction is open to negotiation of many variables. Under this scenario, haggling (negotiation) is not only expected behavior but becomes the norm. This is not the case in consumer markets, where each transaction is small and the large number of transactions make haggling inefficient and ineffective.

SUQ HAGGLING

In traditional Arab culture, the process of haggling serves many purposes. One important function of haggling is that it provides a structured opportunity for both sides to get to know each other as individuals. Both parties are saying many things to each other within the process: that I respect your needs, but I expect you to make certain adjustments in order to respect mine; that I need to know who you are as a person in order to do business with you and will make judgments based on your response to what I say and do. The bargaining part of the process is often conducted with a background of lavish entertaining and the serving of refreshments, frequently in a setting where both parties take the necessary time to learn about each other, their backgrounds, and their activities. The participants' respective status, family, and friendship connections are often revealed through the haggling. An understanding of the process and its implications can be a critical component to successful business dealings in cultures where the process is expected to be followed by all parties doing business.

The *Suq* model (*suq* means market in Arabic) of haggling relies more on personal relationships, obligations, and social tradition than legalisms or formal written contracts. The *Suq* model probably evolved within ancient nomadic caravans, during times when encounters were not frequent and even economic meetings such as bargaining and transacting business provided rare opportunities for social engagement and conversation. *Suq* haggling is a social process with goals more oriented to pursuing and establishing personal relationships than toward reaching agreements. Whereas, in general forms of haggling the end agreement or outcome of the transaction is of primary importance to the participants, in *suq* haggling the means employed are often of equal or greater importance than the ends. In the *suq* model of haggling, the seller welcomes the buyer into his shop or home and addresses him in a familiar kinship manner to indicate respect. Both buyer and seller typically wax elegant, to signify common interest and mutual trust, although little of this exchange is ever taken seriously.

The difference between the *suq* model of haggling and haggling in general is that with the former it becomes a passtime, an activity for its own sake wherein the latter is a more formalized process in which the goal is to reach a mutually profitable conclusion as quickly as possible. The *suq* version of haggling is oriented toward being more of a social activity rather than an economic one. It is the means and not the end that is the key to a properly executed *suq* haggle. The objective is not so much to come to agreement but to focus on the social ramifications of the agreement process. Whereas in general forms of haggling, the objective is to attain an agreement as speedily as possible—the sooner the better is the maxim of conduct. *Suq* haggling, by way of contrast, in its truest sense is "talk for talk's sake," directed toward renewing or creating social relations, rather than reaching a goal. This is especially the case when the goal is already well understood by both parties before the haggle begins. In general, *suq* haggling occurs between two parties, usually two individuals or their agents while an "auction" or a "market" requires many parties to be present in order to function efficiently (Quandt, 1987). *Suq* haggling in its classic sense is a social activity under an assumed economic cover. Traditional cultural *suq* hagglers are most commonly found in the Arabic world. Although, the Orient is known for its hard bargaining, since most transactions there are primarily economic in orientation and lack the necessary social underpinnings, they cannot be considered examples of true *suq* haggling.

ADVANTAGES OF HAGGLING

Haggling offers some advantages to both the buyer and the seller. From the buyer's perspective, haggling affords the opportunity to get a lower price by refusing the seller's initial offer. This also allows the seller to size up the customer and change his tactics in order to entice an unenthusiastic customer. The seller's main problem is keeping other customers from noticing any price discrimination. If another buyer picks up on the results of a prior sale, it may severely compromise the bargaining position of the seller. Haggling also gives the customer a feeling of some control over the price to be paid. For the seller, a commitment to a higher price is to his advantage in an individual transaction, but he may risk losing customers if he shows no price flexibility.

Apparently, social advantages are of paramount importance during haggling interactions between vendor and customer, when they both seem to relish the give and take of the elaborate ritual enacted before a final (probably known in advance) price is agreed upon. If this is the case, individuals who are more likely to experience social isolation and its attendant loneliness (e.g., the elderly, singles, the powerless, and the economically disadvantaged) should predominate at haggling events, an observation that is confirmed in some recent studies of flea markets (Sherry, 1990; Belk, Sherry, and Wellendorf, 1988).

WHY DOES HAGGLING PERSIST?

One reason is that much of the world is not "modern." A large part of the globe is still in the process of development. In developing countries, traditional culture dominates social interaction among people. Within the give-and-take aspects of haggling the seller is afforded a unique opportunity to promote his product and the buyer can have a voice in its selling price. Several conditions and perceptions encourage haggling within traditional societies.When there are perceived differences in quality, haggling allows a buyer to get a better deal. When there is a danger of getting adulterated goods and a lack of formal regulation, only the consumer can inspect the items and determine whether they are worth the asking price. The onus is upon the consumer to validate the transaction, buyer beware. If the consumer purchases risky items, the reward for his risk-taking lies in the lower price.

As regulation becomes more common to these cultures, haggling may give way to less aggressive practices such as traditional price negotiation for expensive items. Considering the slow pace at which cultural idiosyncrasies evolve, any change in these practices is expected to be slow (Atcheson, 1992).

MARKET   CHARACTERISTICS

In many developing countries, where a majority of consumers cannot read and write, goods often do not have price tags, and advertised prices may not have much meaning to the average consumer in these markets. In these markets, haggling traditions provide strong influence over the manner in which many goods are marketed. In some cases, variations in quality and the absence of standard systems for the establishment of weights and measures make it difficult to implement a "one price" system. The initial price offered by the consumer betrays the level of experience with similar goods. Some consumers may get more out of haggling than others because of differing experience levels, social or economic status, and the ability to speak the language used to make the sale.

Haggling is an activity Westerners generally have little experience with. Haggling to many Westerners means being argumentative and verbose in the negotiation process. This is not haggling as it exists throughout most of the world. Haggling is a unique mode of communication prevalent in many developing nations that are potentially new and growing markets for the United States and other Western countries. Since it is a cultural manifestation that has been present for generations, it will be necessary for firms that enter such markets to adapt their selling styles to fit into the culture.

In haggling, it is the nonverbal, the context of the situation that becomes critical. Agents of the firm must understand the gameplaying and social connotations of the haggle ritual to be effective and to reach the final goal. By being respectful of the business customs of the land, the haggle, and understanding the finer nuances of the haggling ritual, the firm and its agents will win the respect of the other side. As a result, a relationship develops and the long term will be profitable indeed for the firm with the wherewithal to have taken the time and resources to have properly conducted the haggling negotiations.

11

Country Study: Indonesia

WHAT INDONESIANS ARE LIKE

Nearly 200 million Indonesians call the thousands of islands of Indonesia home. The national motto is "unity in diversity" or *Bhinneka Tunggal Ika*. Living up to that motto is a formidable challenge, considering that the country has about 300 different ethnic groups. Among the better-known ones are the Achenese, Badui, Balinese, Bataks, Bugis, Dayaks, Minahasa, Minangkabu, and the ethnic Chinese. The official language of Indonesia is Bahasa Indonesia, essentially Malay-based, which is spoken by seventy percent of the people. Most Indonesians perceive that knowing it is necessary to get a better job, social status, and prestige. The use of Bahasa Indonesia has helped promote some semblance of national unity, although it has not entirely replaced the more than 200 provincial dialects that are being used. English is officially the second language, and a sizable (but aging) minority still speak Dutch. (The Netherlands used to be colonial masters of Indonesia.)

Indonesians are ninety percent Muslim, five percent Christian (mostly Roman Catholic), and three percent Hindu and Buddhist. A strong underlying influence in the religious life of Indonesians is animism, or the belief that supernatural forces are at work influencing one's destiny. Thus, Indonesians are greatly preoccupied with activities that seek to divine the will of the spirits and appease their wrath. An outside observer will notice practices involving magic, sorcery, and mysticism. Business executives influenced by animism plan their activities according to supernatural conditions most favorable to them.

For instance, an executive who wants to take a trip holds a *selamatan*, a communal feast to pacify evil spirits, especially *naga*, or the serpent deity, who once protected Buddha from a great storm. If *naga* is in the way of the executive and the destination, the trip is postponed until *naga* has moved to another spot. A *dukun*, or witch doctor, performs the complex task of charting the movements of *naga*.

Three social classes predominate in the two main types of urban centers in Indonesia: (1) metropolitan cities such as Jakarta and Surabaya on Java, Medan on Sumatra, and Ujung Pandang on Sulawesi, and (2) regional towns like Malang and Bandung on Java, Jambi and Banda Aceh on Sumatra, and Balikpapan in Kalimantan. The first social class is the elite. Three elite groups predominate. The first group is composed of the higher-ups in regional towns, who combine both the Western style of living and the traditional norms of their ethnic regions. Mostly Javanese and those retired from government service, these persons were educated in the Dutch colonial era and held positions in the colonial administration. They were active in the nationalistic phase of the country's political development and participated in the quest for independence. After independence, they occupied high positions in society that were once the exclusive ranks of the Dutch colonizers. They highly value university education, civil service, and authoritarian/hierarchical managerial practices.

The second elite group is composed of those who, like the members of the first group, were active in the quest for independence but were not quite as well educated. They were also more strongly influenced by their ethnic cultures even as they tried to blend Western influences into their style of living. Although they flaunt the external trappings of Western-style conspicuous consumption, deep inside, they do not subscribe to modern patterns of thinking and behavior.

The third elite group is younger. It is the first generation of post-independence Indonesians. They differ radically from the first two groups in that they are more strongly oriented toward a metropolitan culture, are motivated much more by entrepreneurial gains rather than by joining the civil service, are less concerned with the traditional criteria for social status, and are more driven to attain financial security for their spouses, children, and themselves. Unlike their older counterparts, they are less attached to members of their extended families and are less bound by colonial attitudes that assigned undue importance to foreigners. They are more confident in dealing with foreigners and perceive themselves as equal to them.

The second major social class is the middle class. It consists mainly of mid-level civil service personnel, skilled and semiskilled workers and merchants engaged in petty commerce. Caught in a bicultural life, they combine values of both the metropolis and their ethnic origins. Some members of this group include those who have university degrees, the Chinese and Arab minorities, and the wealthy *santri* who can afford expensive Western goods but who are not admitted into the higher elite circles because they are perceived as unsophisticated. The lower class is composed of the illiterate street peddlers, laborers, servants, and other lowly groups. They usually live in crowded and unsanitary village units called *kampongs*.

The religious sense of the Indonesians as expressed by their animism is also reflected in their political ideals. Former President Sukarno enforced the "Five Principles" or *Pantja Sila* in his effort to base the Indonesian identity on high principles: (1) belief in a Godhead that is One, (2) nationalism, (3) humanity or internationalism, (4) democracy, and (5) social justice. Later, he added five more principles to constitute the "Manipol" (Political Manifesto) or the USDEK, as they are known in short: (1) U for *Undang-Undang dasar 1945*, the 1945 constitution; (2) S for *Socialisme a la Indonesia*; (3) D for *Demokrasi Terpimpin*, "Guided Democracy"; (4) E for *Ekonomi Terpimpin*, "Guided Economy"; and (5) K for *Kepribadian Indonesia*, the Indonesian identity. Sukarno strongly believed in the magic potency of these slogans. The country's P-4 Programme tries to ensure that all government employees, executives in government businesses, educators, and high school and university students understand and practice these concepts. Indonesians manage their affairs using the social concept of *gotong-royong*, or the spirit of working together to reach common goals. So pervasive is the concern for harmony in the group that consensus is almost always sought in the decision making process at the village level. Among families, the spirit of *gotong-royong* is expressed by decision-making that is done for the good of all its members. Poorer members of the family expect to be assisted by their wealthier relatives—for instance, by finding work for them.

Traces of cultural tension in the managerial profession exist. Some managers, especially the Bataks and Minahasa, can be fiercely nationalistic and want to employ only native Indonesians. A smaller group, executives who have had the benefit of international exposure in Dutch elite schools, for instance, are more aware of the concept of global interdependence in business. Therefore, they are more open toward adopting international business practices. But, in general, all groups of Indonesian managers consistently strive hard to measure up to the difficult work required to attain the Western standard of living they want.

On the whole, a big shortage exists of the skilled manpower needed to meet the needs of the Indonesian economy's projected and stepped-up investments for the rest of the twentieth century. The government has offered tax breaks to foreign firms willing to provide on-the-job training to *pribumi* (or truly ethnic Indonesian) workers. It hopes this will alleviate the shortage of technical and managerial skills.

Labor unions are not too effective because their major weapon, the strike, is illegal. Unions are under the control of the political parties they are affiliated with, and this is where their real power comes from. Dues are very low, so workers usually join more than one union in order to express the wide range of their political beliefs.

Indonesia has many social problems. First, there is the Chinese problem. Many Indonesians resent the economic power of the wealthy Chinese. They continue to wield considerable economic power even after the government made rural Chinese close up their shops and move to cities, restricted the entry of Chinese students in the universities, and harrass them with penalties for unfair business practices. The Chinese have circumvented many restrictions, including those that did not let them hold import-export licenses and those that excluded them from obtaining government contracts. Many changed their Chinese surnames to Indonesian surnames in order to keep a low profile. Many Indonesians perceive standard Chinese business practices as being unfair—such as keeping long hours, living on the business premises, and entering into multiple collusive arrangements among themselves. Government laws discriminate in favor of the majority of the population, the *pribumi*, who are somewhat economically disadvantaged. For example, the government owns the majority of the shares in domestic industries, the Chinese twenty-seven percent, and the *pribumi* eleven percent.

Another social problem arises from the clashes between the Muslims and other ethnic groups. And finally, there is the big problem of providing education to the population. The availability and quality of education just can not seem to catch up with the country's burgeoning population. (It was growing at an annual rate of over two percent.) Indonesia, like many other developing countries, has a tradition of large families due to its Agrarian background. Although it is now in the process of industrializing and the agricultural share of its GDP rapidly declining, traditions die hard. The high fertility rates are to be found in the rural and mostly poor regions of the country. The affluent or growing affluent share of the population is seeing its birth rate decreasing. Indonesia, like many other developing countries, is seeing its population grow in the segment that can least afford it—the uneducated, unskilled, poorest in the country.

INDONESIAN NEGOTIATORS AND YOU

Preliminary Considerations

Indonesian Negotiators: Certainly, there are business opportunities in Indonesia for foreigners. Generally speaking, Indonesians need technical know-how, capital investment, and equipment. But you will face restrictions and problems when you do business with them. For instance, only Indonesian nationals holding current fiscal certificates are allowed to import. Furthermore, foreigners are not allowed to export or to distribute or market goods and services. You will have to find an Indonesian willing to be your distributor if you want to sell there. The government may let you establish a representative office and give technical advice to your importer-distributor, along with help on marketing, advertising, and after-the-sale service.

Other major problems that you will run into are related to the government's intensive efforts to keep foreign capitalists from exploiting the nation's resources: (1) You have to give a certain amount of equity to Indonesians, but the rules for doing this are inconsistently applied. (2) Political patronage strongly influences the selection of local partners for business projects. (3) Foreign enterprises can not borrow from Indonesian banks. (4) Indonesian labor laws are extremely protective of their people—in order to dismiss an employee, for example, you have to get permission from the local labor office.

If you are seriously considering doing business with Indonesians, you will have to think about how to handle the many situations where the use of "grease" money is called for. You will also have to deal with many politicians because local politics are inextricably linked with the economy. Do not think you can avoid "grease" and politicians—you can not.

You: Study the current business environment there and watch how other foreign businesspeople are doing, particularly in your industry. Weigh the costs of doing business there against the gains you expect, taking into account the restrictive policies and inefficiencies you will encounter. In particular, look into the Foreign Capital Investment Law, which strongly protects Indonesian interests. Take a very close look at the sections covering the industries foreigners can enter, time limits on business projects, encouragement of the "Indonesianization" of foreign companies, and the limited legal rights of foreign ventures. These points will assist you in your pursuit of the Indonesian marketplace.

Sensitivities in "Breaking the Ice"

Indonesian Negotiators: Like other Southeast Asians, Indonesians are very personal when they interact with their countrymen and with foreigners. Trust building is a careful process that involves people-oriented socializing and a lot of "playing by ear," or trial-and-error gut feelings. In the initial stages of your business relationships, Indonesian hosts like to spend some time getting to know you personally. They will ask you for details about your personal life, so do not be surprised. They belong to a hierarchical society, so authority figures or their representatives will be participating at all introductory meetings. Finally, they greatly value smooth social relationships based on warmth and good will.

You: If you expect to do a lot of business in this part of Asia, you will need to become accustomed to the "personal prying" of your hosts. If you are used to the impersonal and efficient processes of business practices in developed countries, you will have to change your style. Put together a package of information about your private self that you are comfortable in sharing. If you are basically assertive, learn to back down; proceed according to the cues your hosts give you. Do not stress how good you and your compay are—this does not project too well here. You may come across as a person who exhibits his or her superiority far too much. Indonesians are very cautious in their dealings with foreigners as a result of their unhappy experience as a colony of the Dutch. They are afraid of being taken advantage of, so emphasize their needs when talking to them. Being informed about the latest government policies will leave a good impression on them.

Local   Representation

Indonesian Negotiators: Indonesians are more comfortable in dealing with foreigners when they communicate through a local third party. This is understandable—not only can they express themselves in their native language, but they can also use the local business practices they are comfortable with.

You: Plan ahead. Find a local representative. This is a must in Indonesia. So much business is conducted in the native tongue that language problems alone are enough to stump even the most competent foreign business executive. You may be fluent in many languages but it is the idioms, slang, dialects that will defeat you. Do not take chances, use a local representative who is fluent in the local dialect of the language and is knowledgeable of the culture.

Sales Presentations

Indonesian Negotiators: The top-level decision-maker prefers to meet with foreigners during the initial visit. Their team is better able to follow your presentation if it is amply supported by vivid visual details, so use a slide presentation, and include those graphics in your written presentation.

You: Plan ahead for the audio-visual materials and equipment you will use there. Focus on reliability of use, after-the-sale service, and attractive price ranges, not on labor-saving efficiency. (Labor is cheap in Indonesia.) Align your incentives according to the government's investment preference.

Decision-Making Process

Indonesian Negotiators: On your first visit, you will be met by the leader of the Indonesian team. Although Indonesians are basically a hierarchical society where decisions of those in positions of authority are honored by those in subordinate levels, great effort goes into seeking a consensus (*mufakat*). The decision reached by the top person in the corporation is not necessarily the final decision, though. The government is often involved in approving business projects. Sometimes a proposal that sailed smoothly through all the corporate levels may have to be sent back for reconsideration if the government office evaluating the proposal is not totally pleased. Not understanding the technical parts of your proposal also costs additional time. These delays will test you, but be patient. Do not pressure the Indonesians for a decision. They react negatively to these kinds of efforts. There will be times when even intermediaries can only be of so much help. All you can do is be patient and wait.

A crucial point in your negotiation is reached when the subject of giving grease money, or *sogok* (money under the table), *pungli* (unauthorized assessments), or *korupsi* (corruption) comes up for consideration (and it will come up). Demanding such payments on the side is very much a part of doing business in Indonesia, even though the government is doing all it can through its *KOPKAMTIB* clean-up program. Although they are basically rational and Western in their approach to business, Indonesian executives are also very much influenced by local superstitions in making their decisions. They engage in elaborate rites to appease evil spirits so their business activities may be successful. Failures and obstacles may indicate that the gods are not pleased or that some rule has been violated.

You: Make sure that your top executive is present both at the first meetings and during the final rounds when the end is in sight. Emphasize the main concept and the benefits of your proposal in your first visit with their leader. Leave the technical details for later meetings with operational managers and technicians. Make allowances ahead of time for the additional time required for the next rounds of negotiations in case your proposal is not approved by the government. Do not apply pressure on them. Whether or not you use "grease" money will depend on your ethical standards. Surely, this is one issue that should have been thought about long before you began your negotiations. Do not presume you understand everything about the way Indonesians make decisions. Local animistic practices may make a lot of their decisions seem unintelligible to you. Respect their decisions, and do not push for explanations.

Points of Contention

Indonesian Negotiators: They evaluate bids based on the quality of your product, delivery terms, reliability of after-delivery service, price, your performance record, and the quality of your sales presentation. The Indonesian government has not been too easy with credit terms for firms who engage in foreign trade. Letter of credit (LC) procedures are hardly encouraging. Banks do not accept irrevocable LCs with built-in terms. At the time the LC is opened, they require twenty-five percent of the value of the transaction as deposit in settlement currency—one to two percent monthly cost.

You: Always seek the advice of an experienced intermediary. Your local agent will make a big difference by way of enhancing your sales presentation and interpreting the other side's business signals. Make sure your price quotations are in both Indonesian rupiahs and your currency. Include c.i.f. terms and a close estimate of the tariff duties due. (You will not know for sure because of the *sogok* you will have to pay.) This is usually a considerable amount, since the government uses protective tariffs in place of import licenses.

Seeking the "Right" Connections

Indonesian Negotiators: Getting a local representative to act as your intermediary is a must if you want to succeed in business in Indonesia. There are three major groups you can turn to for support: (1) The president and his close associates, (2) government officials from prestigious families, and (3) *Tjojok Chinese.*

The first and primary group consists of President Suharto himself and his associates, friends, and relatives. They are the most powerful group in the country. Some of those who are in this exclusive network are the president's three sons, Sigit Harjojudanto, Bambang Trihatmodjo, and Hutomo Mandala Putera, and such influential Indonesian-Chinese tycoons as Liem Sioe Liong and Mohamad Hasan. The Suharto sons have established a complex network of businesses, giving them an important hand in the most significant commodity and service sectors of the economy. Their businesses are supported by state contracts, government decrees, and licenses giving them the right to produce, import, and distribute goods and services. They have the power to: (1) assign import licenses to a single company, (2) control imports by dividing quotas among a few importers, (3) appoint a few "approved traders" to distribute products, (4) enforce investment licensing to protect existing companies from new competitors, (5) designate local joint-venture partners for major foreign investment projects, especially in public works, and (6) grant semi-exclusive rights for service contracts. Because of the strong link between politics and business, foreigners should keep a close watch on the players in the political power game. Joint-venture projects are directly affected by any change in players.

The second group of influential locals are the professional government administrators and technocrats, usually from the traditional and prestigious families. The third group is made up of Chinese power brokers known as Tjojok Chinese. These are specialists in working with government bureaucratic procedures. They know what forms to fill out, whom to contact, what offices to visit, who expects *sogok*, and the best approach to make to a particular person. Many Chinese are also prominent in the fields of finance and investments.

You: It is important for you to establish connections through any or all of the three main conduits of power. Power brokers expect reciprocity in their dealings with those who need their support. Exchanging favors or facilitating the deal with *sogok* are accepted practices in this respect.

Communication Style

Indonesian Negotiators: Indonesians strongly believe in staying in harmony with nature and with everyone and everything that is part of it. Pleasant interpersonal relationships, soft-spokenness, and trying to please characteristically mark their way of interacting with people. They have great concern for maintaining face or avoiding being placed in a position of *malu* or embarrassment. Thus, they are averse to people who shout, criticize in public, and talk with loud and grating voices. Subordinates in businesses, government, and society in general practice *sembah*, or respect for superiors. They are not supposed to question a superior's decision. So delicate are they in their communications that there are twelve ways to say "no" and six ways to say "please." Indonesians are trained to practice *hormat*, or the conscious effort of honoring the other person—he or she must be made to feel good and important. You will like that about them.

You: You will need to understand the complicated social rules that govern personal interactions in Indonesia. It is so easy to offend the locals through careless spontaneity. Westerners especially, who are used to the cut-and-dried direct approach back home, may find it difficult to trust a people that can not come right out with a "no." They take great pains to avoid a confrontation, so they do not say "no" very often. For example, they may even disappear from negotiating sessions if they have to give you unfavorable news. Negotiators who are used to fast decision making must curb the tendency to apply pressure when feedback is slow in coming.

Sealing the Agreement

Indonesian Negotiators: As a rule, they want the details of agreements put in writing so they can review them before signing. Written contracts have usually connoted mistrust in the past, although they are beginning to appreciate the opportunity for further consideration that written contracts give them. They think of contracts as instruments to assure cash flow and financial gain. When relations are good between you, they may suggest that you forward the written contract to the top decision maker. Do not misinterpret this as final approval—all it indicates is that you have the support of the negotiators at that particular level. You will still have to sell your proposal to higher decision-making levels. The top person in the corporation is not necessarily the final decision maker, however. Big projects usually need to be reviewed by government agencies.

Indonesians are not rigid in implementating contracts. They are aware that some details may be overlooked in the contract, and so revisions will have to be made. When cases of conflict do arise, arbitration may be resorted to rather than outright legal action. If you have to go to court, remember that contracts are interpreted according to communal law and the local civil code, which is patterned after the Dutch model.

You: You'll need a lot of patience and staying power to endure the tedious process of moving your proposal through the different levels of decision making. After moving through several levels, it is easy to be deceived by appearances that an agreement has finally been reached, especially because their communication style and social behavior favor smooth interpersonal relationships. The challenge to you is not to assume anything until the very last person in the chain of command has affixed his or her signature to the contract.

Specific Tactics Used by Indonesian Businesspersons

(1) Ask the Seller for a Lower Price: Indonesian negotiators may pull a fast one by asking for extra concessions which they will call "minor" after the bargaining sessions are over and shortly before they sign the contract ("the nibble"). They may also gather competing sellers in one place at the same time and negotiate with them simultaneously. Some of them will "low-ball" you by making it appear that their demands are low, but in actuality, they will ask for clauses such as inflation protection, cost-plus, and so forth, which really will cost you a lot. Some try to impress you with their credentials to get you to give them concessions—they want you to think they are valuable potential customers. Almost always, they will try to get you to improve your offer. If they are not that aggressive, they will simply stall for time or exercise patience while waiting for you to relax your initial demands and lower your prices.

(2) Ask the Buyer to Pay More: Indonesian sellers will make high demands on you. This leaves them a lot of room to negotiate on price and other terms. They may even gather a number of buyers together and negotiate with them at the same time to give themselves more leverage. They like to use similar technique—directly mentioning to you that other buyers also want the same goods badly. After they have already agreed with you on the terms, they may ask for more money or some other concession from you before they deliver the merchandise. Indonesian negotiators may also like to tell you they have been long-time and reliable suppliers to many customers and so you should increase your offer. As the negotiations proceed, they will seize every opportunity to nibble concessions from you. If you happen to be tough, they may try saying "Yes, and . . ." This avoids any kind of direct disagreement with you. Then, when it is timely, they will reaffirm their initial terms without having ruffled your feathers. If they think they have little to lose, they may offer to split the difference between their offer and your offer. If they want to play it tough, they could turn

the tables on you and get you to explain why they should sell to you instead of to other buyers. If negotiations stall and the discussions seem to hold no promise, they are willing to simply abandon the negotiation.

(3) Ask the Boss for a Raise: Indonesians send messages about their desire for a raise through colleagues close to the boss to test the boss' reaction before they actually talk to the boss about it. This way they can prepare themselves in advance for potential objections the boss may have. To make the raise appear insignificant, they will also talk about the raise in terms of funny money. Sometimes, they will apply pressure by making the boss feel guilty if a raise is not granted.

(4) Ask the Boss for a Promotion: Indonesians use the record of their past accomplishments and performance to negotiate a promotion with their boss. They also leak information about their achievements through the grapevine to enhance their image. If they already occupy high positions in the company, they may apply pressure by pulling rank and reminding the boss of their importance.

(5) Ask the Boss to Change Their Holiday Dates: Most Indonesian executives would be patient with their bosses and continue lobbying for a change of date even after an initial refusal. To facilitate the changing of the boss' mind, they would even perform tasks that are far beyond the call of duty. Doing this will also make their boss look good. If they are on the cautious side, they might ask their colleagues to find out what their boss thinks about the change of date before they talk to the boss about it themselves. Or they may approach the situation logically and ask their boss to look at personnel records to find out the precise dates of past holidays they have taken and current holiday dates their colleagues are taking. If their request is reasonable, the recorded dates of holidays taken by them and their colleagues will prove it. Or they may use some other issue at work as leverage for them to get their boss to concede to changing dates; for instance, they could agree to do additional work or work overtime without pay in exchange for the approval. If they have a great deal of influence and power in the department, they could be aggressive about their request and assume a "take-it-or-leave-it" attitude. If the boss refuses their request, they may not be as productive or as willing to do what the boss wants in the future. If the boss refuses to approve the change, they may decide to be absent anyway and try to get someone else to do their job in the meantime. Or they could make it appear that they have given up trying to change their boss' mind after an initial refusal, and in the meantime try to find someone else in the company who will back them up.

REFERENCES

The section "What Indonesians Are Like" was adapted from:

Bunge, Frederica M. ed. *Indonesia: A Country Study* (Washington, D.C.: Foreign Area Studies-The American University, 1983), pp. 101–105.

Bureau of Public Affairs, U.S. Department of State, *Background Notes: Indonesia* (Washington, D.C.: U.S. Government Printing Office, December 1985), p. 1.

"Curse on the Economy," in "Survey Indonesia: The Extended Family," *The Economist,* 15 August 1987, pp. 12–14.

Draine, Cathie and Barbara Hall, *Culture Shock! Indonesia* (Singapore: Times Books International, 1986), p. 8.

Grant, Bruce *Indonesia* (New York: Melbourne University Press, 1965), pp. 33, 65, 66, 91, 92, 95, 96, 138, 172.

Johnson, Rossall J., Dale L. McKeen, and Leon A. Mears, *Business Environment in an Emerging Nation* (Evanston: Northwestern University Press, 1966), pp. 15–18.

Lanier, Allison R., *Update: Indonesia* (Chicago: Intercultural Press, 1978), p. 10.

Mintz, Jeanne S., *Indonesia: A Profile* (New York: Van Nostrand Company, Inc., 1961), pp. 24–25, 61, 143, 185, 191.

Sievers, Allen M., *The Mystical World of Indonesia: Culture and Economic Development in Conflict* (Baltimore, Md. : The Johns Hopkins University Press, 1974), p. 14.

"Preliminary Considerations" on the Indonesian side was adapted from:

"Doing Business with Indonesia," *World Executive's Digest*, October 1981, p. 66.

Draine and Hall, *Culture Shock! Indonesia*, p. 198.

Lanier, *Update: Indonesia*, pp. 4–5.

Price Waterhouse, *Doing Business in Indonesia* (Tampa, Fla.: Price Waterhouse, 1986), pp. 14–15.

Sievers, *The Mystical World of Indonesia*, p. 267.

"U.S. Concerns Seek to Convince Indonesia to Ease Regulations on Foreign Business," *Wall Street Journal*, 21 April 1981, p. 37.

The section "Sensitivities in 'Breaking the Ice' " was synthesized from:

Draine and Hall, *Culture Shock! Indonesia,* p. 192.
SRI International, *Doing Business in Indonesia* (Menlo Park, Calif.: SRI International, 1987), pp. 3, 9, 10.

The sections "Local Representation" and "Sales Presentation" were organized from:

Price Waterhouse, *Doing Business in Indonesia,* p. 35.
SRI International, *Doing Business in Indonesia,* pp. 4, 13, 14.

The section "Decision-Making Process" on the Indonesian side was synthesized from:

Draine and Hall, *Culture Shock! Indonesia,* p. 205.
Lanier, *Update: Indonesia,* p. 9.
SRI International, *Doing Business in Indonesia,* pp. 11, 12, 16.
"Uneasy Indonesia: Is the 'Wahyu' Moving On?" *Wall Street Journal,* 16 March 1981, p. 23.

The section "Points of Contention" was developed from:

Price Waterhouse, *Doing Business in Indonesia,* p. 34–35.
SRI International, *Doing Business in Indonesia,* p. 14.

The section "Seeking the 'Right' Connections" was adapted from:

Bunge, *Indonesia: A Country Study,* p. 196.
Business International Corporation, *Doing Business in the New Indonesia* (New York: Business International Corporation, 1968), pp. 13–15.
"Curse on the economy," in "Survey Indonesia: The Extended Family," *The Economist,* pp. 12–14.
"Indonesian Decrees Help Suharto's Friends and Relatives Prosper," *TheWall Street Journal,* 24 November 1986, pp. 1, 22.
Johnson, et al., *Business Environment,* p. 32.
SRI International, *Doing Business in Indonesia,* p. 19.

The section "Communication Style" on the Indonesian style was adapted from:

Draine and Hall, *Culture Shock! Indonesia*, pp. 38–42.
Grant, *Indonesia*, pp. 99–100.
Lanier, *Update: Indonesia*, pp. 41–45.
SRI International, *Doing Business in Indonesia*, p. 13.

The section "Sealing the Agreement" on the Indonesian side was developed from:

Price Waterhouse, *Doing Business in Indonesia*, p. 36.
SRI International, *Doing Business in Indonesia*, pp. 17–18.

12

Country Study: Germany

WHAT THE GERMANS ARE LIKE

Germany has been considered an exemplary country, not only for having spectacularly overcome the ravages of World War II, but also for quickly rising as one of the more advanced countries in the world. A number of factors account for this: An initial boost was given by the United Nations Relief and Rehabilitation Aid and the Marshall Plan. A high rate of reinvestment of profits followed the initial infusions brought by both aid monies. Later, Chancellor Erhard transformed the West German economy into a socialist market economy, which released the country from the tight economic controls of the Hitler regime. In addition to judicious management, hard work, and ingenuity, the West German economy at that time was not hampered by government regulations, rationing, price and wage controls, and debt. Also, business owners, managers, and the labor sector were all eager to cooperate to reconstruct the economy—so much so that they postponed demands they would have otherwise made of each other. The reunification of Germany in 1989 was another milestone in German history.

The "Americanization" of Germans quickly followed prosperity and transformed them into heavy-spending consumers. At first, they purchased household goods, appliances, cars, and so forth, to replace worn-out models. But with the sharp increase in disposable income, their appetite for new and better things became an insatiable drive for acquisitions. Aggressive advertising constantly prods German consumers to fill up their shopping trolleys, have dinner in fast-food outlets, listen to rock music, and wear the latest in designer blue jeans.

Contemporary German society is urban, industrial, and middle class. German industrial workers are among the best paid, highly skilled, and disciplined workers in the world. They are merging their ranks with technical-administrative white-collar employees. German society is also divided by age. Foreigners who visit even for a short time quickly note intergenerational differences in attitudes. Older Germans, those born and raised before 1945, view political stability and prosperity from the point of view of the economic chaos of the 1920s. Those born after 1950 have known only unprecedented affluence. In short, the generation gap is based on the two groups' different experiences of economic well-being.

Significant changes in German society began when it shifted from an agricultural society to a nonagricultural one after World War II. Educational achievement is the ticket for all Germans, as it enables them to move upward through the different levels of social classes. University education is essential to acquiring prestigious positions that pay well. Although the country's educational system is supposed to provide universal basic education to the masses, it gets extremely selective and limited at the higher education level. Usually, those who succeed in attaining higher education come from the upper middle- and upper-class families.

The elite group in German society is a small and powerful coterie. It is marked by its diversity: It includes high-ranking civil service executives, trade union officials, university professors, top members of the officer corps, industrial and financial leaders, politicians, and even artists and writers. As a whole, members of the elite support stability. The members of the old elite come from the extremely wealthy groups—very few trace their roots from lower social ranks. However, after World War II, the ranks of the elite expanded to admit new members—those who were university-educated. By the late 1980s, nearly two-thirds of the elite came from families that have long been entrenched in either business or the civil service. Only one in ten of the elite members had a father who was a manual worker.

Members of the elite who belonged to the industrial and financial sectors have the most diverse backgrounds. These are probably the ones you will negotiate with the most, too. There are about 600 of them. There are those who trace their beginnings from the remnants of the old aristocracy. Some are heirs of nineteenth-century industrialists and financiers. The so-called "salaried-rich" technocrats run enterprises. And there are several post–World War II multimillionaires. All of this diverse elite group form a cobweblike network of interlocking directorates, supervisory boards, and holding companies at the apex of the German economy. Members of the bureaucratic elite, in contrast, form a more homogeneous group. About ninety-eight percent of these members are university-educated, just as their parents were, who more likely were civil servants as well.

Germany saw the demise of the old bastions of aristocracy such as the members of the bureaucracy, family owners of industrial empires, and the Prussian army as members of the new elite emerged. Members of the "new ruling class" now include heads of institutes, service firms, professional associations, industries, and government agencies. Wealth and high incomes are not the only qualifications for power and influence in society—one must actually have command over a certain group of people. Positions of power are no longer inherited except for a few. The old aristocratic names like the Krupps and the Stumms are still remembered because signs over industrial plants bear them. The wealth that the new ruling class amassed for themselves brought them spectacular pleasures that they enjoy privately. Owning Mercedes Benz motor cars, Chris-Craft cruisers, summer houses in places like Lake Lugano in Switzerland or the Costa Brava in Spain, and mansions with swimming pools and parks has been quite common among them.

The new rich may not flaunt their wealth, but they still enjoy displaying their honors and titles. They love to be decorated with honorary doctorates or to be appointed honorary consuls. It is said that the buying and selling of honorary consular titles is in itself big business. Big business tycoons maintain a patronage system in their companies to enhance their status. This also gives them an outlet for their humanitarian impulses. One executive even gave away his photographic equipment company to his employees.

The post–World War II period marked the emergence of the middle class. During this period, the members of the "old" middle class—the small-scale merchants, tradesmen, and farmers—declined, while the number of salaried employees increased. Just as in the elite group, the middle class has different levels. Those belonging to the higher level of the middle class seem to be merging with the managerial and professional members of the elite. Those belonging to the lower level are the highly skilled workers, craftsmen, foremen, and clerical employees.

About one-half to two-thirds of the population belongs to the working class. It is made up partly of skilled workers, craftsmen, factory foremen, sales clerks, and low-ranking clerical help, who overlap with the lower middle class, plus others, including transportation workers, and those who work in the growing services sector. However, the skilled, semiskilled, and the unskilled workers in industry, mining, and agriculture comprise the bulk of the working class. Growing prosperity in the economy has closed the gap somewhat between the middle and working classes.

German workers have a big say in the way companies run their businesses because of the nation's "codetermination" policy. This gives the workers seats on management boards in many industries. Unions and workers in Germany are said to have the most comprehensive codetermination rights in the world. Codetermination is not the same thing as participation, though. Participation implies that employers must *inform* and *consult* with employees or their representatives before they implement certain policies. Codetermination is stronger than that. It implies that employers may implement policies only with the *consent* of the workers or their representatives. The law says that companies employing more than 1,000 workers must give one-third of the seats on their boards to labor representatives. The number of seats may vary depending on the industry concerned. The executive committee must include a labor director appointed by the union to handle the current issues between management and labor.

Through the years, the government modified the law and extended its coverage to many different industries. The government will eventually give smaller unions outside of the largest German labor federation, known as the German Federation of Labor or DGB (*Deutscher Gewerkschatfsbund*), better chances of securing works council seats. It will also create spokesperson committees for managerial employees. The DGB consists of seventeen unions. Its ultimate goal is to achieve full economic codetermination for all employees and their unions through Economic and Social Councils that it wants to establish on the federal, state, and regional levels. It will probably achieve this goal, since labor leaders, most of whom are university educated, are highly respected by German society.

During the 1950s, and up until sometime in the 1960s, labor-management relations were generally peaceful. German workers enjoyed a fairly high standard of living, compared to their situation immediately after World War II. They used a consensus approach to bargaining, and it worked very well in those days. But labor-management relations eroded in the 1970s, and throughout the 1980s and into the 1990s, therewas a more marked increase in labor disputes. This occurred partly because of the country's worsening economic problems. Observers have noted a deterioration in the work ethic that may be behind the country's unemployment problem. Workers resist relocating to areas where the jobs are. They prefer to stay in the places where they grew up. These displaced industrial workers are simply unwilling to take low-paying service jobs. In the early 1990s, Germany's unemployment figure stood at over nine percent of the workforce. At the same time, the nation's economy is burdened by the fact that it has the highest employment costs in the world. The unions are strongly against making the adjustments required should the government decide to restructure industry. That may be unlikely, because Germany still regulates its major industries. The country's rigid labor laws make it unattractive for foreign investors to hire Germans. The unions and national associations of a particular industry negotiate wages at the national level. And the laws make it difficult to fire workers.

A small segment of the German workforce is made up of foreign workers, called *Gastarbeiter* or guest workers, who were hired specifically to do the dirty work. The more affluent natives had shown no interest in these menial jobs since the mid-1950s. The Yugoslavs, Greeks, Iberians, Italians, and Arabs who make up this segment of workers have been subjected to prejudice and are not integrated into the mainstream of society. Many decide to stay and get married in Germany. Since they work in order to support their relatives back home, they are unable to raise their own living standards in Germany and continue to be poor. The government continues to be challenged by the social problems spawned by their presence. The most difficult problems are the education and employment of the children of foreign workers and the housing congestion. In the mid-1970s, Germany began to limit migration into the country and encouraged the return of migrant workers to their own countries.

Because of the outmoded educational system in their universities, more and more young German managers are obtaining their university degrees and certificates with accompanying technical degrees from business schools in the United States or from one of the better institutions in Europe. These managers alsorely heavily on in-company training. They are exposed to modern business methods in subsidiaries or branches of multinational corporations (MNCs) in Germany. Subsidiaries of American MNCs play key roles in the motor car manufacturing, petroleum products, electronics, and data processing industries. As a result of all this exposure, German executives use modern managerial and marketing methods. They practice humanistic managerial styles that encourage the delegation of authority, cooperation, and teamwork with their employees, and they negotiate with labor leaders at a high level of professionalism. The more progressive managers have increasingly been shedding traditional organizational structures and are adopting the American model of Strategic Business Units (SBUs) targeted at specific markets.

About eighty percent of top managers in Germany have attended universities, and about fifty percent of them hold doctorates in their particular fields. The title "Dr." carries considerable weight in the business world. Germans consider two to three years of actual experience essential to qualify for a managerial post. With all the training required, young German managers can realistically be expected to start their careers at age thirty-five. Most managers have had training in scientific management: about forty percent of them have an engineering background, and about twenty percent are economists. he older executives lived through the devastation of World War II. Although there is a considerable gap in knowledge between the older and younger executives, the former are treated with respect and are looked upon as "counsellors" of the company. German companies honor their older members and are not anxious to see them leave, even with an incoming crop of sharper young executives. Problems that grapple younger executives include marketing, salesmanship, motivation, efficiency, ecology, long-range planning, and financial control. Some American executives who have worked in Germany find their executives very "Americanized" compared to their counterparts in other European nations.

In general, German managers have worked in more than one firm, although they tend to specialize in a particular industry. Younger German executives are getting more mobile, but on the whole, they are still relatively less mobile than Americans. The German business magazine *Capital* revealed that eighty percent of the top jobs in ten of the largest German companies were held by executives who had worked *only* in that company. In a different survey of 2,200 executives, twenty-nine percent remained in one firm; fifty-three percent had worked in one or two firms; and only eighteen percent had worked in three or more firms. There is still some stigma attached to transferring jobs.

Young German executives are even more status conscious than Americans. Work is an important source of their fulfillment, self-esteem, and status. They value their company's loyalty to them, and their social security system recognizes their need for security by protecting executives and employees against unreasonable dismissal. In turn, the company appreciates loyalty on the part of its employees and executives. Mutual trust is highly valued in Germany business practices. Although there are traces of the old Prussian virtues of obedience, discipline, sense of duty, and orderliness, younger executives also seem to have a greater sense of freedom. They try to satisfy their personal priorities first.

Greater wealth and consumerism has led to a decline in the people's drive to work, especially since the 1970s. Many now say that Germans work to live, instead of living to work. Liberal company policies that allow more vacation time, flexi-hours, and more holidays have encouraged this change in attitude. Rank-and-file workers in Germany have longer vacations than workers in many nations have. The legal minimum is twenty-five to thirty weekdays for workers under eighteen years of age and eighteen weekdays for all other employees. On top of that, there are about ten to thirteen public holidays in a year. Executives are allowed four to six weeks time off. In over 20,000 private and government organizations, employees can choose the time period within which to work.

Men still predominate at work. Women, as a rule, are paid lower and tend to be concentrated in less prestigious and less fulfilling jobs. In the early 1980s, the unemployment rate for women was twice that of men. As a result, many women gave up, backtracked, and assumed "back-to-the-kitchen" attitudes once again. German males still take pride in the fact that their wives do not have to work. Perhaps women schooled in the notion of domestic dependence consent to remain on the sidelines. The business environment practices "tokenism" in granting managerial positions to women. Qualified ones still get inferior positions, and the laws on sexual discrimination in the workplace are not very explicit or punitive. Trade union have not supported women unless they were already employed. As *Emma*, the largest women's magazine in Germany, put it: "Women got only what men left, the crumbs that fell from the table." To illustrate, look at the data processing industry: The more mechanical jobs are reserved for women. They are the first to be laid off in cases of slowdowns.

In the meantime, women have not made too many efforts to better themselves by training in better skills or voicing their complaints against the system. The female director of the Hamburg Senate's Office for the Equalization of Women once said, "I am afraid we will still have to wait hundreds of years if we think that we can improve the situation of women by changes in the consciousness of men." She sees legal penalties, such as fines for sexual discrimination in jobs, as one of the more effective ways of dealing with the problem. The problem of female equality is not limited to Germany. It is a worldwide problem. By way of contrast, in comparison to other countries, Germany may be regarded as a virtual woman's paradise. Still, this is not to say that Germany does not have its gender problems (it does) and it must resolve these in the coming decades.

GERMAN NEGOTIATORS AND YOU

German Language

German Negotiators: Many Germans speak   excellent English, whereas it is rare to find a non-German who speaks excellent German. The German language is difficult, and only an unusually well-prepared negotiator will take the trouble to study the language ahead of time. The southern parts of the country—Bavaria, Baden-Wurttemberg, Rheinland-Pfalz—have their own dialects   different from another variety called "high German." The *Plattdeutsch*, which is spoken in rural areas, is closer to English but is still difficult to decipher for English-speaking people.

You: Your investment in learning the language depends on the nature of your negotiations, your future relationship with them, the length of time you will be working with them, your motivation, and your time, among other factors. Learning the language through formal training and such informal means as German newspapers, books, television, movies, and so forth, will definitely add to your negotiating strength. Do not overlook using translators, no matter how proficient you are in German. Even if the Germans know you understand German, they can not help but caucus among themselves in the negotiating room in your presence. This gives you the advantage of overhearing the tactics they intend to use.

Technical Orientation

German Negotiators: Germans are very pragmatic people, and they look for concrete, technical evidence of excellence and superior performance in products. They do not get carried away by promises showcased in elaborate presentations. They have great awareness and exposure to what is best in the market. They are always looking for products that are better than the best and that they do not produce or have access to yet.

You: Your product or service must be *proven* to be superior in order for it to sell to the   Germans. Arm yourself with all the data and documentation you can, with benchmark results of tests conducted to show flawless performance of product features, durability, life, efficiency, economy of energy use, and so forth. Better yet, orchestrate a demonstration of your product or service at their plant or office. Give them 100 percent guarantees on your products and service by trial-offer periods with money-back guarantees for them. If you are selling high-technology products such as computer software and hardware, have some of your technical personnel work with their computer staff for a certain period of time so that they can test how compatible your offerings are with their setup. Films and well-illustrated manuals and handouts are also good to use. Use case studies and testimonials—tell them about how your clients have successfully used your products and services. Give them names they can contact. They will be even more impressed with you if you give them a balanced presentation. Tell them the conditions under which your product will not perform well. Show how you will try your best to avoid such unfortunate occurrences as long as they cooperate by following operating instructions.

Germans Do Their Homework

German Negotiators: Do not be surprised to find out just how much your German counterparts know about your firm and its products and services. Negotiating is not a haphazard activity for the Germans, and they prepare for it as methodically as the typical way they approach their day-to-day problems. Not only do they research you—they also research your competition, and they do not hesitate to use whatever leverage they have, such as prices, for example. They will remind you of your competition.

You: You should study their firm thoroughly, too. Find out what their real needs are, their future direction, and their bottom line. You can do this if you have sources that can give you this information ahead of time. Also, know your relative position of strength or weakness, not only in Germany, but in the world market. Just how much do you have to offer compared to your nearest competitors? How will you design your set of concessions in exchange for being given consideration vis-a-vis your competitors? How much do you need their business? How much are you willing to invest in terms of concessions to win them over?

Germans Are Hard Bargainers

German Negotiators: The lowest price and prompt delivery dates matter a lot to German negotiators. Since they are a people who are always on target in almost everything they do, they have little tolerance for delays in delivery. They protect themselves way in advance for this eventuality by inserting stiff penalty clauses for late deliveries. They almost always want generous credit terms. They will not overlook the costs of indirect components or the hidden costs of operating and maintaining products as they bargain with you for the lowest possible price. Be assured that they will be armed with the knowledge of your competitors' prices to give themselves more room in getting the best price out of you. They will not fail to ask for warranties or guarantees either.

You: If your firm delivers superior products and has an efficient system of delivery, there should be no extraordinary problems in dealing with Germans. If your firm enjoys cost advantages over your competitors, you will have more leeway in putting together an attractive package that will earn your clients savings or give them more value in the use of the products and services they buy from you. Of course, do not forget the bottom line—the low price with which you can close the deal. The rest is icing on the cake for them.   And when you are bargaining with them, please be aware that they are sensitive about being compared with the French and British. So do not do this.

Hierarchical Decision Making

German Negotiators: There is a big gap between the top and bottom in larger German corporations. Regardless of the size of the organization, decision making is centralized, and power remains at the top, as a general rule. The pervasiveness of authoritarianism and paternalism in Germany, despite its exposure to modern managerial techniques, encourages this kind of centralization. One person decision making, though, is even more common in medium- and small-sized firms.   Remember this always, even though these smaller firms seem easier to approach because there are not too many layers to penetrate. Larger organizations use committees to arrive at decisions. Germans tend to arrive at decisions rather slowly.

You: For expeditious business negotiations, try to develop contacts in the top layer of the German organization, particularly in what they call the *Vorstand,* where the most important decisions are made. However, communication between layers in the organization is so poor and information so well-guarded that you will have to make more effort getting the information you need than you would in other countries. You may find that it takes more time to get things done in German companies because of their rigidity in following their job descriptions. They are reluctant to perform a function that is not within their assigned duty. This inflexibility and the lack of information flow will challenge your ability to make things happen.

You will have to learn some basic German terms. In a large company, the group that ultimately decides the daily operational matters and international deals is the *Vorstand,* or the German executive committee or board of management. The chairman, or *Vorsitzender* or *Vorsitzer,* presides over the committee. Other companies may have one or more *Geschaftsfuhrer* or managing directors/general managers in place of the *Vorstand.* Middle management presents their recommendation to the *Vorstand,* where final decisions are made. These decisions are later handed down to lower-level managers to implement.

Codetermination and German Trade Unions

German Negotiators: German management defers a lot more to their employees than managers do in other countries. In Germany, whoever the trade union appoints as its official representatives become very important people. Managers have to discuss with trade union leaders any changes in working conditions that result from implementing new proposals or projects. Codetermination requires that these matters are dealt with jointly by labor and management within the *Vorstand,* where a certain number of seats are allocated to labor's representatives.

One particular area of concern is the introduction of new technology in the workplace. In general, trade unions are ambivalent about this. Initially, they have perceived it negatively, denouncing high technology tools as "job killers." However, they have changed their minds and accepted the inevitability of working with high-technology equipment on a conditional basis. The DGB accepts working with high technology if it is "socially controllable." One consequence of this is that unions are demanding to have wider codetermination and veto rights over the use of new technology from the planning stage to the final use, change, and/or extension of new technologies.

You: Give yourself some lead time to allow for extended consultations between labor and management. You may have to extend your network of contacts to include the trade union leaders themselves. You can sound them out on some of the terms covering working conditions previous to the formal negotiations and find ways of improving your provisions and overall presentation.

You must be prepared to deal with the complications involved in introducing new technology. As it is, German firms have argued strongly against technology codetermination, asserting that employees' interests are adequately met by the Works Constitution Act of 1972 and the numerous collective and plant agreements that have been made. German employers have expressed a wilingness to modifying such agreements to accommodate the interests of both workers and management.

Network of Connections

German Negotiators: German organizations pay a great deal of attention to any foreign negotiator who has connections with the "elite." These people can facilitate communications with the organization's top decision makers. In Germany, there seems to be a cobweblike network of interlocking directorates, supervisory boards, and holding companies covering industry, trade, banking, and insurance. Power and influence as such are consolidated in the hands of a small coterie of industrial and mercantile tycoons.

You: You should try to tap into this elite power network. Perhaps people in your own company can help you. You may also initiate contacts by working with industry and trade associations. The primary one is the Joint Committee of German Trade and Industry or *Gemeinschaftsausschuss der Deutschen Gewerblichen Wirtschaft*, which has a very comprehensive membership. There are the seventy-three Chambers of Industry and Commerce or *Industrie-und Handelskammern* in Germany and Berlin. These are other public organizations consisting of all industrial and commercial firms subject to the trade tax. Their principal function is to advise regional government bodies, parliaments, law courts, and other institutions on business and economic questions and to inform their members of new developments in the economy. Other organizations to tap are the Federation of German Industries or *Bundesverband der Deutschen Industrie* and the Federation of German Employers' Associations or *Bundesvereinigung der Deutschen Arbeitgeberverbande.* You can not only gain contacts by looking up these organizations, but their members can also give you valuable feedback on some things that concern your projects.

Waning Work Ethic

German Negotiators: German management gives their workers and executives high pay and very liberal working conditions, such as many holidays, long vacations, and flexi-hours. The German workforce enjoys a high level of prosperity. It does not need to toil long hours, and it is always trying to develop new activities for spending its leisure time. Germans get great personal satisfaction from their individual pursuits. This attitude is especially true of younger workers and executives. This is a major problem in modern Germany with high youth unemployment, high wages, and low labor flexibility. German work rules are inflexible.

You: If you are negotiating about constructing a new production plant, for example, you will definitely be concerned about the high wages and salaries you will have to pay German labor. You will have to give them the same legal amenities that German companies give them. While modern business techniques and production technologies should eliminate the need for "hard work" in the plant, there will still be fewer work days in a year within which to accomplish your targets and plans. Also, it is going to be a lot harder to accomplish ad hoc work if your schedules collide with vacation and holiday schedules of workers and executives.

Age of German Negotiators

German Negotiators: Thirty-five years old is the accepted age for Germans to start their managerial careers following their training.

You: It is recommended that your negotiating team be composed of executives of at least thirty-five years of age to command the respect of the other side.

Time Orientation

German Negotiators: They are more present-oriented than future-oriented. Small- and medium-sized firms especially have a time frame of reference that is less than one year.

You: Stress the immediate benefits of your proposal within a short-term period.

German Written Agreements

German Negotiators: Whenever German negotiators express their agreement orally, they will stick to their word. Ultimately, though, they will put their oral agreements into writing, and, as you might have guessed, all the provisions are quite specific and stipulated. German organizations use their own official forms. You should be aware of certain conventions in the format of these contracts: There are two signatures in the contract. The one on the right is for the functional or department specialist whose area is directly affected by the agreement. The one on the left is reserved for whoever has the binding authority. You may find a *"ppa."* This means "per procura," or that the *prokurist* (or holder) is the one with the authority to act for the principal in all business matters arising out of the agreement. The *prokura* must be entered in the local Commercial Register. Sometimes, a firm will have several *prokuristen.* Sometimes, too, one of them will act together with the firm's partner or manager. When this happens, you will again find double signatures, with the letters "ppa." and "i.V." before them. "i.V." means "*in Vollmacht*," or that the employee signing the contract has been authorized to act as an agent for the firm in his or her specific field of expertise. If you see an "i.A." or "*im Auftrag*," that is "by order of" or "on behalf of." This means the person signing has been authorized by his or her superior to do so, but this person has not been given the power of representation. *Vorstand* members, or a *Geschaftsfuhrer*, may sign agreements without any of these conventions, since it is their job to represent the company in these matters. Occasionally, though, they will still need board approval or will have to have some other top-ranking official countersign.

You: Study these formats and conventions together with your lawyer. It is always better to have the assistance of a German lawyer in drafting the contract and checking that its provisions conform to your oral agreement. Be precise in your wording of the contract. The Germans will especially appreciate that.

Conventions of German Correspondence

German Negotiators: Business letters written by Germans may have two signatures at the bottom. The one on the right usually is that of a functional specialist, and the one on the left is that of a person with authority. Rules of the company require that if the subject of the letter covers overlapping areas, representatives of the departments involved should sign the letter. Sometimes, some company members are authorized to act only in conjunction with another or must be supported by another member of the company.

You: If you need to write a German firm and you do not know anyone there yet, address the letter to the firm itself or to the specific department you are concerned with: Write "*Sehr geehrte Herren!*" or "*Sehr geehrte Damen and Herren!*" (Ladies and Gentlemen:). If you already know someone there, it is best to address him directly at his department with: "*z. Hd. Herrn...*" (*zu Handen Herrn...* —attention Mr...). Then one should address the person using his name: "*Sehr geehrter Herr...!*" Occasionally, you may receive letters signed by Germans who do not type their names below or whose signatures may be too difficult to read. This is done intentionally, not only in Germany but in many other countries. If this happens, look for the reference number or initials below the letterhead and write the firm, asking for the identification of the persons who sent you the letter.

REFERENCES

The section "What Germans Are Like" was derived from:

Berhahn, Volker Rolf, *Modern Germany: Society, Economy and Politics in the Twentieth Century* (New York: Cambridge University Press, 1982), p. 228.

Burmeiser, Irmgard, *Meeting German Business* (Germany: Atlantik-Brucke Publication, 1985), pp. 14–16.

Burt, David N., "The Nuances of Negotiating Overseas," *Journal of Purchasing and Materials Management*, Winter 1984, p. 5.

Dornberg, John, *The New Germans: Thirty Years After* (New York: Macmillan Publishing Co. Inc., 1976), pp. 165, 166.

Kirkland, Richard I. , Jr., "Europe's New Managers," *Fortune,* 29 September 1986, pp. 57, 58.

Merkl, Peter H., *Germany: Yesterday and Tomorrow* (New York: Oxford University Press, 1970), pp. 115–116, 118–119, 120.

Morais, Richard C., "The Low-Energy Germany Economy," *Forbes,* 2 November 1987, pp. 116, 118.

Nyrop, Richard F., ed.,*Federal Republic of Germany: A Country Study,* (Washington, D.C.: U.S. Government Printing Office, 1983), pp. 103, 113–118, 120–122.

O'Boyle, Thomas F., "West Germany Refuses to Come to Grips with 'Rigidities' That Slow Its Economy," *Wall Street Journal,* 28 January 1988, p. 20.

Pachter, Henry Maximilan, *Modern Germany: A Social, Cultural, and Political History* (Boulder, Colo.: Westview Press, 1978), pp. 323–4.

Roth, Terence, "German Complacency on Unemployment Dims Hopes Bonn Will Prod the Economy," *Wall Street Journal,* 5 February 1988, p. 20.

Snowdon, Sondra, *The Global Edge: How Your Company Can Win in the International Marketplace* (New York: Simon & Schuster, 1986), pp. 238, 239.

SRI International, *Doing Business in the Federal Republic of Germany* (Menlo Park, Calif.: SRI International, 1978), pp. 12–13.

The section on German negotiating referenced:

Berhahn, *Modern Germany,* p. 244.

Craig, Gordon A., *The Germans* (New York: G. P. Putnam's Sons, 1982), pp. 167, 168.

Nyrop, *Federal Republic of Germany,* pp. 123, 124.

Materials for the section "German Language" were organized from:

Burmeister, *Meeting German Business,* p. 31.
Burt, "The Nuances of Negotiating Overseas," p. 6.
SRI International, *Doing Business in the Federal Republic of Germany,*
   p. 11.

Materials for the section "Technical Orientation" were combined
from:

Kennedy, Gavin, *Negotiate Anywhere!Doing Business Abroad* (London:
   Business Books, 1985), p. 121.
Snowdon, *The Global Edge,* p. 239, 240.
SRI International, *Doing business in the Federal Republic of Germany,*
   p. 9.

Materials for the section "Germans Are Hard Bargainers" were
accumulated from:

Burt, "The Nuances of Negotiating Overseas," p. 5.
Kennedy, *Negotiate Anywhere!,* p. 121.
Snowdon, *The Global Edge,* p. 239.
SRI International, *Doing Business in the Federal Republic of Germany,*
   pp. 13, 14.

Materials for the section "Hierarchical Decision Making" on the
German side were synthesized from:

Burmeister, *Meeting German Business,* pp. 11–14, 22, 23,24.
Burt, "The Nuances of Negotiating Overseas," p. 5.
Snowdon, *The Global Edge,* p. 239, 241.
SRI International, *Doing Business in the Federal Republic of Germany,*
   pp. 15–17.

The section "Codetermination and German Trade Unions" on the
German side was written from materials taken from:

Pachter, *Modern Germany,* p. 325.
Schneider, "The Current Status of Codetermination in West Germany,"
   pp. 10, 11.

The section "Time Orientation" was written from information combined from:

Snowdon, *The Global Edge*, p. 239.
SRI International, *Doing Business in the Federal Republic of Germany*, pp. 14, 15.

The section "German Written Agreements" on the German side was written from materials combined from:

Burmeister, *Meeting German Business*, p. 26.
Burt, "The Nuances of Negotiating Overseas," p. 5.
SRI International, *Doing Business in the Federal Republic of Germany*, pp. 17, 18.

The section "Conventions of German Correspondence" on the German side was written from:

Burmeister, *Meeting German Business*, p. 25.
SRI International, *Doing Business in the Federal Republic of Germany*, p. 3.

13

Country Study:
Saudi Arabia

WHAT SAUDI ARABIANS ARE LIKE

By the mid-1990s, a population of ten million mainly Arabic-speaking people inhabited Saudi Arabia, a place known for the power and opulence that the world's largest oil reserves and a worldwide energy crisis brought about. These factors thrust the kingdom into unimagined prosperity in the 1970s. Although Saudi Arabia is the largest oil-producer in the Organization of Petroleum Exporting Countries, or OPEC—the largest consortium of oil producers in the world—it no longer enjoys the same level of control it had in OPEC after oil prices fell dramatically in the mid-1980s because of a huge oversupply of oil. Saudi pressure could not hold down the cartel's production. The development of alternative sources of energy such as natural gas, solar energy, and thermal energy, and worldwide energy conservation efforts have dampened what used to be a high demand for the oil that OPEC had to supply. Saudi Arabia's oil revenues have declined considerably since then.

SOCIAL ORGANIZATION

You will find three distinct groups when you visit Saudi Arabia: nomadic and seminomadic pastoralists, settled agriculturalists, and urban dwellers. The nomadic and seminomadic pastoralists group has two important and different subgroups—the camel-raising bedouins and the lowlier sheep and goat herdsmen. The difficult physical conditions in the desert, such as aridity and limited water and pastures, which made cultivation almost impossible, led to a complex tribal organization. Herding their animals, using the techniques of pastoral nomadism, became not only their means of livelihood, but also and more importantly their way of life.

The kind of animals they herd determine both their livelihood and their social standing: Noble tribes of highly warlike and mobile members take great pride in their herds of camels. The next level consists of sheep and goat herdsmen and tribesmen with small holdings in the oases. The lowliest group is made up of servants and artisans employed by the herders. More important, though, than the kind of animals herded, the true power comes from claims to wells, waterholes, pastures, and oases in one's territory or *dira*. Due to the scarcity of these resources, the tribal groups always try to maintain friendly relations with owners of the *dira* to get their permission to use pastures and wells. The tribes, therefore, try to have as wide a circle of friends and contacts as possible to assure their long-term survival under conditions of perpetual drought.

Tracing one's lineage is very important to the nomadic tribes, because common descent provides a tie that allows one group to request aid from another. Choice of leadership also largely depends on one's kin and relations. The head of the nomadic group, or *shaykh*, is chosen by heads of the families that belong to the requisite descent position. Traditionally, they chose a man known for his courage, leadership, and luck in battle. In more contemporary times, however, the last requirement has been replaced by the man's ability to wield influence and deal effectively with government bureaucracy and the royal court. *Shaykhs* hold on to their positions tightly because of the social influence, power, and perquisites that accompany it. They also strongly resist efforts of mainstream society to assimilate the tribes.

With increasing modernization, the sense of romanticism and glory that accompanied the image of the bedouin is slowly fading. Nevertheless, Saudi Arabians continue to regard their bedouin ancestry with great respect and pride.

The way that settled agricultural communities are organized follows that of the nomadic tribes. Descent from common ancestors and lineages determine the organization of the village. It also makes trading easier, and it entitles the village to depend on its relations outside the village for help and protection—and get it. Your personal identity and your status depend on your position in a lineage and that lineage's position in the village. Villages from different lineages, though, still maintain strong bonds of friendship and unity based on long acquaintance, common economic interests, and, in the past, the need for common defense. The village headman, just like his counterpart in the nomadic tribes, is chosen by consensus from a leading family where the position is traditional. His *majlis*, or tribal audience or meeting, usually consists of all adult males and leaders of important village groups. The headman represents the village to the central government.

Saudi towns and cities are usually classified according to those inside or outside the *Hejaz*. Those outside the *Hejaz* are the big villages that are agriculture-based. Their social relations are linked to their lineages. People in these areas tend to shun foreign influence. On the other hand, the *Hejaz* cities, consisting of the religious centers of Mecca and Medina, are more open and cosmopolitan on account of the constant traffic of Muslim pilgrims from around the world, some of whom have remained to study, work, or die on sacred ground. Over time, the *Hejaz* cities became increasingly busy commercial centers marked by the heterogeneity of its population and highly developed trades and crafts.

MAJOR SOCIAL INSTITUTIONS

The three most important social institutions in Saudi Arabia are the family, their religion, and the House of Saud.

The Family

The family is the center of social life and the main source of values for Saudi Arabians. They trace their kinship patrilineally, which means that household ties are based on blood ties between men. An average household is large and is made up of a man, his wife or wives, his married sons with their wives and children, his unmarried sons and daughters, and occasionally, a few other relatives such as a widowed or divorced mother or sister.

Saudis strongly value loyalty to their family. This overrides all other social obligations. A person's status in society is based much more on kinship lineage than on individual achievement. Your honor and dignity are largely affected by the social reputation of your family and your lineage. Because family loyalty is so strong, most other forms of behavior derive from this social reality, including nepotism in the workplace. An observer is bound to find family members and relatives employed in the same business organization and even holding high positions. One Saudi man describes the situation this way: "Objective considerations are of a secondary importance in determining the selection of employees and in assuring the necessary cooperation within the organization. It is common to see many friends and relatives of top officials working in their ministries, departments, and divisions." Another observer comments: "A young Saudi with a Harvard business degree must still deal with a highly personalized and family oriented business environment in which personal trust is as important as efficient cost accounting."

Another important social value that stems from family loyalty is the subordination of individual interests and personal advancement to the group's obligations and interests. Conformity and acceptance of authority are commonplace.

The Islamic Religion

Saudi Arabians place a high value on their Islamic religion, which is more than a religion. It is a comprehensive guide for all social behavior, a total way of life. "Islam" means submission to God, and one who submits is a Muslim. Muslims fervently believe in only one God, Allah. The words of his prophet, Muhammad, are regarded as coming directly from God. They were compiled into what became known as the Koran or *Quran*. The five duties of the Muslim are the recitation of the creed *(shahada)*, prayer five times a day *(salat)*, almsgiving *(zakat)*, fasting *(sawm)*, and pilgrimage to Mecca at least once in a lifetime *(haj)*. Muslims fast for one month during *Ramadan*, the ninth month of the Muslim calendar, to commemorate the revelation of God's law to Muhammad. When Muslims fast, they completely abstain from eating, drinking, smoking, and sexual activity during the daytime hours.

The Saudi Arabian government is a staunch enforcer and protector of the social institutions that were formed as a result of the country's religious obligations. The Koran is the nation's constitution, and the *sharia*, the comprehensive system of religious laws that regulate community life, is the basis of its legal system. Specific institutions, such as the Ministry of Pilgrimage Affairs and the Committee for Public Morality, have been set up to make sure Muslims observe Islamic religious practices.

Society as a whole reinforces the government's religious control. Businesses close during prayer times. The mass media is heavy with religious material. Social and peer pressure make Saudis fulfill their religious obligations. They devote themselves intensely to their religion. When they say "God willing," they firmly believe that only God decides what events should take place or how life should unfold.

The House of Saud

Two groups make up the highest power of the land: the members of the House of Saud, consisting of the older surviving sons and other male descendants of King Abdul Al Aziz, and the *ulema*, or the group of religious leaders and Islamic scholars who are advisers to the king. Saudis recognize King Abdul Al Aziz as the father of their nation, and give his surviving sons unquestioned loyalty and obedience.

This is how King Abdul Al Aziz unified a widely disparate collection of tribes that were strongly resistant to any integration efforts. He conquered the natural barriers to unification—great distances and lack of contact—with modern technology, especially modern weapons and communications facilities, to persuade the Saudis to accept his authority. He also exploited communal loyalties by marrying daughters of tribal leaders whose military alliance and support he sought. He saw a great opportunity in using religion as a unification tool, and so he sanctioned the activities of the Wahhabi movement, which had wielded its influence since the mid-1700s. He championed Islamic purity and used it for his own vested interests by getting tribes to crush his enemies, using the excuse of defending the faith. Eventually, he gained control of the *Hejaz*, or the Red Sea coastal region where Jeddah, Mecca, and Medina are located. Then he sought the alliance of merchant families. He won them over, and they became part of his army. Skillfully combining coercion and financial rewards, he succeeded in getting the bedouins to settle down and abandon their nomadic ways. Through the *majlis* or tribal meeting, the king reinforced acceptance of him by the power centers and people in general by keeping his doors open to citizens who had problems. In order to reach those far away from him, he expanded the postal service and telegraph systems. His government offered alternative means of earning money for the tribesmen, who became motivated to take on other occupations. They became traders, soldiers, drivers of vehicles, and so forth. In time, the tribesmen gave up their claims to their *dira*, or water and grazing rights, in return for money payments.

Social Stratification

The top of the elite level is occupied by members of the House of Saud—the male lineage of descendants of King Abdul Al Aziz and their relatives. There are several thousand members today, the result of intermarriage with members of the more prominent tribal groups. The lower level of the elite group is made up of rich businessmen and landowners, high-ranking officials of the government and military, and leading members of the *ulama,* or religious advisers. The dramatic increase in oil revenues in the mid-1970s created massive wealth for big businessmen, especially government contractors and concessionaires of important foreign brands of manufactured goods, and key government officials who took advantage of the government's hurried efforts to develop the country. Most members of both levels of the elite group speak English and were educated in the West.

The government's efforts to modernize and develop the country prompted people from the nomadic tribes and the settled agricultural communities to migrate to the towns and cities. The development efforts created economic activities that gave these people the opportunity not only to survive but also to gain wealth. They became professionals, small businessmen, and government workers. These people make up the newly emerging middle class. They compete with members of the traditional middle class, who are mostly graduates of the religious school system, for positions of power and authority. Over time, technical knowledge and education is slowly replacing family connections in determining success in the workplace.

The lower class is made up of the bedouins and other unskilled hands who did not adapt to the government's modernization drive. They were forced to move into towns because they could not return to their nomadic ways after selling their animals and spending their capital. The bedouins do not have the education or the skills that an industrializing country needs. In addition, they refused to do what they considered menial jobs, the only ones they were really qualified for, because doing this kind of work was inconsistent with their past high social status. Other members of the lower class are foreigners, such as workers from Yemen, the Philippines, and the Sudan, hired to take on jobs Saudis considered beneath them.

Push Toward Modernization

One of the significant effects of the financial boom brought about by the oil revenues that began pouring in in the mid-1970s was the exposure of Saudis to Western education and ideas. The first few years of the oil boom was an important period of transition. There was a heavy inflow of foreign ideas and cultural practices as wealthy Saudis traveled and studied abroad and as expatriate managers, technicians, and consultants moved to Saudi Arabia. While the opportunities for corruption of the nation's culture increased with exposure to foreign ideas, the government stepped up its efforts to maintain the social and religious conservatism. King Faisal reminded his people to maintain their ways of dressing, decorum, and modesty. But some members of the elite who studied abroad and bought property in the lands of their studies became bicultural—acting like Westerners when out of the country and switching back to their traditional ways when back home. This presented the country with both multiple advantages and disadvantages. Being bicultural enabled those Saudis to better communicate the others from around the world, to better understand other cultures and societies. This enabled business transactions to go more smoothly as well as providing more effective outcomes from such business enterprises. On the other hand, exposure to foreign ways often caused Saudis to wish to incorporate the foreign ways of doing things into their daily existence. Such methods often conflicted with the teachings of the Koran and Saudi traditions.

Exposure to mass media from abroad, made possible by modern communications technology, is another problem for the government to contend with. Content is often racy and exposure to which may upset the social conservatism. But local communications networks are easier to control than groups of Saudis going abroad or communities of expatriate managers and technicians. These groups have a heavy influence on the Saudi population through person-to-person contact.

A welcome change in the area of modernization is the increasing educational opportunities for Saudi women. The situation of women in Saudi Arabia is peculiar. Women are second-class citizens in Saudi Arabia because the Koran very specifically indicates such a status. Society looks upon women as weaker than men in mind, body, and spirit. Women are thought to be incapable of the more challenging tasks because of their "emotional" nature. Having sons is a supreme concern of married women, because this raises their value in society. A woman's influence is greater in the home rather than in the workplace. Mothers are very influential with their sons, and the close relationships that develop between them is a perfect opportunity for mothers to wield the control society otherwise takes away from them. The government now allows women to go to school, and the response to professional alternatives opened to them in the teaching and medical fields, for example, has been very positive. In keeping with society's requirement of segregating men and women, universities use closed-circuit television to permit male educators to teach a class of females. Over time, the local educational system will catch up with the needs of the country. When that happens, the need to send people abroad for further education will decrease. There will be more local people qualified to teach and provide the education needed for development.

SAUDI ARABIAN NEGOTIATORS AND YOU

Business Opportunities

Saudi Arabian Negotiators: The rapid economic development of Saudi Arabia means substantial business opportunities for foreign business executives. The government is by far the most dominant market in the country. It seems especially interested in acquiring operations and maintenance services, labor-saving equipment, agricultural machinery, irrigation systems, arid land-use technology, computer technology, electric and nonelectric machinery, pollution control devices, control systems, and other specialized ancillary services.

You: You will need to negotiate with each individual government agency because Saudi Arabia does not have a centralized office in charge of tenders and contracts. In particular, study Royal Decree Number M/14, which describes such important details as methods of procurement and performance, contract awards, advance payments, fines due to delays, contract forms, and so forth. Another document, Ministerial Resolution Number 2131/97, includes the rules for the implementation of tenders. It describes the manner of advertising tenders, the process of submission, the bid evaluation process, and deadlines for submission, among other concerns.

Local Decision Making

Saudi Arabian Negotiators: The decision-making process is centralized in Saudi Arabia and confined to very specific levels. Control rests with members of the House of Saud, senior goverment officials, and the commercial elite. Older decision makers are largely influenced by highly personal factors, such as trust and their impressions of you. They do not have as much education and technical knowledge as the younger members of the elite. Although the Saudi government bureaucracy is getting bigger, only a few key officials are significant in terms of decision making. Ministers and lesser technocrats are vitally important to the king and his advisers. Their positions in power depend a lot not only on how they perform their duties, but also and perhaps more importantly on the goodwill and positive relations they are able to maintain with members of the ruling family. Many of these technocrats and highly placed government officials use their bureaucratic positions as stepping stones to gain leverage in terms of contacts and influence with the upper echelons of the elite before they move into the private sector. Social cliques exist in the more traditional offices where former schoolmates, relatives, and friends get together for playing cards and socializing. Members of these cliques also create power blocs in the decision-making process and tend to influence each other's votes over an issue.

You: Enlist the support of your agent so you can identify who holds the decision-making power in matters that concern your business. One of the difficulties of doing business in Saudi Arabia is finding the precise people who make these decisions. Although there is a growing number of technocrats who occupy management positions in both the government and private sector, you will have to make sure that their actual authority corresponds with their title or function in the company. It may or may not. Cultivate your contacts in the top bracket of the organization you are dealing with. Decision making is centralized in Saudi Arabia.

Reaching an Agreement

Saudi Arabian Negotiators: Saudi Arabians indicate that a firm agreement has been reached with a handshake or oral commitment. As a rule, they do not like lengthy and tedious contracts, which they feel only imply mistrust. This does not mean, though, that they will not be very careful in drafting a tight contract with detailed, specific terms. The legal consultants of both sides usually draft the actual contract. Once the contract is signed and business activities begin, the foreign party must register with the Ministry of Commerce.

When disputes arise over compliance with the terms of the agreement, the provisions of Royal Decree Number 32 apply. The Committee of Commercial Disputes, which consists of two *sharia* judges and one legal adviser, makes judgments in cases of commercial disputes, except those related to the insurance business. Cases involving commercial fraud are governed by the Regulations for the Control of Commercial Fraud issued under Royal Decree Number 45. Either party can approach the king to appeal the decisions of the Committee of Commercial Disputes. The king will seek the opinion of the Ministry of Commerce before settling the matter.

You: Exercise great care in drafting contracts and in complying with tender specifications—this will help you avoid future disputes. Observers note that foreign parties are usually at a disadvantage when involved in disputes with Saudi businesses and especially so with the government. It is best to avoid getting into this no-win situation with the government. In cases where no resolution of the dispute is in sight, the local *sharia* adjudication takes over.

Establishing Contact and Making Presentations

Saudi Arabian Negotiators: The Saudi Arabian government prefers to deal directly with other governments when selling crude oil, and, in exchange, it offers to deal with the particular country's private companies in specific projects. The government announces its calls for tenders and invitations to bid through its embassies abroad. A committee composed of members of the Saudi contracting party needs a majority vote in order to award a contract. Awarding a contract does not by itself indicate a sale, though. The committee can rescind the award for a number of reasons and reopen the call for bids. These committees favor Saudi bidders.

You: Unless you represent a construction company, your team does not have to register with the appropriate ministry before making a bid. Construction companies need to register with the Ministry of Public Works and Housing before making a bid. Once you register, the ministry includes you in its list of approved contractors. It is a requirement to work with a local agent when you start your business activity in Saudi Arabia. The cost of entering the Saudi Arabian market is high. These are heavy startup representation costs. Competition with established foreign firms is tough, because these firms have already written off most of their startup costs and have already signed several contracts with the Saudis. It is extremely important for your team to understand and comply strictly with the requirements of tender specifications. Use the services of your local agent to make sure you are following their rules.

Be sure to include top-level executives on your negotiating team. They should have enough decision-making authority to sign deals with top negotiators in both the private and government sectors. We advise against including females on your negotiating team. This will complicate matters. Saudis consider females subordinate to males, and they will probably have a difficult time dealing with social mores that give women equal status to men. Prepare your team and materials very well before you make your presentation. This is usually scheduled after the Saudi negotiator has read your proposal. Make sure you translate all your written materials and documents into both Arabic and English. As much as possible, bring tangible prototypes or models representing the product or service you are selling. Use vivid visuals with a lot of animation. This can be done today with computer graphics, software, and the latest audio-visual equipment. The Saudis respond better to tangible visual materials rather than to abstract words.

One of the things your team will have to get used to is the constant traffic of people that pass through offices in Saudi Arabia. You may want to divide your presentation into several brief modules, not only to accommodate these interruptions, but also to give your audience a chance to clarify concepts and meanings as you go along.

Communicating   Effectively   with   the   Saudis

Saudi Arabian Negotiators: It is important to be aware of Saudi Arabian sensitivities. Generally, the Saudis are not confrontational. Because of this, they will not be open and honest about their problems and complaints. The ways they say "no" are indirect—they will delay matters or avoid being accessible. Their society is largely shame-oriented, and so they suffer more from being found out rather than from actually violating a social norm. Therefore, they place a premium on putting on appearances and preserving their favorable social image. They dislike arrogant and harried behavior on the part of their business visitors or partners. This kind of behavior suggests that visitors consider themselves superior and the Saudis not important enough to spend time with. Initial conversations with Saudis are usually spent talking about personal matters. They value spending a lot of time getting socially and personally acquainted with their potential business colleagues. Occasionally, you will catch them in moments of silence.

One important thing foreigners have to learn is the way Saudis use social space. Watch their social behavior in their offices. They observe the same social mores that they use in their *majlis* system of tribal meetings. In the early days, subjects had access to their leaders through the *majlis* system—the leader had an open-door policy, and anyone who had a problem could approach him personally and meet with him in his tent. This pattern is still used in modern offices. Saudis value their family members, relatives, friends, and countrymen so highly that they are willing to interrupt any business meeting, no matter how important, if these constituents should drop by for any reason. Foreigners should expect to see constant traffic in the Saudis' offices, particularly unexpected drop-ins. Sometimes, you will be exposed to another approach called the *diwaniyah,* where the business is conducted in one of the rooms of the Saudi's house. You will see this done mostly by the older and more traditional businessmen.

Saudis think what can be accomplished in a unit of time depends not so much on a person's effort as it does on God's will. The expression, "God willing," is the Saudi's daily affirmation of this belief. Saudis, therefore, do the best they can in a situation and accept delays and interruptions as signs that God's approval has not been earned. Westerners will certainly find their orientation toward time difficult to adjust to because it is diametrically opposed to their own sense of mastery over nature and life itself.

You: Be aware of the unique social sensitivities you will find in Saudi Arabia. Do not put the other side on the spot by pushing for answers, clarifications, and decisions when they are not ready. Show deference and respect, and respond positively to their need to preserve a good social image. One way of doing this is to avoid using dirty tricks when you negotiate. Another way is to allow lots of time for the other side—your agent, your Saudi counterpart, or your other business contacts—to accomplish what they have to regarding your business requirements. To Saudis, time is a highly malleable frame of reference within which they operate. They do not want to be rushed.

During your meetings, use an interpreter, and make sure your local agent is present so he can help you in clarifying the issues and questions that come up as you deal with the other side. Remember that Saudis appreciate being informed ahead of time about the agenda they will be discussing with you. Before you meet, make sure that all documents are translated into Arabic, English, and your language.

When you are dealing with Saudis who come to your country, you have more leeway. You do not have to observe their social rules. Make sure you follow them when you are in Saudi Arabia, though—for example, never hand the other side documents with your left hand; never expose the soles of your shoes when you sit cross-legged; and so forth. Make sure you brush up on rudimentary matters of Saudi etiquette so you will not offend them. Get your agent's advice here.

Relationship with a Local Agent

Saudi Arabian Negotiators: The government requires foreigners to have either a partnership agreement with a Saudi company or individual, or to be represented by either a commercial agent or a service agent.

A commercial agent may be an importer, distributor, or wholesaler. Royal Decree Number 11 gives details about how you should deal with commercial agencies. Commercial agents must be registered with the Ministry of Commerce. The service agent acts on behalf of the foreign contractor or anybody having a contractual relationship with the government. Royal Decree Number M/2 says several things about service agents. These agents have to be registered with the Ministry of

Commerce. They represent foreign contractors who do not have Saudi partners. Only Saudis may act as service agents. Do not pay your service agents more than five percent of the contract value for services they perform. Disputes between you and your service agent are settled by the government's Commercial Disputes Arbitration Committee. Read the decree for more details.

The younger, better-qualified, and better-educated agents are becoming more selective in their choice of foreign clients. They can afford to be more choosey since they have more to offer—advanced modern office facilities and highly trained office personnel. Ask around. You will find out who are the best full-time representatives in Saudi Arabia. If any of your products, services, or projects have a high technological content, make sure your agent has well-trained technical personnel.

You: In dealing with commercial agents, particularly importers, there are certain things you should look for. Make sure that the Saudi importer you pick has a broad geographic coverage of your target market and excellent contacts. Choose your importers carefully because they usually have a big hand in determining local prices and in promoting your product or service. Go out of your way to nurture your relationships with your importers. This will pay big dividends, because long-term personal relationships are one of the secrets of success in Saudi Arabia. Make sure you fulfill your part of the bargain by filling orders according to specifications, by delivering goods on time, and by complying with the agreed-upon prices.

Most agents you contact will claim that they have good connections. Check out their claims. Ask them for evidence of past deals they have successfully transacted. Spell out all the responsibilities of your agent clearly in the agreement you both sign. Generally speaking, agents are expected to introduce you to their contacts in banks, the government, and businesses, and to establish personal relationships with key people in those institutions. They should advise you on the local business practices and social customs. Since organized marketing information is hard to get in Saudi Arabia, tap their knowledge of local market trends to make up for this information gap. Even when you have an agent working for you, you should assume the main responsibility for such activities as sales and marketing.

Monitor their activities closely. Make sure you have enough bargaining leverage so you will be able to adjust their commission depending on the actual work they do and the benefits they deliver to you. Charge their commission against the money your Saudi Arabian clients pay you. You must keep detailed records of all your financial transactions with your agents. Do not let them make direct or indirect payments to any of the employees of your Saudi Arabian client. It is better for you not to give your agents legally binding powers, although you are traditionally liable for the consequences of all acts they perform on your behalf. Make sure they keep you up-to-date about developments and that they consult with you often about important decisions that you will have to make.

You will have to make certain adjustments for sure when you are working with your local agents—such as allowing more time and being more patient with them in waiting for results. Saudi Arabians do not share the same sense of urgency about the use of time as most westerners seem to have—to them, nothing can rush God's will, upon which everything depends. If things do not work out well between you and your agents, consult the new Commercial Agency Regulations, which spell out valid reasons for ending agency relationships and the damages each party has to pay.

Establishing Connections

Saudi Arabian Negotiators: Saudi Arabians value doing business through people they know and respect. Their culture revolves around family ties and extended family connections. Success in business depends a lot on the connections they make within their own family and institutional networks. With the country's rapid modernization, these traditional values are slowly but surely being replaced by more modern values, such as power based on possession of knowledge or technical information. Traces of traditional values will be a strong underlying current for a long time to come, though.

You: Make sure your agent has significant connections with important social institutions such as the House of Saud, top government levels, the banking system, and big business. Expect your agents to spend a considerable amount of time socializing with their contacts to solidify relationships on your company's behalf. Once they have introduced you to their contacts, take the initiative—share in the efforts of building good relationships by participating in the process yourself. To illustrate the power of having good connections, examine the case of Saudi Pritchard, an Anglo-American company that had business relationships with Prince Abdul-Rahman bin Abdullah. The prince took a fifty percent stake in the company. The company had a difficult time dealing with British banks, who were not keen on backing up performance bonds required by the Saudi government. With the support of the prince's connections who have provided substantial guarantees, Pritchard managed to get the Saudis to cut the bond to ten percent of the value of each year's work, reducing the liability to two percent of the total contract versus the five to ten percent usually required.

Cultivating   Friendships

Saudi Arabian Negotiators: Saudis appreciate the value of investing in friendships to facilitate their business transactions. This attitude goes all the way back to their nomadic days when tribes had to cultivate as wide a circle of friendships as possible, particularly among the more noble tribes. The latter owned and controlled access to waterholes and wells, which were indispensable to the survival of both the nomads and their animals during periods of drought.

You: You should invest a lot of time and effort in cultivating and maintaining friendships in all important sectors—the government, banking system, the marketplace, private businesses, and so forth. It takes time to clinch major deals. You win the trust of Saudis only after a long period of cultivation, even when you have the right contacts. This investment pays off, particularly for subsequent business deals whose gestation times need not be as long.

The   Issue   of   Bribery

Saudi Arabian Negotiators: Even though the government prohibits bribery of public servants in Royal Decree Number 38, the use of facilitating payments is considered to be the norm in Saudi Arabia. Evidence of bribery is extremely difficult to find, though. The procurement law, Royal Decree M/14, prohibits Saudi agents from abusing their authority and acting as intermediaries in deals involving illegal payments. But foreign companies participating in joint ventures are not covered by the legal requirement that the service agent's commission be about five percent of the contract value. Quite often, service agents contact middlemen who, in turn, are paid by them for deals they are able to clinch, and eventually the foreign company pays for all these costs.

You: You must have close control over your agent's activities to prevent bribery. If you are with an American firm, the Foreign Corrupt Practices act of the United States makes you assume full responsibility and liability for *all* the activities of your agent, so make sure you know what your agent is doing. Preventive measures include keeping thorough records of all your organization's financial transactions and not allowing your agents to make payments to employees of your Saudi Arabian clients. Bribery is clearly involved if you pay a middleman or other institutional entities with decision-making powers to grant you business, if the purpose of the payments is to influence them to give you business. Of course, in order for a charge of bribery to be valid, you must be completely aware of all this.

Favorite Bargaining Tactics Used by Saudi Arabians

Saudi Arabian Negotiators: In the construction business, the government prefers to give jobs to Saudi Arabian contractors as long as they can deliver within ten percent of the quality specifications. The Council of Ministers prohibits foreign contractors from using imported materials, tools, and equipment that local sources are able to supply. Foreign contractors are required to subcontract part of the project to local firms.

When it comes to government contract projects, the Saudis are tough negotiators. The government prefers to fix the price of the contract even for projects that will take years to complete. Government negotiators, who are experienced project managers and estimators, make sure that the contract is tightly written with very exact specifications and that the margin for inflation allows for about three to five percentage points below the actual inflation rate. The Saudi government requires that the foreign firm offers both bid bonds (one to two percent of price) and performance bonds (up to five percent of the contract value). Both bonds will have to be submitted in the form of certified checks drawn on Saudi Arabian banks or in the form of a guarantee backed by syndications of several foreign banks, and these must be payable on demand. In addition, the Saudis require guarantees on the performance of all components of a project for at least ten years.

One important issue in bargaining with the Saudis is price. Although the Saudis do not like it when you use hard bargaining tactics on them, they take a hard bargaining stance when haggling with you over prices. Of course, just like many other negotiators, they try to get as many bids and quotes as possible from firms in different countries to enhance their bargaining position. They negotiate from a position of mistrust if you do not already have a long-term relationship with them, and they often maintain that Western international firms charge exorbitant prices. Their frequent experience is that prices tend to be much lower from international firms based in the developing or Asian countries for a project of comparable quality and workmanship. It is on that basis that they often feel they are being taken advantage of by Western companies. In one case, for instance, in 1977, blue-chip international companies submitted their bids for $700 million worth of electrification schemes. The contract involved supplying switchgear, transformers, electric power lines, and diesel-powered generator sets, with extensive engineering work required in Jizan, Al Kharj, Baha, and Asir. The Industry Minister accused these companies of price rigging. He charged that eight of these companies were in collusion in setting their prices. The accused companies were blacklisted and barred from submitting tenders in the future.

The Saudi government likes to use the turnkey approach in huge construction projects. This means the foreign contractor has to turn over the entire physical plant, workforce, and management team to the government when the project is completed. The foreign contractor bears total responsibility for the project.

The Saudis respond favorably to the "power of powerlessness" tactic and often extend their kind consideration to foreign negotiators who are in greater need of winning a contract.

You: If your competitive position allows you to do so, you will want to build in the cost of your agent's commission, your performance and bid bonds, and your penalty guarantee in the price you quote. You can greatly enhance your bargaining position if you demonstrate your serious intention of following up on your commitments. Do this by establishing a presence in Saudi Arabia—set up an office and assign your representatives there. Saudis respond to close and constant personal follow up—not to mere correspondence or long-distance phone calls.

Another significant way you can enhance your company's leverage is to offer specialized and technical training to the local people along with the project and technology you are selling. Technical training and education is one of the government's top development priorities. If your proposal involves technology transfer, be careful about the information you release to the Saudis. The government is still working on patent and licensing legislation. So if you introduce sensitive technology, be aware that the risk of patent infringement is a real threat. Try to build in explicit provisions in the contract regarding the use and protection of patent rights that are involved in the project. Some foreign firms publish announcements concerning their patent rights or copyrights in the *Saudi Official Gazette*, and you might want to do that too.

REFERENCES

The section "What Saudi Arabians Are Like" was adapted from:

Bureau of Public Affairs (U.S. Dept. of State), *BackgroundNotes: Saudi Arabia* (Washington, D.C.: U.S. Government Printing Office, December 1986), p. 1.
Miller, Sarah, "Saudi Politics Won't Push up Oil Prices," *Businessweek*, 17 November 1986, p. 72.
Nyrop, Richard F., Beryl Lieff Benderly, Laraine Newhouse Carter, Darrel R. Eglin, and Robert A. Kirchner, *Area Handbook for Saudi Arabia* (Washington, D.C.: U.S. Government Printing Office, 1977).

The section "Social Organization" was adapted from:

Chesanow, Neil, *The World-Class Executive: How to Do Business Like a Pro around the World* (New York: Rawson Associates, 1985), pp. 113, 114.
Hobday, Peter, *Saudi Arabia* (New York: The Macmillan Press Ltd., 1979), p. 5.
Ministry of Commerce/Kingdom of Saudi Arabia, *Doing Business in Saudi Arabia* (Washington, D.C.: Commercial Office/Royal Embassy of Saudi Arabia, 1982), p. 4.
Nyrop, et al., *Area Handbook for Saudi Arabia*, pp. 134, 136, 148, 149.
The Royal Embassy of Saudi Arabia Information Office, *Saudi Arabia—Education and Human Resources* (Washington, D.C.: The Royal Embassy of Saudi Arabia Information Office, 1985), p. 1.

The section "Local Decision Making" was synthesized from:

Chesanow, *The World-Class Executive*, p. 139.
Hobday, *Saudi Arabia*, p. 81.
Nyrop, et al., *Area Handbook for Saudi Arabia*, pp. 4, 149.
Doing Business on the Arabian Peninsula, Menlo Park, Calif.: SRI International, 1978, p. 16.

The section "Reaching an Agreement" was adapted from:

Business International Corporation, *Saudi Arabia: Issues for Growth*, New York: Business International Corporation, August 1981, p. 116.
Ministry of Commerce, *Doing Business in Saudi Arabia*, pp. 13, 16.
SRI International, *Doing Business on the Arabian Peninsula*, pp. 17, 18.

The section "Establishing Contact and Making Presentations" was developed from:

Business International Corporation, *Saudi Arabia: Issues for Growth*, pp. 114–116.
Chesanow, *The World-Class Executive*, pp. 123, 130, 137.
SRI International, *Doing Business on the Arabian Peninsula*, p. 12.

The section "Communicating Effectively with the Saudis" was adapted from:

Chesanow, *The World-Class Executive*, pp. 115, 118, 120.
Hobday, *Saudi Arabia Today*, pp. 4, 68.
Kennedy, Gavin, *Negotiate Anywhere! Doing Business Abroad*, (London: Business Books Ltd., 1985), pp. 72–76.
Nyrop, et al., *Area Handbook for Saudi Arabia*, p. 5.
SRI International, *Doing Business on the Arabian Peninsula*, pp. 7–10, 11, 13–15.

The section "Relationship with a Local Agent" was synthesized from:

Business International Corporation, *Saudi Arabia: Issues for Growth*, pp. 121–126.
"Doing Business in Saudi Arabia," *World Executive's Digest*, April 1981, pp. 28, 29.
Kennedy, Gavin, *Negotiate Anywhere! Doing Business Abroad*, pp. 72–76.
Ministry of Commerce, *Doing Business in Saudi Arabia*, pp. 6, 12, 13.
SRI International, *Doing Business on the Arabian Peninsula*, p. 20.

The section "Establishing Connections" was adapted from:

Business International Corporation, *Saudi Arabia: Issues for Growth*, p. 118.
Hobday, *Saudi Arabia*, p. 104.
SRI International, *Doing Business on the Arabian Peninsula*, pp. 18–20.

The section   "Cultivating Friendships" was adapted from:

Business International Corporation, *Saudi Arabia: Issues for Growth*, p. 117.
Nyrop, et al., *Area Handbook for Saudi Arabia*, p. 136.
SRI International, *Doing Business on the Arabian Peninsula*, pp. 13, 117.

The section "The Issue of Bribery" was developed from:

Business International Corporation, *Saudi Arabia: Issues for Growth*, pp. 106, 119, 125.
Kennedy, *Negotiate Anywhere!*, pp. 73, 75.
Rossman, Marlene L., *The International Businesswoman: A Guide to Success in the Global Marketplace* (New York: Praeger , 1986), pp. 40, 42.

The section "Favorite Bargaining Tactics Used by Saudi Arabians" was organized from:

Business International Corporation, *Saudi Arabia: Issues for Growth*, pp. 116, 119, 121, 129, 130, 133, 135.
Chesanow, *The World-Class Executive*, p. 138.
Hobday, *Saudi Arabia,* pp. 102, 103, 105.
Nyrop, et al., *Area Handbook for Saudi Arabia*, pp. 5, 6.
SRI International, *Doing Business on the Arabian Peninsula*, pp. 12–15.

14

Country Study:
Hong Kong/China

WHAT THE HONG KONG CHINESE ARE LIKE

Hong Kong has a population of around six million people, ninety-eight percent of whom are Chinese. About half of the Chinese were born in Hong Kong, and the other half migrated from various parts of mainland China such as Canton, Sze Yap, Chiu Chow, Shanghai, and Hakka. The majority of the immigrants come from Kwangtung. This accounts for the strong Cantonese influence among these migrants. The early Cantonese migrants were mostly peasants, small traders, or artisans; recent migrants are much better educated. The remaining two percent of the population consists mostly of non-Chinese people from Britain, India, the United States, Australia, Portugal, Pakistan, Philippines, Singapore, Canada, Japan, Indonesia, and Germany. The people's religious activities are strongly influenced by Buddhism, Taoism, and ancestor worship. A minority follow Muslim, Hindu, Sikh, and Christian beliefs. The increasing number of foreign companies locating in Hong Kong has created a multicultural society that is the basis of the country's modern, cosmopolitan ambience. Cantonese Chinese and English are the main languages, but there is increasing interest in learning Mandarin because it's the main dialect spoken in mainland China. China has opened up her lines for international business through Hong Kong.

The life of the traditional Chinese is centered around the patriarchal family, which is headed by the father, or by the grandfather, if he is still alive. His authority is absolute over all family members. The family is still seen as both the means of economic survival and the focus around which the network of relations within both the immediate and extended family revolves. Confucius taught the Chinese to observe filial devotion and to seek interpersonal harmony in the family. The family is valued as a means to express reverence and accountability to its ancestors as predecessors of the family, to extend the family's reputation, and to ensure perpetuation of its members. The young are taught to honor, respect, and obey the elderly members of the family, particularly their parents.

Well-to-do families pass along their assets along the male line with great interest in helping sons to establish their own businesses or in expanding the family's business. The middle- to low-income groups, in turn, save their limited assets for the education of the eldest son. The daughters of the families do not receive as much attention as the sons; their education is usually inferior to that of their brothers. When they marry, the daughters eventually transfer their loyalties to the family of their husbands. They have been trained to maintain self-control and serve the family until they mature. They are expected to be subordinate to their husbands after marriage.

Another significant institution is the lineage or clan associations. There are many of them. These are groups of families with the same surname who trace their descent through male lines originating from a common ancestor. These associations assist and protect the less fortunate members of the association and maintain the family tradition of honoring ancestors by constructing ancestral halls where rituals and festivals are held. The wealthy members of the clan naturally dominate and use their family and corporate resources to ensure their control and advance their own interests. The poorer members profit not only from the material support they gain but also from the prestige they garner from being associated with their well-to-do relatives. Members of the immediate family, though, see to it that their loyalties to their own family remain intact regardless of the conflicting interests that may exist between their family and the clan. The family always comes first.

Migrant Chinese families who moved to Hong Kong had a strong determination to succeed. This was primarily motivated by loyalty to their family and the fear of shaming their kinsmen in case of failure. Invariably, news about their welfare reached their extended family on the mainland, who depend on them heavily for financial support. The behavior resulting from this kind of motivation emphasized self-control, hard work, abstinence, willingness to save, openness to risk taking, and self-reliance. Somehow, migrant Chinese excelled particularly in the economic activities of their new country.

Of course, the younger generation of Chinese born in Hong Kong have a much different mind set. Their exposure to Western culture and industralization in modern-day Hong Kong has reduced their identification with their family. Instead, they are more aware of their own self-identity, as is the pattern in most Western societies. Rather than being oriented toward the past, in keeping with their ancestral traditions, the young Chinese are more forward looking. Their involvement in such social organizations as their workplace, trade unions, political parties, and so forth, has diluted their loyalty to their family. They are making their own choices of friends, spouses, jobs, and other important matters.

Despite the encroachment of the impersonal ways of twentieth-century modernization and industrialization, Chinese families still continue to be more cohesive units compared to Western families. The father is still the unquestioned head of the household; the young continue to respect the elderly members of the family; and aged parents continue to live at home with their children, especially the eldest son, who risks social sanctions in the eyes of relatives and neighbors if he neglects his parents.

The influence of Confucian tradition, which is strong on the mainland, weakens as Chinese immigrants move to Hong Kong. Confucianism looked down upon material gain earned through commercial activities. But the needs of survival and the modern point-of-view that sought wealth through the numerous options offered by an industrialized economy eventually transformed the immigrant Chinese into a pragmatic economic group. Many become very rich.

The Hong Kong elite, or *kao-chi*, is made up of three groups: the old Hong Kong families, the Chinese industrialists and new rich, and the wealthy foreigner-residents. The old Hong Kong families have more stable bases for wealth, such as land. They emphasize family connections based on marriage and relationships with founding fathers of their families. Some members of these families are of mixed blood (Chinese and European,) and have chosen to retain the Chinese traditions governing family organization. They also continue to practice ancestor worship in their effort to conform to classical practices within the urban setting of Hong Kong. Members of these old families have often been bestowed with honors by the British colonial government, which has often been successful in getting their cooperation in implementing their policies. Having established social and economic prestige on the basis of their historical prominence does not necessarily guarantee the stability of their position in society. Enduring wealth is still the primary basis for social prestige in Hong Kong.

The members of the industrial nouveau riche have emerged only recently. They derive their wealth mainly from speculative enterprises instead of from the more secure forms of investments that the old families prefer. Another difference between this group and the old families is that many of the nouveau riche come from dialect groups other than Cantonese, from which most of the old rich seem to come. As always, considerable strife exists between the new rich and the old. The old are protective of their power and influence and the new wish to use their newly gained wealth to secure that power, influence, and status which they see the old rich having. This is an age-old dilemma which will not be resolved in a fortnight.

Both members of the old and new rich seek additional social prestige by donating significant amounts to charitable associations. They receive a great deal of publicity from their generous deeds, and the media display their pictures and credentials prominently. Fund-raising campaigns are another activity that earns social visibility and approval. But participation in these charitable networks exerts a tremendous economic pressure on the business executive, who is expected to continue donating money even after retirement and to solicit additional money from his friends. Eventually all these activities pay off, and the prominent executive earns the most prestigious position of all in Hong Kong—membership on the permenent board of directors of the prominent clan associations.

The foreigners in Hong Kong are the third wealthy subgroup. Mainly British, this subgroup, led by powerful *taipans*, head British-owned banks, mercantile houses, and financial institutions. Western expatriates benefit from free housing or nominal rents provided by their multinational corporations. They invest part of their money in their home nations, in other countries, and in local investments run by other Western companies. Lured by the cheapness of local labor, quite a number of them have become wealthy by establishing new companies and industries. Expatriates have flocked to Hong Kong in record numbers, attracted by the low tax rate, the work ethic of the population, and the immense opportunities which exist there; Hong Kong is truly a cosmopolitan city.

Those who occupy the lower levels of the elite are professionals such as lawyers, doctors, architects, engineers, journalists, executives, high-level civil servants, and so forth. Their prestige and status are directly proportional to the amount of income they earn. These groups tend to be the up-and-comers, driving toward success without regard to the price it requires. You will probably meet all of these groups as you negotiate in Hong Kong.

HONG KONG NEGOTIATORS AND YOU

Preliminary Considerations: Incentives

Hong Kong Negotiators: Hong Kong has become so economically successful not only in Southeast Asia but throughout the world because of six main reasons: First, there is little government interference in the conduct of business. This results in a minimum amount of red tape. There are no restrictions on ownership or management of foreign companies, and there are no restrictions on foreign exchange or on remittance of profits in and out of Hong Kong. The government has designated Hong Kong as a free port, where controls on imports or exports and reexports are to be determined only by international obligations. There are no import or export licensing requirements for most products, and a simple 0.05 percent ad valorem fee is charged. These incentives are offered to all investors—foreign investors are not given special treatment.

Second, the government imposes low taxes. A flat eighteen percent tax is placed on corporate profits earned in Hong Kong. Profits or income earned outside the colony, including royalties, dividends, sales, and capital gains, are not taxed. Losses may be carried forward yearly without limitation to offset future profits.

Third, Hong Kong supports a modern international financial network in such markets as gold, foreign exchange, and futures trading. A comprehensive array of banking services are offered. Local capital is available at low interest rates.

Fourth, a well-trained workforce is available at wages whose levels are determined by market supply and demand. Minimum wages and labor union activities do not exist in Hong Kong. The workforce offers low-skilled to highly technically oriented individuals—plus able managers, most of whom speak fluent English. The government is investing heavily in technical education and industrial training; each industry has its own training board advisor on planning and training needs. There are two universities and two polytechnic institutions that produce the country's skilled workforce.

Fifth, Hong Kong is strategically located on the western rim of the Asia-Pacific region. It is right next door to mainland China, a major international market. Hong Kong has modern and efficient facilities, including an accessible harbor with the third largest container port in the world, an international airport, and excellent communication systems—telephone, telex, and cable.

Sixth, Hong Kong is an excellent gateway from which to do business with mainland China. Its superior transportation and communication links make it very easy to move around the mainland from Hong Kong. Hong Kong will revert back to the People's Republic of China in 1997, and both economies have been integrated in many ways. China has grown from Hong Kong's eighth largest market to its second largest. China's trade with Taiwan, South Korea, and Indonesia passes mainly through Hong Kong. Hong Kong banking institutions have been instrumental in providing capital for China; about eighty percent of all investment comes from Hong Kong. Mainland Chinese business executives have been learning modern methods of conducting business from their Hong Kong counterparts. China's modernization program calls for expansion of trade with countries such as the United States through Hong Kong, where it is more convenient to put up a business base. Hong Kong producers of labor-intensive consumer products have been locating in special economic zones put up by China.

You: You will need to look at these six incentives very closely. Are they applicable to your project? One unavoidable issue that you must consider is the future of Hong Kong. Here are the facts: According to treaty, China will regain sovereignty over Hong Kong in 1997. It will then become a Special Administrative Region of China, enjoying considerable autonomy in managing its own economic, financial, trade, and monetary affairs. According to the treaty terms, Hong Kong's free enterprise system will be preserved along with free trade policies and its existing financial system. The mainland's socialist policies will not be applied to Hong Kong. Its current system of law will be maintained. A fifty-year extension on all land leases expiring in 1997 will occur. The rights of Hong Kong citizens, including freedom of movement of capital, the right to own and dispose of property, the right to a full and prompt compensation for their property, and the right of free movement to and from Hong Kong will be preserved. The million-dollar question is will China follow the terms of the treaty after it takes over Hong Kong or will it impose its own rules and ignore the treaty terms.

There seems to be optimism over the future of Hong Kong even after 1997. Most business executives think that the success of China's modernization program heavily depends on continuing Hong Kong's present economic system, so the chance of any drastic change is low. Many companies have placed their bets on this optimistic outcome, including Exxon Corporation, Japan's Asahi Optical Co., Dow Chemical Pacific, and others. They have increased their investments in Hong Kong. Your company will have to make its own independent estimate and base its calculated risks on that.

Some doubt about Hong Kong's future has emerged due to these significant developments: Although a majority of Hong Kong citizens expressed their desire for elections in 1988, a biased government panel instead concluded that there was little domestic support for 1988 elections, and they were not held. Observers note that this is a clear indication that the British government has given in to mainland objections. China thinks such political concepts as the separation of the executive, judicial, and legislative powers are inappropriate to Hong Kong. The British government has stepped on individual rights by imposing the press-control law, which penalizes journalists who write "false" news. They are assumed to be guilty until proven innocent. So, many feel that China may curtail Hong Kong's political freedoms while maintaining its basic economic system. In the meantime, more and more of the middle class and professionals are fleeing the colony to such countries as Canada and Australia, thus creating a severe brain drain problem.

Finding Local Representation

Hong Kong Negotiators: Hong Kong's Chinese prefer to do business with foreigners through middlemen with whom they have had long-term relationships. There are reliable agents who have good track records and technical selling capabilities.

You: We highly recommend that you find a trading company that specializes in the line of business you are interested in. It will give you adequate market coverage and logistical support. If your company plans to do business beyond the parts of South China that are closest to Hong Kong, then find an agent with offices in the main cities such as Beijing, Shanghai, and Guangzhou in order to get good coverage in the main provinces. Try to get your local agent to spend money on a joint survey of product/service marketability in the areas you have chosen.

Decision Makers in Local Firms

Hong Kong Negotiators: The majority of the firms in Hong Kong—whether they are small sweat shops or relatively large organizations—are still family-owned. Paternalistic management practices still prevail even if a firm's management has been well-trained in modern technology and business practices. The owner and head of the enterprise, who is usually the father or the eldest son, keeps the ultimate authority to make decisions. Some executives accept "tea money" or bribes to facilitate the decision-making process. Although the government has been trying to curb the practice of bribery through its Independent Commission against Corruption, some degree of it still goes on. The Chinese New Year season is often used as the occasion to give extravagant gifts to favored business contacts to maintain positive relationships. However, when an enormous amount of money is spent on gifts, they can be considered bribes. There seems to be more restraint nowadays on the amounts spent and the kinds of gifts being given. Some top executives have donated their gifts to charity to avoid embarrassing their donors. Society tends to tolerate the use of bribes in expediting legitimate services. Business executives who gain their wealth through illegitimate means gain acceptance of society if they later transfer their wealth back to a respectable business or donate it to charitable organizations.

You: You will need to establish your relationship with the top person early in the game. Do not expect the lower levels of managers to have a significant role in the decision-making process. Chinese tradition is exacting in terms of deferring the decisions to the top executive, so do not expect lower-level managers to express their own views about your proposal or to lobby on your behalf with the head of the company. You may have to work with them a lot, though, especially if your proposal is technical. If your project involves relatively new technologies, you will need to be understanding about the lack of familiarity and expertise. You may even find that some of the people are unqualified for the job. This happens because of the predisposition of management to hire relatives, mainly to help them, even if they do not have the necessary qualifications. You will have to define your position about the use of "tea money" to facilitate decisions favorable to your proposals.

Enhancing Relationships with *Guan-xi*

Hong Kong Negotiators: The Hong Kong Chinese value personal and long-term relationships based on *guan-xi* or "special interpersonal relationships." Implicit in *guan-xi* is the trust that the other party will not do or say anything that would make the Chinese lose face. Also implicit in this relationship is the expectation that both parties are willing to give each other special consideration and even protection. The obligation to grant these considerations is even heavier on the party who is perceived to be in a superior position. It turns out, then, that *guan-xi* works to the benefit of the inferior party, since it can summon obligations and even accuse the superior party of not living up to expectations if the latter refuses the inferior party any favors. (This is related to the "power of powerlessness" tactic.)

One easy way of establishing trust is to use Chinese interpreters. Local business executives find it a lot easier to deal with interpreters who are Chinese like themselves, and they will seize the opportunity to express their desires to your interpreter. In fact, it is common to find Chinese executives exerting undue pressure on Chinese interpreters to emphasize special considerations they want from you.

You: You need to be sensitive to words and gestures that may make the other side lose face. This is the very least you can do to establish *guan-xi.* But you need to do more. One way of cementing *guan-xi* is to invite your hosts to your home country—ask them to visit your headquarters. One executive did this, and he used the opportunity to acquaint the Chinese with American quality standards and taste preferences. But be careful when you say that you will help your Chinese counterparts. Such pronouncements are taken seriously within the context of *guan-xi,* and if you are not prepared to grant the favors they ask in the future, your chances of building *guan-xi* will be seriously hurt. In fact, this gives the Chinese justifiable reason to complain that you are not living up to the expectations of *guan-xi.* If you are a Canadian working as a manager in Hong Kong, for instance, your Chinese subordinates may expect you to help them and their family members find ways and means to work or study in Canada.

Handling the Delicate Matter of "Face"

Hong Kong Negotiators: The Chinese recognize two basic kinds of face: (1) *Mien-tzu* is face within a social context. You gain face when you observe society's rules in maintaining face, and when you acquire status symbols. (2) *Lien* stands for moral integrity. Violating this causes personal pain in the form of guilt. There are no observers in the case of *lien*; only you are aware of your violation of your inner standards. The Confucian tradition is largely responsible for the practices that many Chinese use to maintain face: concealing emotions, maintaining impersonal expressions, avoiding open and direct confrontations, using face-saving devices such as third parties to resolve conflict, and observing decorous social manners. Confucius also taught the Chinese that a person who causes another to lose face suffers a worse loss of face—that of being considered a barbarian and ignorant of the ideal code of behavior. Saving another's is prized much more than telling the truth. Usually the person whose face was saved is socially indebted to reciprocate the gesture in the future should the other person be in a similarly awkward social situation.

The degree to which face must be observed depends on the kind of business situation you are involved in. For instance, in Hong Kong's volatile financial world, the business executives are increasingly Westernized, and it has become a luxury for them to observe rules of face. Sandra Lui, a Hong Kong finance executive, says, "Where money is concerned, people no longer attach importance to face. They want to get their money back—and that means you sometimes have to be harsh." On the other hand, Dennis Lam, managing director of an investment firm, has had different experiences: He notes that bosses tend to use their subordinates to ask their clients difficult questions or to say no on their behalf. In this setting, face is still a vital consideration in maintaining good business relationships. George Vinson deals a lot with manufacturers. He comments that in handling a situation where you must reject a batch of goods, it is important to meet with the suppliers, explain your reasons tactfully, and then ask them to resolve the situation. Here, saving face is still important.

You: You should be especially sensitive to the need of the Chinese to save and maintain face. Occasionally, you may be in a situation where they try to save *your* face. Simply be aware of this possibility and accept the gesture gracefully. Remember that the penalty for causing another to lose face is double. Do not put your counterparts on the spot. Do not criticize or confront them in public. Use trusted go-betweens to build your case with them if communications seem to be breaking down. Do not ask them questions that will force them to say "no" in public. In general, maintain a mild and moderate demeanor. Be tentative about statements they make. Be aware that since they are under tremendous pressure to maintain face, they may often say things that please you or often agree with what you said. Some practical ways you can give the other side face are the following: Recognize your client's family and its achievements. Attend social functions even if you do not feel well just to show the other side that you care enough to show up even at the cost of inconveniencing yourself. Continue to give the other side allowances—such as generous credit terms—especially if the are experiencing hard times. You will be relieved to find some sophisticated Chinese executives with considerable Western exposure, who can deal with you more directly than other Chinese and handle Western impersonalism with ease. There is growing familiarity with the West and the cultures of the West among the sophisticated Chinese executives. Many of them were educated in the West and feel comfortable in Western environments. But it is hard to know who these people are.

Arriving at an Agreement

Hong Kong Negotiators: Formal agreements are executed by the Chinese in writing often in the presence of lawyers. Services of a nonprofit organization called the Hong Kong International Arbitration Centre is available for settling commercial disputes.

You: Establish sufficiently strong relationships with heads of family enterprises and businesses so you will be able to interpret signals about whether or not your proposal has been accepted. Find yourself a good local lawyer to help you draft and interpret any formal agreements that need to be written.

Specific Negotiating Tactics

These are the favorite tactics chosen by Hong Kong executives that are used in particular business situations.

(1) Ask the Seller for a Lower Price: As buyers, the Hong Kong executives tend to remind you of their competition to get you to lower your price. They place high demands on you, perhaps by offering a very low Hong Kong dollar figure in the beginning. Some try to win every minor concession they can from you while working on the major concession on price. Purchasing managers consult their records and base their current bid on the historical trend of prices you used to charge. Others make their price request seem insignificant by using funny money. Some give you deadlines, after which their price offers expire. They will tell you their budgets constrain them to work within certain amounts only. They will even highlight their position of weakness and show you that if they pay your high asking price, they may go bankrupt and not give you any business in the future. Others use the take-it-or-leave-it stance with just one price offer.

(2) Ask the Buyer to Pay More: As sellers, Hong Kong executives will try to get the highest price from you by using funny money, being firm about their asking price, constantly exerting pressure on you by using hard-sell techniques, and reminding you that other buyers are interested in the product or service as well. To make their product or service look extra good, they may get a prestigious person to recommend the use of the product or service or create an unusually impressive image using unsubstantiated information. Others will base their bid for higher prices by showing you records of their expenses. They will show you the costs that went into the making of the product or service. The more patient sellers will not close any deal immediately and will wait you out until they find your prices are more acceptable.

(3) Ask the Boss for a Raise: Hong Kong executives stress their record of performance and accomplishments when they ask for a raise. They will not hesitate to make high demands on their boss, praise themselves, and remind their boss of their talents and contributions to the company. They will keep the pressure on when negotiating for a raise. If their bargaining leverage is not strong enough, they will try these other tactics instead: They will point out what the company may stand to lose more by "exploiting" them and not giving them a raise, for instance, by saying that morale and productivity will decline. Those who are more cooperative will be patient and wait their bosses out until the initial objections to their request have subsided.

(4) Ask the Boss for a Promotion: Hong Kong executives use here many of the same tactics they use to get a pay raise: Looking at past records of performance, keeping the pressure on their bosses, keeping their demands high, praising their own talents and contributions to the company, and being patient in waiting out a more opportune time to request the promotion. In addition, they improve their image by using their colleagues to leak information to their bosses about their more recent contributions. Many are candid and approach their bosses in a straightforward way and discuss why they think they deserve a promotion. They placate the boss and facilitate the process of granting them the promotion by promising a better performance in the future.

(5) Ask the Boss to Change Their Holiday Dates: Hong Kong executives do not hesitate to use pressure, make high demands, concede on other matters related to the change in holiday dates, and even stage office antics—like appearing fatigued and in very bad shape just to get their bosses to change their holiday dates. Those who are more rational simply consult the company policy covering the changing of dates and calmly admit that they had made an error in signing up for the initial dates. Or they are very straightforward—they tell their boss their reasons. To facilitate the negotiation, they like to use the department's record of their past and future vacations and work out an agreeable schedule. In anticipation of rejection from their bosses, some use "powerlessness" by saying that the company has more to lose if they are forced to take a holiday within the initial dates because of prime work scheduled on those days. Those who prefer not to confront the boss directly may pass information to the boss through their colleagues. The leaked plan to change their holiday dates tests out the boss's initial reaction to the request. They could also create a situation favorable to the change by getting the support of other executives in the company. They may also promise their boss better performance in the future if the change is allowed.

REFERENCES

The section "What Hong Kong Chinese Are Like" is derived from these sources:

Ambrose, Y.C. King and Rance P. Lee, *Social Life and Development in Hong Kong* (Hong Kong: The Chinese University Press, 1981), pp. 6, 214.

Jarvie, I.C., ed. *Hong Kong: A Society in Transition* (London: Routledge & Kegan Paul, 1969), p. 186.

Peat, Marwick, Mitchell & Co., *Investment in Hong Kong* (Hong Kong: Peat, Marwick, Mitchell & Co., April 1986), p. 29.

Price Waterhouse, *Doing Business in Hong Kong* (Tampa, Fla.: Price Waterhouse, 1986), p. 4.

Salaff, Janet W., *Working Daughters of Hong Kong: Filial Piety or Power in the Family* (New York: Cambridge University Press, 1981), pp. 42, 43, 44.

The section "Preliminary Considerations: Incentives" on the Hong Kong side was synthesized from:

"Big Business Sees Profit in a Chinese Flag over Hong Kong," *BusinessWeek*, 8 October 1984, p. 55.

Gorman, Thomas D. , "Hong Kong/China '86: Opportunities for Growing American Businesses," *Inc.* , May 1986, pp. 142, 144.

Government Information Services, Hong Kong, *Hong Kong Now* (Hong Kong: Government Information Services, Hong Kong), pp. 1, 12, 13.

Hicks, George L., "Hong Kong's Hopes of Freedom Are Fast Fading," *Wall Street Journal*, 28 December 1987, p. 13.

Hicks, George, "The Selling Out of Hong Kong," *Wall Street Journal*, 15 June 1987, p. 23.

The Hong Kong General Chamber of Commerce, "Setting-up Business in Hong Kong" (Brochure) (Hong Kong: The Hong Kong General Chamber of Commerce, April 1985), p. 1.

Hong Kong Industrial Promotion Office, "Main Factors Contributing To Hong Kong's Eminence As a Manufacturing Base," (Handout) 1987, pp. 1-4.

Hong Kong Government Industry Department, *Industrial Investment Hong Kong* (Hong Kong: Government Printer, April 1985), pp. 2, 3.

Kronholz, "Few in Hong Kong Still Trust Promises of Britain and China," *Wall Street Journal*, 13 April 1987, p. 13.

Levin, Burton , "Hong Kong and China: The Ties That Bind," (Handout of the American Consulate General), 15 May 1986, p. 3.

Maremont, Mark "The 'Brain Drain' Crippling the Colony," *Businessweek,* 25 January 1988, p. 50.

Peat, Marwick, Mitchell & Co., *Investment in Hong Kong,* p. 7.

The section "Decision Makers in Local Firms" on the Hong Kong side was organized from the following materials:

Geiger, Paul and Richard Geiger, *The Development Progress of Hong Kong and Singapore*, London, 1985 pp. 56, 112, 123.

Jarvie, *Hong Kong: A Society in Transition*, p. 205.

Kay, Michele, *Doing Business in Hong Kong* (Hong Kong: South China Morning Post Limited and American Chamber of Commerce in Hong Kong, 1976), pp. 28, 29.

The section "Enhancing Relationships with *guan-xi*" was adapted from the following:

Pye, Lucian, *Chinese Commercial Negotiating Style* (Santa Monica, Calif.: Rand Corporation, January 1982), pp. 62, 63, 86, 89, 90.

Yao, Esther Lee, "Cultivating Guan-xi (Personal Relationships) with Chinese Partners," *Business Marketing*, January 1987, p. 62.

The section "Handling the Delicate Matter of 'Face' " was adapted from the following sources:

Bishop, Vonnie, "The Changing Concept of 'Face,'" *World Executive's Digest*, February 1985, pp. 50–53.

Bond, Michael H., and Peter W. H. Lee, "Face Saving in Chinese Culture: A Discussion and Experimental Study of Hong Kong Students," in Ambrose Y. C. King and Rance P. Lee, *Social Life and Development in Hong Kong* (Hong Kong: The Chinese University Press, 1981), pp. 289, 291.

Geiger and Geiger, *The Development Progress of Hong Kong and Singapore*, p. 38.

Jarvie, *Hong Kong: A Society In Transition*, p. 140.

Pye, *Chinese Commercial Negotiating Style*, pp. 32, 89–90.

Snowdon, Sondra, *The Global Edge: How Your Company Can Win in the International Marketplace* (New York: Simon & Schuster, 1986), pp. 78, 80.

Yao, p. 64

15

Country Study: Australia

WHAT AUSTRALIANS ARE LIKE

Australians are known to be rugged, direct, and tough-minded people, quick to assert what they perceive as their rights—occasionally, at the expense of others. They have very strong positive feelings for egalitarianism. This goes far beyond making sure everybody has equal opportunities in life. There is a dark side, however, to Australia's view of egalitarianism. It means equating the legitimate authority of your boss with oneupmanship, leading to almost a perpetual state of anarchy in unionized workplaces. It means discouraging nonconformity even to the point of withholding recognition for outstanding performance or ability on the job. A union official once tried to reduce the pay of a teacher who had a rare master's degree to that of a bachelor's degree holder because he thought all pay differences were unfair. Rewarding the teacher with the master's degree was far from his mind.

The dark side of Australia's obsession with egalitarianism is inextricably interwoven with its strong unions. This has dragged Australia down to a lowest-common denominator level of equal social misery. An editorial in the *Sydney Morning Herald* talked about egalitarianism and Australia's "union masters" this way: "Union organization and politics are sacred cows and must not be questioned. Trade-unions are the backbone of Australia and can do no wrong. In this brave new Australia of union mastery, with people increasingly allowed to travel, to work at their normal jobs, and to meet their legitimate needs only by courtesy of trade-union leaders, equality is certainly the watchword. There is an equal opportunity *not* to use public transport, *not* to drive one's car, *not* to book a seat in an aircraft, the list is almost endless. "Let's all be miserable together." It would make a good motto for present-day Australia.

Until progress and affluence increased the size of the middle class and the affluent, almost all Aussies treated each other as "mates." (Today, mateship is still important, but it is not universal as in earlier years.) Mateship is an outgrowth of the unique Australian experience of surviving the isolation and privation called for by pioneering the bush. So great was their need for support in an isolated continent that they quickly learned to live together. Settlements of friendship, caring, and trust stem from these experiences.

Australians love to have fun, especially outdoors. They have the right climate and environment for it: Long stretches of sunny beaches are close to most Australians, since almost all of them live in the five major coastal cities—Sydney, Melbourne, Brisbane, Adelaide, and Perth. It is one of the most urban nations in the world. They are so leisure-oriented that it is hard for them to understand why one should live to work. They work to live. They would rather be carefree and throw the price of success—strains and tensions—to the winds. Their very high marginal tax rates also stifle any motivation they might have to work hard.

This does not mean they are not striving for progress, though—the economic evidence shows otherwise. For instance, they came out of the 1983 recession with rapid growth. But they will not push themselves beyond a certain point. They certainly will not drive themselves the way the Americans and Japanese do, for example. There *are* progressive and success-driven members of the population, but they are a definite exception. Observers note that increased prosperity has made the younger generation even *less* oriented toward hard work, if that is possible, even as they continually push for higher pay. Hardly anybody will work overtime—the high marginal tax rates leave little to take home. Instead, most people take the short route to more money by gambling on horse races, dog races, poker machines, and lotteries. When they want extra time off, they will duck some significant issue and simply go on strike. They are not penalized when they do this, because most of the time, they do not lose pay for striking. Strikes do not last long. But they occur often. When one of the authors lived in Sydney, the *Sydney Morning Herald* newspaper reported that there were an average of fifty strikes a day in Sydney (population 2.5 million) alone:

Last week was a quiet week for strikes. Some of the strikes were: One involving about 14,000 meat and transport workers over three issues. Meat supplies have been cut drastically. If it is not settled by next week, Sydney faces a meat famine. About 4,000 members of the Storemen and Packers' Union imposed a series of rolling strikes and an overtime ban in the bond, produce, drug, hardware, softgoods, and grocery sectors. Shortages of many lines are expected. The oil dispute has cut bus services, rail services have been slashed by 50 percent, and heating oil and petroleum products are very scarce in some states. About 300 nursing aides have been on strike for a week for a pay raise. Construction of the natural gas pipeline is held up by a month-old strike. This strike is in support of traveling time, more leisure time, wage increases, and other conditions. About 800 members of the Electrical Trades Union went on strike in protest at the suspension of 40 fitters who refused to comply with new timekeeping procedures. Six women secretaries employed by the Builders Union went on strike for five days in support of an over-award payment demand. National strikes in railway and building workers were postponed, but they are scheduled within the next few weeks.

And that was a *quiet* week! Australia is the second most unionized nation in the world. For many years, it lost more days to strikes per resident than any other nation. Its unions are *extremely* powerful, and this limits management's negotiating options with you. For example, look at what happened when the insurance companies' trade association began its advertising campaign against the federal government's plans to start its own insurance company. It claimed this was the first step to nationalization of all industry: Since most businesses obtain financing from insurance companies, businesses would become dependent on government financing to survive, according to the ads. Supposedly, this dependency would occur because the government insurance company eventually would force private insurance firms out of business. Nationalization of dependent firms would be the next step. The ads ended by saying, "If you don't want to see Australia turned into one giant post office, write the Prime Minister." The communications workers unions were insulted by this remark, although postal service in Australia at that time *was* quite poor because of continuous strikes—five during a ten month period in Sydney alone, not counting other cities. The unions gave the insurance companies an ultimatum—change the ad, removing all references to the post office, or all communications would be cut off—no telephone service, no mail deliveries, no telegrams or telexes. The powerful coalition of money-rich insurance companies capitulated immediately. The unions in Australia, some feel, actually run the country. Many similar examples can be told.

Many reasons exist for their strike-proneness. No matter what they are, labor-management relations were always bad. Both sides had "us against them" attitudes from the very start. In the sheep industry, for instance, labor resented management's harsh policies, and management resented labor's intransigence. Although Australia was no longer a penal colony by the 1800s, many workers still had the convict mentality of despising their bosses, who they felt had taken the role of the British soldiers who had ruled them under martial law. This tradition of animosity has given the nation's workers a well-deserved reputation as hard bargainers.

The situation had improved somewhat by the early 1990s. There is some evidence that the incidence of long, bruising strikes has been reduced slightly, because the government, unions, and businesses are agreeing somewhat more often. However, this does not mask the fact that the quality of industrial relations and grievance handling has not improved. There is still an urgent need, by world standards, to correct the mechanism of arbitration. This is putting it mildly, considering the fact that Australia's unions still get away with what other nations might feel are laughable demands. For example, Qantas Airways passengers were stranded in Sydney overnight in 1986 after flight attendants walked out because they did not like the "unsanitary hot towels" the carrier was using. The same year, Ansett Airlines' flight attendants won their case when they threatened to stop service if they were not allowed to wear short-sleeved shirts during the Easter holiday period. In 1981, workers building an entertainment center near Sydney's Chinatown demanded that they be given "tea money" every day by management in exchange for this inconvenience: Smelling the appetizing aromas coming from neighboring Chinese restaurants created a "hardship in the gastronomical expectations of their employees."

The great power and influence of their union movement makes it the unseen third party at all negotiatins you will have with Australians. Management's signature is meaningless if the unions do not go along, too. They have the ability and the will power to press their demands regardless of their effect on the country as a whole. And you are the foreigner, so they will care even less about how you are affected. Do not rely on arbitration to help you, either. Australian law was originally intended for wage claims and other issues to be determined on their merits through arbitration, using logical economic principles to evaluate them rather than succumbing to coercion or pressure. However, the government's Arbitration Commission has consistently backed down on this principle by giving in to the unions' high demands that wages be increased and that strikes be used whether necessary or not. As unions continue to monopolize power, the government's Arbitration Court has lost its ability to discipline recalcitrant unions. Enforceable work contracts have become a thing of the distant past, and trade unions have emerged as the only organization not subject to effective legislative or judicial control. They continue to wield power, using ploys such as strikes, work bans, and other disruptive activities. Watch out for them. They should be a major factor in your negotiating plans.

Australia is quickly molding itself into a multiethnic society. Immigration has been essential to the development of the country ever since the first British settlements in the 1700s and 1800s. For many years, the government followed a "White Australia" policy on immigration. This policy discriminated against Asians and even non-British Europeans. In the 1970s, though, their policy changed, and today there are many "New Australians," especially Greeks, Turks, and Italians. You will also find Maltese, Polish, Ukrainians, Lithuanians, Latvians, Estonians, Serbs, Yugoslavs, Spanish, Portuguese, Dutch, Germans, and French people, along with such Asian nationalities as Japanese, Indonesians, Indians, Koreans, Filipinos, Sri Lankans, and Malaysians.

Australia is not a "melting pot." Its "New Australian" immigrants were not ready candidates for assimilation. So, the government encouraged a multicultural society rather than push for homogeneity. The country now has ethnic television and radio stations broadcasting in languages other than English. There are many newspapers and magazines in more than twenty-five languages. Even so, many immigrants, especially their children, tried to absorb as much as they could of the Australian culture. Many Australians of British descent never fully supported the new immigration policy, though. Old prejudices die hard. Opinion leaders noted that multiculturalism was being achieved at the expense of social cohesion. Opinion polls showed that people wanted the new immigrants to "fit into" Australian society as soon as possible.

Things are changing, though. Opinion surveys now indicate they prefer immigrants with skills the economy needs, and only six percent favor a "Europeans-only" policy. This is clearly a break from the earlier prejudice favoring only whites. The change in their outlook is probably due to the fact that more immigrants are coming in from Asia, especially refugees. Asians are doing fairly well in Australia; they do not line up for welfare support, nor do they present social problems by drug trafficking, for instance. Native-Australians perceive them to be "drycleaned and industrious," disciplined, and orderly—but not sociable enough. Still, only twenty-three percent strongly support letting more refugees in. They would much rather have "suitable" people with relatives already in Australia.

Australians are egalitarian by nature. People seem to have easy and amicable relationships with each other. For instance, passengers like to sit beside taxi drivers; they feel tipping is offensive; and they do not look down upon manual labor. But the reality is that there are class distinctions. It is easy to spot the differences: Members of different social classes work at different jobs, live in different areas, recreate in different pubs, send their children to different schools, and so forth. Members of the upper class are the most wealthy, well-educated, prominent people who hold positions of power and status. Family background and occupation count more than wealth in gaining recognition in this class. They are highly concerned about sending their children to the "right" schools to perpetuate their positions in the upper crust. There are many more British Protestants than Irish Catholics. Cognizant of their position, they do not observe social egalitarianism and can be blatant in promoting snobbery and class-consciousness. It is said, though, that the social barriers they erect are notas forbiding as in Britain.

Membership in the growing middle class is wide-ranging: white-collar workers, small farmers, tradesmen, shopkeepers, foremen and supervisors with executive power, and some skilled workers all belong to this group. Economic progress gave them more buying power, and they joined ranks with other industrialized countries in the world marked by heavy consumerism. In this "up-market" consumer society, the middle class has whetted its appetite for more of the best television sets, VCRs, motor cars, furniture, swimming pools, and the like. Desires are endless.

The "mateship" ethic—a militantly fair treatment of others, male friendship, disdain for authority, crudeness, and contempt for pretense—is now linked more with the behavior of the working class. It is composed mainly of semiskilled and unskilled workers, farm laborers, shearers, truck drivers, railwaymen, road laborers, and so forth. Working-class Australians are glorified in the media as "the common man." Many of them fit the "Ocker" stereotype. An *Ocker* is a native male Australian who puts on a heavy Australian accent (and acts crudely) to intentionally distinguish his speech (and actions) from the more cultured British accent (and manner of behaving). He is a heavy drinker and gambler who loves spectator sports. He does not care about cultivating the upper-class British accent, which might bring him respectability, and he looks down on those who do. (For years, many Australians, perhaps ashamed of their origins as a convict colony, tried to cultivate a British accent.) Many ads glorify the *Ocker*. One advertising executive described *Ockerism* as reflected in television commercials this way: "The *Ocker* must have the ability to shout 192 words in 30 seconds and repeat a simple sales message 18 times in that period. He must have the natural talent to burp on cue, and although a beer gut and broken nose are not essential, they are a definite aid to his career potential."

Australia is a very male-dominated, "macho" kind of society, even though there have been some government and media efforts to boost the status of women. One of the authors had the opportunity to interview several expatriate women professionals in Australia in the mid-1980s. Here are a few statements from them on the view that male Aussies still place women in a subordinate position:

"I left the U.K. 10 years and two months ago, went to New Zealand for three years, and then on to Australia . . . I consider myself a permanent Aussie now . . . it took me a long time to make friends and a long time to be accepted in *any* office. You're only a girl, and they want to know how long will you stay here, or will you just get married and leave quickly. If a man is ambitious, it's great, but if a woman is ambitious, she's a bitch. There are many more opportunities for men than for women, so you have to promote yourself more than a man does."

"I was at the University of Michigan on staff as a doctor, and my department chairman knew the head at Royal Melbourne Hospital. . . . There are very few female M.D.s [here]. . . . it's the old boy buddy system, a close-knit group of macho males who keep women subservient. Now, the men at work are very friendly, but this friendship didn't extend past the workplace."

"Before you come out [to Australia], make sure you know people who will sponsor you so you can get a job. You'll get the rudest awakening when you come here, though, because of the extreme male chauvinism. . . . Women are second class citizens here, especially with my own colleagues."

"In 1980, I moved to Australia . . . the longer you live here, the more you realize that you have less in common with them. . . . And Aussie men are far behind the times. They have no respect for women."

"I've spent the last four years in Australia. . . . Men in Australia are more chauvinistic than in the U.S. Why, the secretaries here are expected to serve tea and biscuits to their bosses in the afternoon."

The labor government of the early 1970s secured equality of pay for equal work and made it easier for women to get divorced. Women still hold most of the lower-paying jobs, though, and one survey in the early 1980s indicated that there is a two-to-one support for the view that a woman should put her husband and children ahead of her career. Things are changing, but it is still very slow. Newspapers and talk shows on televison and radio are discussing substantive issues concerning the feminist movement that society has ignored for years. Equal opportunity boards are now available for redress when women are not given the jobs for which they are qualified. Women are holding more prominent positions in Parliament, in business, and in media. Membership in women's organizations is growing, so this direction probably will not be reversed.

AUSTRALIAN NEGOTIATORS AND YOU

Progressive Attitudes

Australian Negotiators: Australia likes to call itself "the lucky country." Its residents do enjoy the fruits of progress and affluence. Exceptionally enterprising and progressive business executives understand what it takes to compete internationally. You will meet many of them as you negotiate.

You: If you are negotiating with a progressive firm, you will not have to worry as much about unions overturning the final agreement. It is still wise not to step on their toes. But do not let that keep you from emphasizing the strong points in your negotiating position—how an agreement will lead the other side to greater competitiveness, performance, and success.

Making the Right Connections

Australian Negotiators: The hub of economic activity is mainly the southeastern corner of the country, in both Sydney, the well-known metropolis where about twenty percent of Australians live and work, and Melbourne, the financial center, where another twenty percent are. The business elite is a tight circle of people who know each other quite well. Most of them are over fifty years old. Members of their "Old Boy Network" are always exchanging opinions and socializing. A connection you make with one member may very well lead to another. Acquaintance with a business executive is a clear asset for gaining entry into the inner circle. Knowing politicians will not help you as much, because they are not as influential in business as they are in government.

You: You may not have a difficult time getting your foot in the door even if you deal only with a younger executive. They are pretty much straightforward and will evaluate your proposal on its merits alone. However, you will make things a lot easier for yourself by contracting with a local agent who has a close relationship with the power network. These agents usually offer a full line of services—marketing, financial, quality control, storage, transportation, and so forth—that you can make use of. Maintain your relationship with your agent once you have found a good one, for they are invaluable and difficult to find. The better ones are headquartered in Melbourne and Sydney.

The Formal Presentation

Australian Negotiators: Australians are direct by nature and prefer that you mention everything in your presentation. They have a good international communication system, and so they are exposed to the best products on the world market. Therefore, they demand high and consistent quality, regular supply, availability of parts, and excellent maintenance service.

You: Pay attention to the export mechanics in your presentation. You must draft your proposal including c.i.f. terms, since freight to that faraway part of the world accounts for a considerable part of the total cost. Also make sure you state the f.o.b. foreign port price for the accurate billing of customs and duty rates. Units of measure should conform to the metric system, naturally. Normally, you can expect to be paid for what you exported to Australia not later than six months after the goods have arrived. Other arrangements outside of these usual terms must have the approval of the Reserve Bank of Australia. This is usually granted if the terms of payment are in accordance with standard international practices for the products involved. Finally, when you draw up your market profile for your products or services, make sure you take Australia's multiethnic nature of the market into consideration. You may even have to translate instructions for use into Greek and Turkish.

Bargaining Guidelines

Australian Negotiators: As a rule, Australian business executives do not want to spend too much time bargaining. They prefer a straightforward presentation with a minimum of playing games. Although the government recognizes the importance of foreign investment in the development of Australia's economy, it is also keen on ensuring Australian participation in these investments. It looks particularly close at the potential opportunities and economic benefits to be generated by your project and the equity participation terms stipulated. The government follows certain guidelines. For example, it requires seventy-five percent Australian equity and control in uranium projects and fifty percent for other natural resource projects. Restrictions on foreign investment are in force in banking, finance, insurance, the media, civil aviation, and real estate. The Foreign Investment Review Board decides promptly—the average processing time is only thirty days.

You: The opening price quotations you make will have to be close to the final price you are willing to accept—otherwise, you lose all credibility. Emphasize how your project falls within the development guidelines of the government. Reassure them about a fair participation in the project for their side.

Decision Process

Australian Negotiators: Senior and top executives are the main decision makers in Australia. Technical experts are also consulted for highly specialized projects. Family boards dominate in family-owned enterprises. If you are negotiating with lower-level executives, they will have to consult often with their bosses, and so final decisions may not be arrived at as quickly as you would like.

You: Your contacts with the top echelon of the business you are negotiating with will be enhanced by the presence of a local contact or agent. They are especially helpful in answering questions and resolving conflicts during negotiations. You should allow a lot of time for waiting for the other side to decide. Hard-sell tactics and pushing for a decision do not usually work.

Reaching Agreement

Australian Negotiators: They like to shake hands with you—hard—to indicate an agreement. Eventually, they will seal the business relationship with a contract. Business contracts can be quite detailed. Once they are signed, they are not likely to be changed before implementation.

You: Use the services of Australian lawyers here. They will make sure that all the terms and conditions important to you are covered in the contract.

HOW TO TALK WITH AN AUSTRALIAN

Communicating with an Australian business executive poses special problems. Apart from the fact that you will have to get used to their unique accent which is not quite British nor American, here are seven guidelines that will help both of you get to know each other better:

(1) Keep an Equal Footing

Australian Negotiators: They want to be talked with as equals; they resent condescension of any kind. Even if they know your accomplishments, they will not be particularly impressed by them and will not make them the basis of the initial phase of your relationship.

You: Relate to the Aussie in terms of your person rather than your accomplishments or work—save that for later when the context of the conversation is appropriate. Share your feelings and opinions about things, jokes, and so forth. Turning on your competitive mode would be especially offensive to them. There is no need to prove yourself to them without their asking—and they probably will not. Keep the atmosphere informal and be comfortable and direct with them. Do not patronize them—do not offer help, sympathy, or solace unless asked.

(2) Inner-Directedness

Australian Negotiators: They evaluate each person in terms of their own personal reactions, feelings, preferences, and expectations of that person. They are less influenced by your status and accomplishments—in other words, by your external presentations. Effective interaction with Australians is therefore important in winning them over.

You: Recognize their complexity. Meeting with them is a good opportunity for you to get away from the uninteresting small talk that is usually used to open conversations. Instead, use the meetings you have with them to really get to know them.

(3) Catch Their Attention

Australian Negotiators: Australians typically do not like meeting with accomplished but colorless people. They want more in terms of what you have to offer as a person.

You: One way for you to let them know who you are is to take a definite stand on an issue. Do not be verbose when you do this, though. State your reasons clearly and succinctly. There will probably be no need for you to defend your stance.

(4) Little Need to Be Liked

Australian Negotiators: One strength of the Australians is that they do not really need for you to like them. Therefore, they do not try hard to be accepted or to influence others.

You: You do not have to try hard to make the Australians like you either. Trying to please and playing games will be futile.

(5) Comfortable with Conflict

Australian Negotiators: Another strength is the relative ease they have in dealing with conflict. They expect it in most transactions in life; they are familiar with it whenever they deal with unions; they are not at all put off by it; and they are quite capable even of enjoying it, to the point of intentionally creating conflict at times just to engage the other side. They admire people who can handle conflict with style. Negative reactions evoked by conflict do not bother them too much.

You: Accept the Australians as they are, allowing room for idiosyncratic and unexpected behavior. Understand that conflict is their way of adding spice to life. Use conflict yourself in a constructive way. Australians may start badgering you with derisive comments and criticisms, all in the spirit of fun, simply to get you to budge a little from your position. Do not feel bad when this happens. Do not feign agreement with them just to correct the situation. Simply state your beliefs firmly and leave it at that. Meanwhile, take advantage of the opportunity to learn more about them, for an interesting sparring session will very likely motivate them to share important opinions with you.

(6) Australian Sense of Humor

Australian Negotiators: Australians are likely to tease you once in a while, just to break the ice or to get to know you better. It is a great way for them to probe you and find out how resilient you are.

You: Practice sparring with the Australians. Above all, enjoy it. Use self-deprecating humor to bring you both on an even keel, especially if you are American or British. Many Australians think the Americans and British bask in their own sense of superiority. Laughing at yourself could very well dispell this notion.

(7) Mild Undertones of Inferiority

Australian Negotiators: They are quite sensitive about their historical past, as early Australia was built by the efforts of convicts. Also, Australians often subject themselves to excruciating comparisons with the British and Americans—a fruitless effort and somewhat contradictory with their strong sense of independence, but they do it anyway.

You: Develop a genuine interest in Australian culture and current events. Find an area that truly interests you—like the poems of Banjo Patterson or how jackeroos (cowboys) work on the stations (ranches)—so you can project your enthusiasm when you share your thoughts with them. Deemphasize areas in their past that might touch local sensitivities; emphasize the positive, progressive aspects of their growth. And never compare them with the British or the Americans.

HOW TO DEAL WITH THE WORKERS

If you are thinking of setting up an organization or facility in Australia, there are special considerations you will have to think about in dealing with the Australian workforce and mentality. We have already discussed how powerful the unions are. Keep that in mind as you read these five guidelines that will help you ensure successful working relationships with employees in an organizational setting.

(1) Dealing with Authority

Australian Negotiators: Australian workers are wellknown for their extreme egalitarian attitudes that result in breaking hierarchical barriers, including those erected by the flow of authority. They prefer to be treated as equals. The tradition of "mateship" also got them used to cooperating with each other on an equal footing.

You: Collaborate with your workers. Do not expect all your orders to be heeded blindly. Adopt a participative management style.

(2) Preference for Personal and Democratic Managerial Style

Australian Negotiators: Australians react to people's character rather than to their authority or status. Also, "mateship" has gotten them used to relating to their fellow workers in a very personable way, even to the extent of taking care of each other. When they are on the job, they do not think they are just doing a job for a boss. They prefer a collaborative approach—they assume management gives equal consideration to their interests and welfare in every decision made. On the job, they are at their best in a relaxed, democratic atmosphere.

You: If you accomplish your goals as a manager by merely imposing your authority, it will work by itself. Take care of your personal relationships with each one of your subordinates. Keep an "open door" policy. Respect their opinions and suggestions. Do not expect them to put you on a pedestal and defer to you. That is against their egalitarian way. Keep a flexible organization, allowing room for movement and changes. Deemphasize rules and regulations; use your creativity to accomplish the same goals through means other than rules. When it is time to relax, do it with your employees.

(3) Inattention to Work Standards

Australian Negotiators: Work standards do not motivate them to work harder. Their productivity is more a result of the sense of satisfaction and rapport they feel on the job.

You: You can not run a company without standards of performance. Use them, but make sure you have discussed them with your subordinates ahead of time and that they have accepted these standards. Do not base your expectations just on these standards. Maintaining a good relationship with your employees is the key. Simplify procedures that monitor their performance. Emphasize good relationships, not control.

(4) More Good Times, Less Hard Work

Australian Negotiators: A lot has already been said about Australians' love for good leisure times and how they do not care for putting in extra efforts on the job. The economical rationale is obvious for this worship of leisure and away from extra work: since the Australian rarely gets to keep much of any money made by overtime work, the incentive to do so is minimal. Until the tax laws change to lower the marginal rates, do not expect this trait to reverse itself. This, of course, does not apply to the few exceptional executives who are steering their economy toward higher standards of productivity and success.

You: Agreed-upon time limits for work need to be observed. Work schedules need to be worked out with your employees, taking their personal needs into account. Work out with them an ideal pace of work that supports optimum productivity without unduly straining them. Incentives that would provide additional leisure time or time off would be quite interesting and motivating to the typical Australian worker. Instead of offering additional pay for overtime, consider offering time off instead.

(5) Managing the Militant Labor Unions

Australian Negotiators: Labor unions have considerable power in Australian society, as we've said earlier. Although it is common to blame Australian workers for their irresponsible behavior, perhaps weak and remote management should also accept part of the blame. Strong management can make a difference.

You: Dealing with Australian labor is one of the most serious concerns you will need to plan and prepare for in setting up your business organization. The lack of any disciplinary power from the Arbitration Court or from any part of the federal, state, or local government, puts you in a very difficult position. Hiring strong managers with effective links to labor union leaders and members will be crucial. You will have to develop your own arbiters of power to deal with aggressive labor demands. Forging strong relationships with their leadership and a constant monitoring of the attitudes, feelings, needs, and suggestions of your workers through surveys, interviews, and consultations with your labor relations manager will be extremely important. Make absolutely certain you do this. If you do not, your business will get into trouble quickly.

SPECIFIC TACTICS

These are the favorite tactics chosen by Australian executives to use in typical business situations.

(1) Ask the Seller for a Lower Price: In dealing with sellers, Australian buyers can be difficult. They like to remind you of your competition and make it appear that other sellers are offering them better terms. They will definitely reject your first price offer and ask you to do better than that. They consistently keep the pressure on through various ways and simply will not give in. They like to try other ploys involving histrionics. For example, they will tell you their well is dry"—that financial constraints prevent them from accepting the going price. They like to fake it and give the appearance that they have more information about your product or service than they really do. Sometimes, they try to threaten you by predicting a disaster for you because they will not recommend your products and services anymore to their friends if you do not agree to their price concession.   When they are in a more cooperative mode, they are willing to be patient with you. Or, they also like to take the other extreme, offer a "take-it-or-leave-it" figure once and for all, and just walk away if no agreement is reached.

(2) Ask the Buyer to Pay More: When they are selling to you, Australian executives are equally tough. They will insist on maintaining their asking price and not give in to your bargaining efforts. To support their bid for their initial asking price, they will tell you that there are others who are interested in buying their product or service, or that they are already carrying and selling the best brand for this particular product or service. It may happen that it is a seller's market and there's a shortage of the product or service involved. If this is the case, and if they hold a monopoly position in the market, they may even try turning the tables on you and get you to justify why you deserve the product more than other buyers.

They also like to use low-pressure tactics. For instance, they will let you see their accounting records reflecting costs to prove to you that they are not charging unreasonable prices. They will also listen to you, note your objections, and then try to defuse them, one by one. They also like to use funny money to make it appear that their price is reasonable. If it is a buyer's market and sales are not going too well, they may become more laid back. They may just stall for time, be patient, and not close at any price until later on when the market changes, especially if they're not that hungry now for your business.

(3) Ask the Boss for a Raise: Generally speaking, most Australians like to use their record of accomplishments and performance in negotiating for a pay raise. They will more likely continually exert pressure on their boss, though. They will stick to their high salary demands and justify their claims by reminding their colleagues and boss how valuable they are to the company. They also like to use other tactics with less pressure, such as talking openly with their boss and building a straight case for their pay increase. They also listen carefully to their boss's reactions and work on objections systematically. Some of them will approach their bosses through an emotional route, building or reinforcing positive relations with them first and then making them their allies before making their request for the pay raise.

(4) Ask the Boss for a Promotion: Just as in asking for a raise, Australians like to use the company records that show their contributions and performance to support their bid for a promotion. They will assert their rights to this promotion by putting pressure on their boss until they are heeded. They will not give in to the boss' initial objections. Especially if they are already key managers, they will keep reminding their boss of just how important they are to the company. Some of them may have pending offers of a higher position or better pay from another company. In this case, they may take the risk of turning the tables on their boss, mentioning the fact that they have an offer from another company, and allowing their boss to persuade them to stay with the company.

Sometimes, they like to use softer tactics. For instance, often they will bring up their desire for a promotion and discuss it openly with their boss. Then, they listen intently to their boss' feedback and work diligently on defusing the objections. Sometimes, they are patient and wait to bring the matter up again when the timing is more favorable. At times, they will go above and beyond the call of duty and perform extraordinary tasks to improve their image and bargaining leverage. And they will even try to reposition their bosses by treating them as their mentors and asking them for suggestions on how they could get the promotion they want so bad.

(5) Ask the Boss to Change Their Holiday Dates: Most of the Australian executives like to plan ahead by anticipating their boss' objections and defusing them. Many of them like to put pressure on their boss, and not listen to objections from their boss or from their colleagues. They try to make their boss feel guilty somehow for disapproving the change in dates. Australians simply admit they made a mistake in submitting wrong dates in the first place. They negotiate if there is no reason for the work to be hampered because of the change in dates.

REFERENCES

The section "What Australians Are Like" was derived from these sources:

Brooks, Geraldine, "Aussie Workplace: Theater of the Absurd," *Wall Street Journal*, 6 April 1987, p. 16.

Carroll, John, ed., *Intruders in the Bush: The Australian Quest for Identity* (New York: Oxford University Press, 1982), p. 145.

Gunther, John, *Inside Australia* (New York: Harper & Row Publishers, 1972), p. 38.

McGregor, Craig, *Profile of Australia* (Chicago: Henry Regnery Company, 1967), p. 43.

Preston, Richard, ed., *Contemporary Australia: Studies in History, Politics, and Economics* (Durham, N.C.: Duke University Press, 1969), pp. 244, 245.

Renwick, George, *INTERACT: Guidelines for Australians and North Americans* (Yarmouth, Maine: Intercultural Press, Inc., 1980), p. 13.

Younger, Ronald M., *A Concise History: Australia and the Australians* (Australia: Hutchinson Group Pty. Ltd., 1982), pp. 892, 938, 939.

The section on negotiations was derived from:

Brooks, Geraldine, "Aussie Workplace: Theater of the Absurd," p. 16.

Caves, Richard E., and Laurence B. Krause, *The Australian Economy: A View from the North*: p. 303, 304.

"Doing Business with Australia," *World Executive's Digest*, February 1982, p. 92.

Schmidt, Klaus D., *Doing Business in Australia* (Menlo Park, Calif.: SRI International, 1980), p. 6.

Snowdon, Sondra, *The Global Edge: How Your Company Can Win in the International Marketplace* (New York: Simon & Schuster, 1986), p. 159.

16

Country Study: Philippines

WHAT FILIPINOS ARE LIKE

Filipinos, all fifty-seven million of them, are mostly of Malay stock and belong to a young democracy that is the product of many years of Spanish and American colonization. One writer says the country "lived in a convent for 350 years and then in Hollywood for fifty years." Filipinos belong to a country with one of the highest literacy rates in the world (eighty-eight percent), and where English is spoken very fluently by the well-educated ones. In spite of the presence of eight major indigenous languages and a number of minority groups such as the Muslim Filipinos in the south, the assimilated ethnic Chinese, and scattered pagan ethnic tribes in the interior, there is a relative sense of homogeneity among the majority of the lowland Christian Filipinos, who are about eighty-three percent Roman Catholic. To foster cultural unity, Tagalog (or Pilipino) has been designated the national language, with English as the secondary language. The Philippines is unique in Asia in the sense that its peoples reflect a blend of both Eastern and Western influences (mainly American) in its culture.

Foreigner businesspersons will be pleased to find that the larger corporations, especially those in the Makati district of the metropolitan Manila area, operate very much like American firms. The younger, more modern managers are educated in prestigious local private and public institutions, such as the Asian Institute of Management, Ateneo de Manila University, La Salle University, and the University of the Philippines, whose M. B. A. and management training programs are patterned after the American system. The more well-to-do ones obtain their training abroad, particularly in the United States. You will find, though, that even as younger managers strive to adapt Western, particularly American, ways of doing business, ingrained native values still operate in varying degrees. You will encounter four very important social values when you negotiate with Filipinos: (1) *utang na loob;* (2) *amor propio, SIR, pakikisama, and Hhya;* (3) *suki;* and (4) family loyalty.

(1) Filipinos have an immediate appreciation of the basic negotiating concept that nothing in life is free. *Utang na loob* describes the value placed on receiving help or favors from someone else—usually from your family, circle of friends, and business associates. When you receive the particular benefit in whatever form—be it money, facilitation through the bureaucracy, or any kind of social support, whether or not it is freely given—you are bound by social obligation and gratitude to repay the gesture some time in the future. *Utang na loob* derives from the nation's underdeveloped state. Due to the high level of poverty and the difficulty of getting support from the government bureaucracy to meet personal and social needs, Filipinos have learned to find persons who have the power, access, and linkages to decision makers who are in the position to grant housing, business, or scholarship loans from a development bank, to secure medical or social benefits from the social security office, and so forth. The country is so underdeveloped that government and even private bureaucracies can not give services to all who are entitled. So scarce are the resources of these organizations that the few who are served consider getting the service a favor. Because of the value attached to *utang na loob*, Filipinos consider it a compliment to be thought of as someone who is reliable in meeting his or her obligations; conversely, it is an insult and affront to be considered ungrateful and reneging on these obligations.

(2) To a foreigner, it appears there is a lot of "dancing around" in dealing with Filipinos socially. This perception is somewhat accurate because of the value attached to *amor propio*, smooth interpersonal relationships (SIR), *pakikisama*, and *hiya*. All four concepts are related. *Amor propio* refers to the Filipinos' great concern for maintaining dignity and honor in the eyes of the public they are exposed to. Filipinos use their own version of face-saving, which they abbreviate with the acronym SIR (smooth interpersonal relationships), by seeing to it that conversations and business meetings go smoothly by avoiding open confrontations and argumentativeness. They feel they are saving both their faces and those of their guests by

creating appearances of harmony and good relations. Thus, they will not openly disagree, they will not use euphemisms and indirect speech, they will flatter you, and, when it is absolutely necessary, they will tackle a serious disagreement by bringing in a third party to smooth out an otherwise thorny encounter. *Pakikisama* is the value placed on going along with what the group wants so as not to displease anybody and stick out like a sore thumb. *Hiya* literally means shame, and Filipinos at times go to great lengths to avoid situations that would put them on the spot and perhaps evoke rejection and, therefore, shame. For instance, they avoid standing up for their rights, they do not assert their privilege to apply for a loan, and so forth. It can even be a situation so minor—like meeting a foreigner—that makes unfamiliar Filipinos so shy and hesitant to talk about themselves candidly. All this happens because of *hiya*.

(3) In the marketplace, the *suki* system works to create stable relationships between buyers and sellers. If you are a regular buyer from a store, the owner considers you a *suki* if you purchase your goods from him or her regularly. The *suki* system works extensively and creates a network of unwritten contracted relationships between wholesale suppliers and retailers, retailers and customers, and small tradesmen like tailors or drivers and their customers. If you are a *suki*, there is an unspoken expectation that you buy the goods or services regularly and occasionally recommend them to your friends. In return, you get extended credit terms, goods of consistently high quality, and special treatment when being attended to.

(4) Filipinos are loyal to members of both their immediate and extended families. They express this sense of loyalty and support by hiring their relatives, especially in companies they own and run. The scarcity of jobs and the difficulty of breaking through both the government and private company marketplace increases the need for this kind of special patronage. Placing their relatives in strategic managerial positions also ensures business owners that they have sufficient control over their operations. Owners of huge corporations, who belong to the traditionally rich oligarchy, like to appoint their nearest kin, like a son or daughter, to occupy top executive positions. Other than these exceptionally high-level positions, traces of nepotism aren't too visible in the lower levels of big and well-known corporations, such as the San Miguel, Benguet, and Ayala corporations. More impersonal Western methods are used to staff the rest of the organization. Nonetheless, as a general rule, the extended family and taking care of all family members within a business is the business norm in the Philippines.

The core of the elite of Philippine society is composed of a few families whose wealth and reputation can be traced back to the eighteenth century. Their regional strongholds were initially based on their landholdings. Today, many of the top political figures, absentee landlords, and big business executives come from those families. This exclusive upper class makes up three percent of the country's population. They hold most of the wealth and have access to government favors. The height of the skewed dominance of the upper class was during the Marcos Era, 1965–1986. Graft and corruption reached their peak during this administration, which promoted its own brand of crony capitalism. Its main purpose was to enrich the friends and relatives of ex-President Ferdinand Marcos, and, of course, Marcos himself. The country's laws and public agencies were absolutely abused in the process of creating private empires. The Aquino government thereafter started to dismantle the corporate empires spawned by these cronies by confiscating their assets and premises. Most of the sequestered companies were put up for sale by the new government in an effort to privatize their productive capacities. Meanwhile, members of the disenfranchised elite fled the country and found refuge abroad. Unfortunately, the same type of graft and corruption that existed during the Marcos reign reasserted itself late in the Aquino reign and is currently very visible. For instance, some of Aquino's relatives were implicated in a number of shady deals: Her brother and his wife were implicated in a scam involving Australian gambling syndicates who needed licences to operate in the Philippines. This incident, among others, thoroughly embarrassed Aquino, who did not hesitate to order government officials to prosecute even her own relatives.

Things have changed, but there is still an elite. The "new" elite is composed of some of the traditional elite who remained in the country and who were either uninvolved in the clandestine network of business dealings of the previous government, or who were involved but were "pardoned" by the new government. Other members of the "new" elite are newly assigned government officials who were previously regarded as "powerless glorified technocrats" under Marcos. They were not quite as wealthy as the Marcos cronies. They seem to be the main bastions of power as the government seeks solutions to the country's enormous problems.

There are three other important segments in the upper class that you need to know about. One segment consists of many American and Spanish citizens who played significant roles as bankers, financial experts, business executives, manufacturers, industrialists, importers, and exporters in the local economy, while retaining ties with their native countries. Then, there are the Philippine-born pure-blooded Spaniards and Spanish *mestizos* (mixed blood), who descended from the elite class. They first emerged during the Spanish era that ended in 1898. Since then, they were socially protected and maintained by the sense of exclusivity and prestige associated with their origins. The third segment, consisting of the wealthy Chinese *mestizos,* is not quite as socially visible and prominent as their Spanish counterparts. Through generations of intermarriage with the locals and an increasing degree of cultural assimilation, the later generations of Chinese *mestizos* concentrated in Manila and other large cities as they became powerful channels of trade and commercial activities. Quietly, they amassed great wealth, and some of them have become dominant in finance, banking, and manufacturing.

Members of the small middle class ascended to this level mainly through education and the subsequent business and political opportunities available. Though entrepreneurship is supposed to be a main route to vertical mobility, opportunities for gathering capital were restricted because the country's resources were increasingly controlled by the few families who held them. Today, the middle class consists mainly of small businesspeople, small property owners, professionals, civil servants, teachers, merchants, tradesmen, and clerical workers.

Sixty percent of the population consists of those who have incomes below the official poverty line. This is the lower class. Their average family size is six. The very poor are in both urban and rural areas, and they lack full-time jobs. Those who do have jobs are mostly domestic helpers, peddlers, laborers, drivers, and minor clerks. The majority of the unemployed live in squatter areas scattered throughout the metropolitan areas.

FILIPINO NEGOTIATORS AND YOU

Gaining Entry through Power Brokers

Filipino Negotiators: Filipinos slant their decisions in favor of those they are familiar with or who are at least connected in some way to their network of business contacts, friends, or family relations. It is largely a personalistic society, where scarce resources such as money, other forms of financial support, and social support are distributed through person-to-person linkages bound by patron-client relationships. Because of this, you will find it to be a rather complex system that provides you service only if you are at the right place, in the right time, with the right contacts. The right contacts are especially valuable to whoever wants to get new business, and they are also helpful in getting favorable decisions on any proposal. The relatives of President Aquino emerged as members of the new political and economic elite following the local elections of January 1988. The pattern observed is reminiscent of that which Marcos capitalized on, but to a much lesser degree.

You: To enter the Philippine market either as a buyer or seller, you must find a good local contact. In dealing with the government bureaucracy, you have to be represented by a registered agent. Get recommendations from local trading companies, import-export firms, and Filipino consulates abroad. Get an agent who is well-connected with the industry and particular firm you are interested in. Your agent is valuable to you in at least six ways: obtaining permits, cutting through bureaucratic red tape, getting credit and foreign exchange, being introduced to key decision makers, maintaining smooth communications, and expediting your negotiations by acting as a third party when problems occur and when issues need to be reclarified and reinterpreted. Their fees are negotiable, and usually they are open to other incentives that foreign executives are in a position to give.

You must not only find yourself a registered agent—you have to keep yourself up-to-date. Acquaint yourself with the changes in the political arena and identify the rather rapid changes in power networks. Even as the government makes strong efforts to rid itself of the graft and corruption that maintained the Marcoses and their cronies, there are still signs that government officials are involved in brokering large business deals. In the Philippines, political and economic power go hand in hand. That has not changed, and probably never will change. So we advise foreign business executives to cultivate many contacts on all sides of the political spectrum. Do this becauise of the volatile nature of the country's politics and the relative instability of tenure of its appointed and elected officials.

SIR: The Oil That Lubricates Business

Filipino Negotiators: Filipinoshighly value SIR (smooth interpersonal relationships) not only among themselves but also with foreigners. Their society is permeated with a great deal of personalism. For example, they want to know all the details of your whole personal life, even if these do not have anything to do with your business transaction. New business relationships are usually preceeded by long social conversations focusing on the personality and personal circumstances of the person they are getting to know. Filipinos express this kind of personalism in the effusive smiles with which they greet you. They smile not only to set the stage for mutually profitable relationships but also for amiable relationships. Part of the price Filipinos pay to maintain SIR is putting a lot of extra effort into circumlocutions. They avoid open confrontations as much as possible and do not like public criticism. When either one happens, they are extremely sensitive to maintaining their *amor propio*, or personal dignity and honor—their local version of saving face. They also want to save the face of the other side, which is why they will hardly be forthright and frank with objections and criticisms. You will have to do some probing to find out negative things.

You: You will have to do a lot of adjustment and mental rehearsals, especially if you come from Western countries where impersonalism and controlled body language is the norm. For one thing, you will learn how to smile more, or at least you will learn how to be comfortable with dealing with a lot of smiles. Plan ahead of time which aspects of your personal self you will share in the candid conversations that are preludes to your new business relationships. Back off and find appropriate ways (and times) for airing disagreements with the other side. Remember the delicate matter of preserving their *amor propio*. Do as much as you can to make them look good. Remember, to win their trust, you will have to orchestrate your senstivities so that they are attuned to these particular needs that most Filipinos have.

Fine-Tuning Your Sales Presentation

Filipino Negotiators: Top-level Filipino negotiators appreciate an elaborate presentation that emphasizes the important benefits of your proposals. Audio-visual aids that help highlight the history of your company, your strong product lines, and your good service will greatly aid your presentation. Back up your claims by testimonials and documents showing customer satisfaction. To make it easier for them to read and understand your proposals, use local standards for units of measure and local currency. For instance, state your monetary terms in pesos, c.i.f. Manila. Filipino business executives also appreciate any additional incentives your company may offer them to sweeten your proposal.

You: Plan ahead for the right audio-visual materials and equipment to use just in case they are not available on the premises of the other side's company. Filipinos react favorably to vivid and colorful methods of displaying information. Be sensitive to their economic problems by gearing the benefits of your proposal toward short-term gains to the country. Highlight those gains that are consistent with the government's plans for recovery. Because of the shortage of economic resources in general and foreign exchange in particular, consider offering generous pricing terms and financing if you can. If you are selling products, emphasize those with well-known international brand names, especially American brand names. Filipinos are exposed extensively to American advertising in their media. Invitations to visit your office back home and observe your plant operations are welcome incentives for top-level executives. They love to travel abroad.

Exploring Business Opportunities

Filipino Negotiators: For many years, the Philippines has maintained a liberal attitude toward foreign investment. Tax exemptions, financial and technical assistance, and packaged investment incentives are available to those who are interested in ventures that conform to the government's priorities. Some of these incentives include: Nationality requirements for producers and exporters of preferred products have been relaxed. Income tax has been reduced. The Central Bank has eased its rules covering remittance of profits and dividends and repatriation of capital. Immigration rules for foreign investors and Filipinization requirements have been relaxed. Aliens are now allowed to participate in the rice and corn industry under certain conditions. Become familiar with the Investment Incentives Act (RA 5186) and the Export Incentives Act (RA 6135). They will tell you more about the benefits and incentives the government gives to firms involved in preferred areas of investment.

You: Foreign investors have extra leverage in the Philippines because of the country's urgent need for capital and earnings. An important result of the government's efforts to confiscate the businesses owned and managed by Marcos and his cronies was the availability for sale at bargain prices of hotels, factories, and other companies. This was part of the government's privatization program. Investors could easily knock off twenty percent of the acquisition costs of these businesses by using debt-equity swaps: After buying Philippine loans from foreign banks at a discount, an investor can trade them for equity in Philippine businesses. As a buyer of Philippine businesses or products, you can expect to be given extra attention and special treatment. But when you are selling, do notexpect the same amenities. In fact, you will have to plan ahead of time to find a way to get through the local business network. In short, it is a *buyer's* market and not a *seller's* market. They do not have much foreign exchange and will not part with it very easily.

Representation During Your Negotiation Sessions

Filipino Negotiators: Attendance at introductory meetings by top-level local executives will depend on the appropriateness and effectiveness of your contacts. If your contacts do not have friends within the interlocking system of decision makers in the company you want to deal with, lower-level executives will most likely attend the first meetings to filter out the beneficial aspects of your proposal. They will pass on that information to their bosses.

You: It is a good idea to have a team of experts represent your firm. How many? That depends on what you are proposing. If the negotiations are expected to take a long time, have enough on your team so they can alternate during the sessions. Your inactive members can observe the sessions. It is crucial, though, for your top-level executives to participate in the final rounds of the negotiations, especially near the conclusion and successful close. Offering concessions and incentives is most timely at this stage of the process, and both sides should be in the position to grant them immediately.

Decision Making, Filipino Style

Filipino Negotiators: Although the largest corporations train their executives in the most advanced Western management methods, most of them still use centralized decision-making processes. The chief executive of public companies makes the important final decisions, but there is a lot of close coordination with the government agencies that oversee their operations. Family-owned private firms, likewise, are closely run by their owners. Still, they have a high regard for what the CEO has to say, if he or she is not one of the relatives. Most of the top executives of these firms, however, are still the family members, and often they control their company with an iron hand. Since jobs are scarce in the Philippines, outmoded techniques of treating workers, for instance by emphasizing penalties rather than rewards, are tolerated by middle-level and lower-level managers.

As a rule, Filipinos have a hard time saying "no." Therefore, they will often smile, say "yes," or give some other positive signal when all the time they meant to say "no" to your proposal. So do not be surprised to find them being roundabout in the way they indicate how your proposal is doing in the hands of the decision-makers.

You: Give them enough room to save face by not pressuring them. Allow enough time for them to consider your proposal. Filipinos are known to squander time, so do not be surprised by many routine delays. Do not show hints of impatience, and do not pressure the other side to tell you what the final decision is. Even though you are not hearing about its progress, your proposal is slowly being processed through channels. Wait for the other side to initiate a discussion about the fate of your proposal. It is OK to ask them to tell you approximately how much time it will take for them to consider the issue. Do not be fooled by what they tell you, though. Most likely, the period of time it will actually take is longer than what they say it will take. Better yet, be direct and ask them when you can check on the progress of your proposal. The usual procedure is to submit a proposal to senior management. They will consider it and then make a recommendation to their CEO. The final decision flows back down from that point.

You will find Filipinos are at home with the tedious process of seeking concessions. They love to wrestle with you for the best deal. Go to the local shops. You will quickly observe how they haggle. It is common for veteran buyers to cut twenty to forty percent off the price of most items. Shop sellers do not seem to mind—they willingly engage the buyer in a tug-of-war for concessions. They do it in their shops, and they will do it with you, too.

Do not overlook the importance of the role played by your contact person or agent throughout your negotiations. To cut short what could be an extremely time-consuming effort of obtaining a favorable decision, enlist the support of a well-connected person right from the start. Ideally, look for somebody with a top-level executive position who belongs to the circle of friends or school mates of the main decision maker in the firm you are wooing. Another complicating factor in dealing with the bureaucracy in large organizations is the existence of the *bata* (*lakad*) system. This refers to the linkages of expediters who work for a particular manager. Because they compete within the organization for scarce resources, managers have to nurture their own connections within the firm. These good connections have at some time or or another benefited from favors done for them by the manager. Try to get to know these important people, too.

A delicate matter that all foreign negotiators have to be discrete about is how to handle incentives, or what in the eyes of others may constitute a bribe. Quite often, obtaining favorable decisions from top executives is expedited by certain percentage shares, commissions, bonuses, or outright bribes. It has been suggested that these be enclosed in a blank envelope or in a briefcase left on the desk of the decision maker. Although the government is trying to get rid of graft and corruption, such institutional practices central to doing business in the Philippines will take a lot of time to eliminate.

SPECIFIC FILIPINO NEGOTIATING TACTICS

(1) Ask the Seller for a Lower Price: When Filipino's are buying, sometimes they will refuse to bargain with you and name their price on a "take-it-or-leave-it" basis. If they do decide to bargain with you, they will be tough and ask you to improve your offer, or they will remind you of your competition. They will insist on their price demands, and if you do not give in, they will try nibbling for concessions on other items such as credit terms, delivery dates, and so forth, just to gain the upper hand. They also like to use use funny money, to get you to think either that the price they are offering is high enough or that the price you are offering is too unreasonable. Sometimes, they will offer to split the difference with you. Another favorite tactic of theirs is to try to soften you by saying that their "well is dry" because their company's rules will noy allow them to spend any more on your product or service.

(2) Ask the Buyer to Pay More: As sellers, Filipino executives like to subject you to pressure tactics. They like to remind you that there are others who would like to buy the same product or service. Sometimes, they will receive all their customers in the same room at the same time and have them see and hear each other bargain. They also like to use funny money either to persuade the buyers that the price they want is reasonable if not cheap, or to show that the price you are offering is too low compared to the quality and value you will be getting. Often, they will try to get you to split the difference with them, to gain some momentum in the negotiation.

(3) Ask the Boss for a Raise: Most Filipinos use the records of their past and present performance and achievement in negotiating for a pay raise with their bosses. This seems like a reasonable and fair enough thing to do. However, they are also capable of exerting extra pressure to push for their raise. They try to keep the pressure on their bosses in

many ways: One way is to remind their bosses of just how important they are to the company and how much they have achieved so far. If they are key contributors to the company, they like to use their leverage to demand many things, the pay raise being only one of them. They will deliberately press for a number of such demands to distract their bosses from the latter's own demands and requirements. If their bosses try to please them, they sometimes will take advantage of this and put on an act to emphasize how much they want the raise.

On the softer side, they often take a less confrontational approach with their bosses. For instance, they will often leak their desire for a raise through another colleague to test how their bosses react. This way, they can change their initial approach if it does not work too well and try something better. Before actually asking for the raise, they like to float information through the grapevine about their most current accomplishments to make them look good in their boss' eyes. Another thing they like to do is to try to improve their relations with their boss and make them their ally before asking for the raise. Once they have told their boss what they want and have learned their objections, they will work on the issues raised by their boss to defuse these objections.

(4) Ask the Boss for a Promotion: Filipinos especially like these three tactics both for asking for a pay raise and a promotion: keep the pressure on their boss, use company records showing their accomplishments and achievements, and remind their boss that they are the best in the company and that they have contributed a lot. Most of them will also make their bosses feel guilty if they fail to get the promotion. Also, they like to use flattery if they know their boss is weak enough to succumb to this ploy.

(5) Ask the Boss to Change Their Holiday Dates: Filipinos like to put on an act to get their boss to approve a change in holiday dates. They also like to surprise their bosses and keep them off balance by creating side issues. They think these issues give them enough leverage to make their bosses feel they owe it to them to approve the change in dates. They also like to improve their relationships with their bosses first and make them their allies before pressing for the change. Finally, they try to get the support of somebody else in the office who is on good terms with their boss to help negotiate the change in dates.

REFERENCES

The section "What Filipinos Are Like" was adapted from:

Bello, Walden, David Kinley, and Elaine Elinson, *Development Debacle: The World Bank in the Philippines* (San Francisco, Calif.: Institute for Food and Development Policy, 1982), p. 185.

Bunge, Frederica M., *Philippines: A Country Study* (Washington, D.C.: Foreign Area Studies-The American University, August 1984), pp. 75, 94

Bureau of Public Affairs (U.S. Department of State), *Background Notes: Philippines* (Washington, D.C.: U.S. Government Printing Office, August 1986), pp. 1, 3.

Guthrie, George M., "The Philippine Temperament" in *Six Perspectives on the Philippines*, George M. Guthrie, ed. (Manila, Philippines: Bookmark, Inc., 1968), pp. 49–83.

Hollnsteiner, Mary R., "Reciprocity in the Lowland Philippines," in *Four Readings in Philippine Values*, Institute of Philippine Culture Papers No. 2, Frank Lynch and Alfonso de Guzman, eds. (Quezon City: Ateneo de Manila University Press, 1970).

Kraar, Louis, "Aquino Needs a New Miracle," *Fortune*, 14 September 1987, p. 90.

Lynch, Frank, "Social Acceptance Reconsidered," in *Four Readings on Philippine Values*, Institute of Philippine Culture Papers No. 2, Frank Lynch and Alfonso de Guzman, eds. (Quezon City: Ateneo de Manila University Press, 1970), pp. 1–64.

Marzan, C.V., "Preferences and Job Satisfaction in Selected Domestic Private Commercial Banks," M.B.A. Thesis, Ateneo de Manila University, Manila, Philippines, 1984.

Morais, Robert J., *Social Relations in a Philippine Town* (Chicago, Ill.: Northern IllinoisUniversity/Center for Southeast Asian Studies, 1981), pp. 21–22.

"Oiling the Wheels of Misgovernment," *The Economist*, 21 November 1987, p. 50.

Silos, L. R., "The Basis of Asian and Western Organization," *Occasional Paper No. 13* (Manila, Philippines: Asian Institute of Management, 1985).

Steinberg, David Joel, *The Philippines: A Singular and a Plural Place* (Boulder, Colo.: Westview Press, 1982), pp. 23–24.

The section on negotiating was synthesized from:

Andres, Tomas D., *Management by Filipino Values* (Quezon City, Philippines: New Day Publishers, 1985), pp. 53–56.

Andres, Tomas D., *Understanding Filipino Values: A Management Approach* (Quezon City, Philippines: New Day Publishers, 1981), pp. 16–17, 99–100.

Bunge, *Philippines*, p. 83.

Miller, Matt, "Local Philippine Vote Marks Resurgence of the Traditionally Dominant Families," *Wall Street Journal*, 18 January 1988, p. 13.

Morais, *Social Relations in a Philippine Town*, pp. 19–21.

Price Waterhouse, *Doing Business in the Philippines* (Tampa, Fla.: Price Waterhouse, 1981), pp. 14, 15, 32.

SRI International, *Doing Business in the Philippines* (Menlo Park, Calif.: SRI International,1987), pp. 2–4, 16.

Steinberg, *The Philippines*, p. 4.

17

Conclusions: Dos and Don'ts of Cross-Cultural Negotiations

International business negotiators are separated from each other not only by physical features, a totally different language and business etiquette, but also by a different way to perceive the world, to define business goals, to express thinking and feeling, to show or hide motivation and interests. The way one succeeds in cross-cultural negotiations is by fully understanding others, using that understanding to one's own advantages to realize what each party wants from the negotiations, and to turn the negotiations into a win-win situation for both sides.

TEN RECOMMENDATIONS FOR SUCCESS

1.   The path to success in negotiations is "prepare, prepare, prepare." Preparation is essential if one is to be proactive rather than reactive. Counterpunching only works when you are prepared before the blow is thrown. Preparation is difficult enough in domestic negotiations, but when the many multifaceted cross-cultural aspects are added the problems and time necessary for adequate planning rise exponentially. Planning means coming prepared technically as well as culturally. Many foreigners come to the negotiating table well prepared technically and operationally and expect you to be likewise. Poor preparation, in addition to being a major obstacle to your success in achieving an agreement, can also have adverse cultural considerations—in the Orient not having the answers or being sloppy

may be a reason to lose face. The Chinese (as well as the Japanese and Russians) usually are meticulous in their preparation and well briefed on technical uses. Any sloppiness in the preparation of their opponent will be used against them. Meetings tend to fail in inverse proportion to the time spent in preparation and in direct proportion to the time spent meeting.

Planning is critical. One should know sufficiently the country and the culture of those with whom one is going to negotiate. Many foreign companies and governments try to turn negotiating sessions into technology seminars. The Chinese have a reputation for making unending demands for technical data (After six weeks of technical briefing by Boeing, the Chinese remarked, "Thank you for the introduction.") During the planning stage, one should establish limits regarding the extent and type of information you will disclose. All members of your team should know exactly what they can and cannot say.

One should also carefully plan the tactics. Certain American behaviors may insult or irritate members in other cultures. Know, beware of, respect, and accept the customs and culture of the other side. It will greatly smooth the negotiation process. Understand and avoid those special meanings and nuances that are inhibitions, turnoffs, or taboos in the other culture. On the other hand, some items will likely facilitate the process; know them too and use them. Just understand, accept, respect, and practice them during your stay. They will appreciate it and respect you for it.

Company representatives should prepare for a long negotiating period; cross-cultural negotiations can often last anywhere from two to six times as long to reach an agreement as it would take domestically. It would be appropriate to take the time to learn about the culture and language of the society you are to meet with. Set aside at least a week for such a study or even a month if it is a major commitment. Another reason for preparedness is to learn about and be able to counter negotiating tactics that may be peculiar to the culture you intend to visit and may have the effect of harming your efforts. Forewarned is forearmed.

2. Extensive preliminary work by subordinates or cross-cultural brokers (go-betweens) is often necessary for a successful outcome of a negotiation. It usually pays to spend what you consider to be an excessively large amount of time upfront with the other side's subordinates and aides and getting them on board and in agreement before the CEOs get together. This is especially true and required if one

is working with the Japanese—their *ringi* system demands this decision from middle management upward. It is necessary to know who are the key gatekeepers and decision makers, where they are located in the organization, and what their authority and impact and involvement on the upcoming negotiations will be. In many cultures, behind-the-scenes actions are more important than the actual meeting—so the actual negotiating meeting can become a mere formality.

In the case of a large company, it is not recommended to send the president or CEO of your company for the first meeting or first contact internationally. If the CEO comes over first, the subordinates can be at a severe disadvantage for completing the work on a favorable and equitable agreement. It is best to use the top executives only for the signing at the end. The procedure for many cultures is having the subordinates work out the details of an agreement and having the corporate directors arrive only at the end for the actual signing. Nonetheless, it is recommended that the company send high-level managers who have sufficient credentials and access to relevant top-level managers at headquarters so as to have the capacity to talk as equals to the top people of both sides during the actual negotiations. Understand what is customary in the culture you are negotiating with and have a clear plan on how you intend to use the CEO's presence in your negotiating.

3. Needless to say, it is advantageous to know the language of the other team. Even If you decide not to use it at the conference, knowing it will be handy. A foreign language can be an awesome barrier, though. Words have different or multiple meanings. Perceptions and concepts starkly differ across cultures. If any doubt whatsoever exists to the meaning of a word or action, ask questions. For your part, paraphrase your response, go slowly, and recap your position often. Eliminate, if possible, the use of jargon, idioms, or slang. Speak clearly, audibly, and slowly. Explain each major point in several different ways, but do not be condescending. Expressions and gestures may be useful in making a point with foreigners and bridging the gap between two foreign languages. In most cultures it is advisable to always maintain a pleasant disposition and not show signs of anger.

Many negotiators typically treat the translation problem much too naively, believing it a problem in linguistics and not in cross-cultural communications. Meaning may be further modified by gestures, tone of voice, and cadence, which are important to the message sent but are not found in straight translations. A truly bicultural interpreter offers multiple benefits. If you do know the language, he can offer you more time to think, and more time to prepare your response and next statement. Even if you do know the language, chances are you may not understand fully the culture and the particular nuances and implied meanings involved. Often, equivalent concepts do not exist between cultures. Detailed probing and illustrations, examples, and explanations must be given to provide complete understanding. The interpreter can be skilled in linguistics but he still may not be familiar in the nuances of negotiation. If you can, hire a bicultural advisor who will, besides the translation aspect, serve as a go-between and cultural broker on how to best prepare yourself and conduct the negotiations. A truly bilingual and bicultural interpreter can help you phrase responses with just the correct shades of meaning and decisively impact the entire negotiation process. It is rare indeed to find a bicultural interpreter who is thoroughly familiar with the business cultures of both sides and not merely the languages. It may be an expensive service but it will yield dividends many times over.

Many American business travelers feel it is unnecessary to learn a foreign language or to employ an interpreter when doing business overseas. This is an example of "penny wise and pound foolish." Using the opponent's interpreter may be unwise, as his level of expertise is suspect and his loyalty will not be to you but to the other side. It is clearly a much better strategy to employ your own bicultural advisor and interpreter who can alert you on the peculiarities of the foreign culture before you commit a faux pas on a seemingly innocent matter. The interpreter can act as coach and should be briefed on all items in advance. This includes giving him a copy of your proposed presentation and any media to study with enough time for him to alert you to any problems he may encounter therein. Ask his advice when stuck on what to do next or if you do not completely understand the other's response.

Do not talk more than a minute or two without giving the interpreter a chance to speak. Allow the interpreter to take notes or even use a dictionary; no one can be expected to be perfectly fluent in two or more languages. Permit the translator to spend as much time as needed in clarifying points when meanings may be obscure. Do not interrupt him in the midst of his translation. If there is heavy work, night sessions, or long sessions with no break, consider two interpreters so they can alternately perform the translation task.

4. Since language barriers will always exist in any cross-cultural negotiations, pictures are worth more than a thousand words. One should plan to support presentations with instructive visuals whenever possible. Photographs, drawings, diagrams, copies of key documents, catalogs, books, even samples of products should be brought if they will help state your case. Bringing an English copy to the meeting is fine if that is all that is available. Many members of other cultures can read English better than they can speak it. But beware: certain colors, subjects, or models can be taboo or distasteful to members of the other culture. Using them can be hazardous to the health of the agreement. Check out your visuals with your bicultural interpreter or an ethnic member of your company's local office to check for any faux pas before you present them. You can always redo them; but once you have presented them, it may have caused irrevocable damage to the negotiating effort.

5. The side that uses time most effectively usually wins. Americans are, in the eyes of foreigners, notoriously impatient, always seem to be in a hurry, and usually must come back with a signed agreement to show the boss the trip was eventful and not just a boondoggle. They can be driven into an agreement they really do not want just to take home a signed document. It is therefore a good strategy not to let the other side know your return plans, to prepare for the long term, and to be patient. The Chinese value patience and will freely use all sorts of stalling tactics and delays. This behavior can also stem from lack of experience, sluggish bureaucracy, subordinates having fear of criticism from above, or just plain slowness in decisions coming down from above. In any case, negotiations can not be rushed, nor should they be.

Be prepared for the long term. Make certain everyone in your organization (including the CEO, the other executives, and the board) are aware of the increased time demands that exist in any cross-cultural negotiation, especially if one is dealing with developing countries. Get them all committed to the long term. Do not create any self-imposed deadlines; they will only come back to haunt you later. If you think you can fly in, negotiate, sign, and fly out the same day or the next, you are in for considerable disappointment, frustrations, and an agreement—if any—that is not in your organization's best interest. Know what to expect and make certain everyone in your organization is aware of these expectations.

6. The use of ethnic American members on your negotiating team when negotiating in an international setting is of questionable value in cross-cultural settings. Many cultures put first allegiance to the ethnic background and second allegiance to citizenship. Put another way, most Chinese believe once a Chinese, always a Chinese and one's loyalty is (or should be) to China no matter where a Chinese currently resides or of which nation he is a citizen. When negotiating in China, Chinese expatriates on a negotiating team are frequently pulled aside to discuss informally and with great insight, items of interest on the agenda. Usually an ethnic American even if of pure ethnic blood and still proficient in the tongue of his forefathers, has usually lost touch with the subtle cultural nuances that are so critical in cross-cultural settings. Unless he can take an active role in the negotiations, it is probably better not to send an ethnic only for ethnicity sake. Use a local who is skilled biculturally if you know him and trust him or hire a native go-between who has been highly recommended. However, if you are negotiating with a foreign government, a American citizen or an ethnic from a third country would probably be more effective than using a government-supplied interpreter or a citizen of that country.

In addition, bicultural persons—persons born in one culture but living and working in another—may be highly effective international negotiators, not because they have substantive knowledge of a relevant culture but because through experience they have learned to communicate and relate effectively to persons from other cultures. Those who have learned to interpret correctly the cultural messages and signals from another group and communicate to that group in its own language are also potentially effective negotiators.

7. Most agreements have long-lasting implications. In many cultures a written agreement is therefore not the culmination of the talks but considered only the start of a longer relationship. To a Chinese, for example, the signing of a contract is not the termination of the negotiations but a prologue to a longer continuous relationship. It sets the stage for a growing relationship in which it will be proper for the Chinese to make increasing demands on the other party. You can expect the Chinese negotiator in the post-agreement implementation phase to continue to press to further his objectives; closure is never fully reached. In Japan and Greece, a contract is considered valid only as long as it serves both parties' interests.

To the Japanese, a negotiated agreement is seen as an indication of the direction to be taken while adjustments and modifications can be made as conditions and circumstances warrant it. An agreement is seen only as the beginning of an adaptive process rather than the end. The American expectation of contractual finality is foreign to the Japanese way of thinking. Japanese negotiators do not mind suggesting major changes even after a contract is signed; this to the American side is considered devious and leads to the conclusion that the agreement was made in bad faith from the beginning. The Russians as well as numerous other cultures interpret a contract strictly or loosely according to whether or not it is in their best interests to do so. Americans and many businessmen in the West believe the signing of an agreement is an indication that all problems under discussion have been resolved. An agreement in many other cultures is open to renegotiation by either party at anytime. It is, therefore, to your benefit that both parties understand and agree over exactly what is the purpose of the agreement, what actions must be taken, and how tasks and responsibilities are to be divided or shared, or to prepare for continuous negotiations.

And finally, get the specifics on paper. The Japanese and the Russians prefer generally worded accords that provide them utmost flexibility in actions. Here one must try to pin down details. If you are working with a culture that likes such general, broadly worded agreements, it would be useful to agree on the details and get them on paper. Otherwise, the other party could come back to you later on with an interpretation of dubious merit that is advantageous to their position and not to yours.

8. Do not be intimidated. How does one respond to end-game tactics? One must be prepared to walk away without reaching an agreement. The other side's advantage in knowing you have promised to be home by a certain time is an advantage to them only as long as they believe you are committed to reaching an agreement before leaving. If they know you are prepared to depart without an agreement, the deadline begins to work against them. At the point when an agreement no longer benefits you, you must be able to walk away without a deal, no matter how disappointed you are.

9. Do not be ethnocentric and view the negotiations in a domestic sense. The strategy of rewarding intransigence with concessions is called "the Jimmy Carter school of negotiations." He never understood that giving things away and appealing to the better nature of the Russians, Iranians, Panamanians, and othes could not possibly work. They had absolutely no incentive to compromise, and every reason to make additional demands. Nibbling is the attempt to make additional demands after the terms have been finalized. People will be willing to make minor concessions rather than jeopardize a deal that has already been made. Some countries try to eke out just a little more, regardless of what the contract says and see nothing wrong with their behavior. Koreans and Chinese are famous for raising ongoing objections to contacts and for insisting upon revision of the terms.

George Kennan, former ambassador to the Soviet Union and a top-level advisor in the State Department, has pointed out that the pattern of unilateral concessions started long before Jimmy Carter. When Kennan was a relatively junior diplomat, he was so frustrated by the American government's negotiating strategy that he sent a full-rate telegram of several thousands words to the State Department. Books on diplomatic history call it "the long telegram." He got their attention and very forcefully argued that the Russians see unilateral concessions not as something to be reciprocated, but as signs of weakness that should be exploited. Alas, later generations of Aemrican leaders (both political and business) have probably never even heard of "the long telegram."

They do not realize that some people will not move without an incentive to do so. Furthermore, simply getting both parties to move is not enough. You want to move toward the right deal, and the first moves can determine both the speed and direction of the momentum. If a public statement is made in the West, it is more binding than a private statement. In Japan, the reverse is true.

10. Know your bottom line. Benjamin Franklin said "Necessity never made a good bargain." What is your BATNA (best alternative to a negotiated agreement)? What is your walking away point? At the point when an agreement no longer benefits you, you must be able to walk away without a deal, no matter how disappointed you are. Have a predetermined point where it becomes preferable not to make a deal and stick to it. Too many executives, having made the decision to do business are so anxious to conclude a deal that they proceed despite the poor agreement reached. Sunk costs are irrelevant. Amounts already invested and effort already expended should be irrelevant to a decision maker. The deal itself should not be the objective. If the deal can not justify itself, the best alternative is to walk away, no matter how great your disappointment.

CONCLUSIONS

In summary, three major rules would start you on the route to success in cross-cultural negotiations:

1. Recognize that a foreign negotiator is different from you—in perceptions, motivation, beliefs, and outlook. Identify, understand, accept, and respect the other side's culture. And be prepared to communicate and operate on two separate and different cultural wavelengths. One should not assume that anything that is acceptable in one's own culture is necessarily acceptable in all other cultures. One must adjust the pace of negotiations to that of the people with whom you are trying to do business. One must always remember that in any negotiations, with anybody anywhere, you have the option of saying no to a deal. Even if one has been working hard for a long time to get the deal, one must accept fate. One must treat everybody with whom you deal with the greatest personal respect. You must be guided by what you feel comfortable doing rather than by what you feel is right or wrong. Good and enduring personal relations between negotiators lead to long-term relationships between their companies and this is how mutual prosperity occurs.

2. Be culturally neutral. Being different does not denote being better or inferior. Do not cast judgment on the other party's cultural mores any more than you would want them to judge your values. It may be true that from a moral point of view some foreign customs may appear senseless, capricious, even cruel and insane to you. But remember you are visiting the country as a businessperson—not as a missionary. You plan to do business there—not to convert the natives to American customs and practices. Recognize that they probably feel the same way about your culture as you do theirs. It may not be necessary to adopt their values as part of your own personal value system. All that is necessary is that you accept and respect their norms as part of their culture.

3. Be sensitive to their cultural norms, dos and taboos. Try to understand what they are and how your behavior may impact them even if it causes you discomfort or emotional stress. Yet it is necessary to accept, and to proceed with the business without showing distress if one wishes to come home with an agreement that is beneficial to both parties and marks the start of a long-term, healthy relationship between two companies from two cultures. One way to bridge cultural differences is to demonstrate interest in, knowledge of, respect for, and appreciation of the other side's culture. Failure to do so can easily be interpreted as an act of cultural superiority and arrogance, a statement

that the other side's culture is not significant or important. Questions about culture framed in an uncritical way show that you find the other side's culture to be interesting, important, and worth learning about. Therefore, the international negotiator should try to learn as much as possible about the other side's culture. Negotiators should be tolerant and respectful of cultural differences. Once differences are understood, negotiators should seek ways of accommodating them. Some islands of cultural commonality should be found and enjoyed together.

Table 17.1 provides a list of mistakes commonly made when negotiating overseas. Table 17.2 provides a list of dos and don'ts when involved in an international or cross-cultural negotiation.

Table 17.1
Common Mistakes Made When Negotiating Overseas

- Failure to place yourself in the other person's shoes
- Insufficient understanding of different ways of thinking
- Insufficient attention to saving face of the opponent
- Insufficient knowledge of the host country—including history, culture, government, status of business, image of foreigners
- Insufficient recognition of the nature and characteristics of the role of government in centrally planned economies
- Insufficient recognition of the relatively low status assigned to businesspersons in many countries
- Insufficient recognition of the role of host government in the negotiations process
- Insufficient recognition of the economic and political criteria in the decision-making process
- Insufficient recognition of the difference between approval at one level and implementation of such approval at other levels of the government
- Insufficient understanding of the role of personal relations and personalities in the decision-making process
- Insufficient allocation of time for negotiations
- Insufficient attention of time for negotiations
- Insufficient attention to planning for changing negotiation strengths
- Interference by headquarters
- Insufficient planning for internal communication and decisions
- Insufficient recognition of the role of the negotiator in accommodating the conflicting interests of his group with those of the opposing groups
- Insufficient recognition of the loci of decision-making authority
- Insufficient recognition of the strength of competitors
- Insufficient recognition and attention to training executives in the art of negotiations

Table 17.2
Dos and Don'ts for Cross-Cultural Negotiations

DOs
- know your substance and be well prepared
- specify clear objectives and know your bottom line
- develop personal relationships but be careful not to be manipulated
- seek opportunities for informal get togethers since it is there that most of the initial contacts will be made
- meticulously follow protocol: foreigners usually are more status conscious than Americans
- understand national sensitivities and do not violate them
- assess the flexibility of your opponent and his obstacles
- understand the decision-making process and build up your position by taking advantage of each step
- pin down details
- understand the negotiating style of the country
- be patient and use time deadlines sparingly
- use media pressure carefully because it could backfire
- be involved in your own decision-making process because this will probably give you an advantage over your counterpart

DON'Ts
- try to look at everything from your own definition of what determines a rational and scientific viewpoint
- press a point if others are not prepared to accept it
- look at things from your own narrow self-interest
- ask for concessions or compromises that are politically or culturally sensitive
- stick to your agenda if the other party has different priorities
- use jargon that can confuse the other side
- skip authority levels in a way that hurts sensibilities of middle-level officials; the top man has the power to commit the organization, but for implementation you require the support of people at intermediate levels
- ask for a decision that you know the other side can not make or is not ready to make
- differ with members of your own team in public
- stake out extreme positions; be consistent in your approach
- negotiate with yourself

Selected Bibliography

Acuff, Frank. (1993). *How to Negotiate Anything with Anyone Anywhere*. Chicago: AMACOM books.

Adler, Nancy J., Theodore Swartz Gehrke, and John L. Graham. (1987). "Business Negotiations in Canada, Mexico, and the United States." *Journal of Business Research*. 15 (October): 411–430.

Adler, Nancy J., and John L. Graham. (1989). "Cross Cultural Interaction: The International Comparison Fallacy." *The Journal of International Business Studies*. 20 (3) (Fall): 515–537.

Altany, David. (1988). "Culture Clash: International Negotiation Etiquette." *Industry Week*. 238 (October 2): 13–18.

Anand, R. P., ed. (1986). *Cultural Factors in International Relations*. New York: Abhinav Publications.

Arbose, Jules R. (1982). "Wise Men from the East Bearing Gifts." *International Management (UK)*. 37/5 (May): 67-68.

Atcheson, Richard. (1992). "Dealer's Delight,"*Travel-Holiday*. 175/4: 39.

Banks, John C. (1987). "Negotiating International Mining Agreements: Win-Win versus Win-Lose Bargaining." *Columbia Journal of World Business*. (Winter): 67–75.

Barnum, Cynthia and Natasha Wolniansky. (1989). "Why Americans Fail at Overseas Negotiations." *Management Review*. 78/10 (October): 55–57.

Beliaev, Edward, Thomas Mullen, and Betty Jane Punnett. (1985). "Understanding the Cultural Environment: US-USSR Trade Negotiations." *California Management Review.* XXVII/2: 100–110.

Belk, Russell W., John F. Sherry Jr., and Melanie Wallendorf. (1988). "A Naturalistic Inquiry into Buyer and Seller Behavior at a Swap Meet." *Journal of Consumer Research.* 14 (March): 449–470.

Binnendijk, Hans, ed. (1987). *National Negotiating Styles.* Washington, D.C.: Center for the Study of Foreign Affairs, Foreign Service Institute, U.S. Dept. of State.

Black, J. Stewart, and Mark Mendenhall. (1993). "Resolving Conflicts with the Japanese: Mission Impossible." *Sloan Management Review.* (Spring): 49–53.

Burt, David N. (1989). "Nuances of Negotiating Overseas." *Journal of Purchasing and Materials Management.* 25: 56–64.

Campbell, Nigel C.G., John L. Graham, Alain Jilbert, and Hans Gunther Meissner. (1988). "Marketing Negotiations in France, Germany, the United Kingdom and the United States." *Journal of Marketing.* 52/2 (April): 49–62.

Campbell, Nigel C.G. (1987). "Negotiating with the Chinese—A Commercial Long March." *Journal of Marketing Management.* 2/3: 219–223.

Casse, Pierre. (1991). *Negotiating across Cultures.* Washington, D.C.: United States Institute of Peace Press.

Casse, Pierre, and Surinden Deal. (1985). *Managing Intercultural Negotiations.* Washington, D.C.: Sietar International.

Dennett, Raymond, and Joseph E. Johnson. (1989). *Negotiating with the Russians.* New York: World Peace Foundation.

Deverge, Michael. (1986). "Negotiating with the Chinese." *Euro-Asia Business Review.* 5/1 (January): 34–36.

Drake, Laura E. (1995). "Negotiation Styles in Intercultural Communication." *The International Journal of Conflict Management.* 6/1 (January): 72–90.

Dreyfus, Patricia A., and Amy Roberts. (1988). "Negotiating the Kremlin Maze." *Business Month.* 132 (November): 55–62.

Druckman, Daniel, Alan A. Benton, Faizunisa Ali, and J. Susana Bagur. (1976). "Cultural Differences in Bargaining Behavior." *Journal of Conflict Resolution.* 20/3: 413–449.

Engholm, Christopher. (1992). "Asian Bargaining Tactics: Counterstrategies for Survival." *East Asian Executive Reports.* (July): 9–25.

Faure, Guy Olivier, and Jeffrey Z. Rubin. (1993). *Culture and Negotiation: The Resolution of Water Disputes.* London: SAGE Publications.

Fayerweather, J., and Ashok Kapoor. (1976). *Strategy and Negotiation for the International Corporation.* New York: Ballinger Publishers.

de Ferrer, Robert J. (1989). "Playing the Away Game." *Marketing.* (February 16): 24–26.

Firth, Raymond. (1966). *Malay Fisherman.* Hamden, Conn.: Archon Books.

Fisher, Glen. (1980). *International Negotiations: A Cross-Cultural Perspective.* Chicago: Intercultural Press, Inc.

Fisher, Roger, and William Ury. (1983). *Getting to Yes: Negotiating Agreement without Giving in.* New York: Penguin Books.

Foster, Dean Allen. (1992). *Bargaining across Borders.* New York: McGraw Hill.

Frances, June N. P. (1991). "When in Rome? The Effects of Cultural Adaptation on Intercultural Business Negotiations." *Journal of International Business Studies.* 22/3 (Third Quarter): 403–428.

Frank, Sergy. (1992). "Avoiding the Pitfalls of Business Abroad." *Sales & Marketing Management.* (March): 48–52.

Frank,Sergy. (1992). "Global Negotiating." *Sales & Marketing Management.* (May): 64–70

Geertz, Clifford. (1963). *Peddlers and Princes.* Chicago: University of Chicago Press.

Ghauri, Perdez N. (1988). "Negotiating with Firms in Developing Countries: Two Case Studies." *Industrial Marketing Management.* 17: 49–53.

Ghauri, Perdez N. (1986). "Guidelines for International Business Negotiations." *International Marketing Review* (Autumn): 72–82.

Graham, John L., Leonid I. Evenko, and Mahesh N. Rajan. (1992). "An Empirical Comparison of Soviet and American Business." *Journal of International Business Studies.* 23/3 (Third quarter): 387–418.

Graham, John L., and Yoshihiro Sano. (1989). *Smart Bargaining: Doing Business with the Japanese.* New York: Harper Business.

Graham, John L., Dong Ki Kim, Chi-Yuan Lin, and Michael Robinson. (1988). "Buyer-Seller Negotiations around the Pacific Rim: Differences in Fundamental Exchange Processes." *Journal of Consumer Research.* 15 (June): 48–54.

Graham, John L., and R.A. Herberger. (1988). "Negotiators Abroad: Don't Shoot from the Hip."*Harvard Business Review,* (July-August): 160–168.

Graham, John L., and J. Douglas Andrews. (1987). "A Holistic Analysis of Japanese and American Business Negotiations." *Journal of Business Communications.* 24/4 (Fall): 63–73.

Graham, John L. (1986). "Across the Negotiating Table from the Japanese." *International Marketing Review.* (Autumn): 58–70.

Graham, John L. (1985a). "The Influence of Culture on the Process of Business Negotiations, an Exploratory Study." *Journal of International Business Studies.* (Spring): 81–96.

Graham, John L. (1985b). "Cross Cultural Marketing Negotiations: A Laboratory Experiment." *Marketing Science.* (Spring): 130–146.

Graham, John L. (1983). "Business Negotiations in Japan, Brazil, and the United States." *Journal of International Business Studies.* 14 (Spring-Summer): 47–62.

Graham, John L. (1981). "A Hidden Cause of America's Trade Deficit with Japan." *Columbia Journal of World Business.* (Fall): 5–15.

Griffin, Trenholme J., and W. Russell Daggatt. (1990). *The Global Negotiator.* New York: HarperCollins.

Grindsted, Annette. (1994). "The Impact of Cultural Styles on Negotiation: A Case Study of Spaniards and Danes." *IEEE Transactions on Professional Communication.* 37/1 (March): 34–38.

Gross, Stein H. (1988). "International Negotiation: A Multidisciplinary Perspective." *Negotiation Journal.* 4/3: 221–232.

Gulbro, Robert, and Paul Herbig. (1996). "Negotiating Successfully in Cross-Cultural Situations." *Industrial Marketing Management.* 24 (March): 1–12.

Gulbro, Robert, and Paul Herbig. (1995). "Differences in Cross-Cultural Negotiating Behavior between Industrial Product and Consumer Firms." *Journal of Business and Industrial Marketing.* 10/3: 18–28.

Gulbro, Robert, and Paul Herbig. (1994). "External Effects in Cross–Cultural Negotiations." *Journal of Strategic Change*. 3/158: 1–12.

Gulbro, Robert, and Paul Herbig. (1986). "Differences in Cross-Cultural Negotiating Behavior between Manufacturers and Service-oriented Firms," *Journal of Professional Services Marketing*. 13/1: 1–14.

Hall, Edward T., and Mildred Hall. (1987). *Hidden Differences: Doing Business with the Japanese*. Garden City, N. Y.: Anchor Books, Doubleday.

Hawrysh, Brian M., and Judith Lynne Zaichkowsk. (1990). "Cultural Approaches to Negotiations: Understanding the Japanese." *International Marketing Review.* 7/2: 1–10.

Heiba, Farouk I. (1984). "International Business Negotiations: A Strategic Planning Model." *International Marketing Review*. 1/4 (Autumn): 5–16.

Hendon, Donald W., and Rebecca Angeles Hendon. (1990). *World Class Negotiating*. New York: John Wiley & Sons.

Herbig, Paul A., and Hugh E. Kramer. (1993). "The Suq Model of Haggling: Who, What, When and Why. " *Journal of International Consumer Marketing*. 2/3: 12–20.

Herbig, Paul A., and Hugh E. Kramer. (1992). "The Dos and Don'ts of Cross-Cultural Negotiations," *Industrial Marketing Management*. 20/2: 1–12.

Herbig, Paul A., and Hugh E. Kramer. (1992). "The Role of Cross-CulturalNegotiations in International Marketing." *Marketing Intelligence and Planning*. 10/2: 10–13.

Herbig, Paul A., and Hugh E. Kramer. (1991). "Cross-Cultural Negotiations: Success Through Understanding."*Management Decisions*. 29/1: 19–31.

Hofstede, Geert. (1992). *Cultures and Organizations.* London: McGraw-Hill Europe.

Hofstede, Geert. (1984). *Culture's Consequences*. London: Sage.

Husted, Bryan W. (1994). "Bargaining with the Gringos: An Exploratory Study of Negotiations between Mexicans and U.S. Firms." *The International Executive*. 36/5: 625–644.

Ikle, Fred Charles. (1982). *How Nations Negotiate*. New York: Harper and Row.

Issac, Berry L. (1981). "Price, Competition and Profits among Hawkers and Shopkeepers in Pendembu, Sierra Leone." *Economic Development and Cultural Change.* 29/2 (January): 353–373.

Jastram, Roy W. (1974). "The Nakodo Negotiato." *California Management Review.* XVII/2 (Winter): 88–92.

Kapoor, Ashok. (1974). "MNC Negotiations: Characteristics and Planning Implications." *Columbia Journal of World Business.* (Winter): 121–132.

Kassaye, Wossen W. (1990). Using Haggling in the Marketing of Goods Internationally. *Journal of International Consumer Marketing.* 3/1: 1–12.

Katzin, M. (1960). "The Business of Haggling in Jamaica." *Social and Economic Studies* 9/3: 1–12.

Kennedy, G. (1987). *Negotiate Anywhere!* London: Arrow Books.

Khuri, Fuad I. (1969). "The Etiquette of Bargaining in the Middle East." *American Anthropologist.* 12/3: 698–706.

Kramer, Hugh, James Gray, and Paul Herbig. (1994). "A Two Way Perspective of Haggling in the Global Marketplace." *Journal of Pricing and Pricing Strategy.* 1/1: 1–12.

Kramer, Hugh E. (1989)."Cross-Cultural Negotiations: The Western Japanese Interface." *Singapore Marketing Review.* IV/1: 23–27.

Kramer, Hugh E., and Paul A. Herbig. (1992). "Suq Haggling." *International Journal of Consumer Marketing.* 5/2: 25–35 .

Lee, Kam-hon, and Thamis Wing-Chun Lo.. (1988). "An American Business People's Perceptions of Marketing and Negotiating in the People's Republic of China." *International Marketing Review.* 5/2: 41–51.

Magenheim, Ellen, and Peter Murrell. (1988). "How to Haggle and to Stay Firm: Barter as Hidden Price Discrimination." *Economic Inquiry.* XXVI (July): 449–459.

March, Robert M. (1983). *Japanese Negotiations.* New York: Kodansha International.

March, Robert M. (1985). "NoNos in Negotiating with the Japanese." *Across the Board.* (April): 44–50.

McCall, J. B., and M. B. Warrington. (1987). *Marketing by Agreement: A Cross Cultural Approach to Business Negotiations.* second edition. New York: John Wiley and Sons.

Messing, S. D. (1991) "The Abyssinian Market Town," in Paul Bohannon and George Dalton, eds. *Markets in Africa*. Evanston, Ill.: Northwestern University Press, p. 401.

Moran, Robert T., and William G. Stripp. (1991). *Successful International Business Negotiations*. Houston: Gulf Publishing Company.

Natlandsmyr, Jan Halvor, and Jorn Rognes. (1995). "Culture, Behavior, and Negotiation Outcomes: A Comparative and Cross-Cultural Study of Mexican and Norweigan Negotiators." *The International Journal of Conflict Management*. 6/1: 5–29.

Nite, Mikhail. (1985). "Business Negotiation with the Soviet Union." *Global Trade Executive*. 104 (June), 27–38.

Oikawa, Naoko, and John Tanner Jr. (1992). "Influences of Japanese Culture on Business Relations and Negotiations. " *Journal of Services Marketing*. 6/3 (Summer): 1–12.

Pascale, Richard Tanner. (1978). "Communications and Decision Making across Cultures: Japanese and American Comparisons." *Administrative Science Quarterly*. 23 (March): 91–110.

Peak, Herschel. (1985). "Conquering Cross-Cultural Challenges." *Business Marketing*. (October): 138–146.

Pye, Lucian. (1982). *Chinese Commercial Negotiating Style*. Cambridge, Mass.: Oelgeschlager, Gunn and Hain Publishers Inc.

Pye, Lucian. (1992). "The Chinese Approach to Negotiating." *The International Executive*. 34/6 (November/December): 463–468.

Quandt, William B. (1987). "Egypt: A Strong Sense of National Identity," in *National Negotiating Styles*, Hans Binnendijk, ed. Washington, D.C.: Department of State, Foreign Service Institute.

Rangaswany, Arvind, Jehoshua Eliashberg, Raymond R. Burke, and Jerry Wind. (1989), "Developing Marketing Expert Systems: An Application to International Negotiations." *Journal of Marketing*. 53/4 (October): 24–38.

Reardon, Kathleen Kelley, and Robert E. Spekman. (1994). "Starting Out Right: Negotiation Lessons for Domestic and Cross-Cultural Business Alliances." *Business Horizons*. (January-February): 71–79.

Riley, John, and Richard Zeckhauser. (1983). "When to Haggle, When to Hold Firm." *Quarterly Journal of Economics*. 98/2 (May): 267–289.

Roberts, Steven V. (1990). "Bush in the Bazaar: the President is Haggling with Hussein, but Does He Know the Rules?" *U.S. News & World Report.* 109/25 (December 24, 1990): 24–28.

Salacuse, Jeswald W. (1991). *Making Global Deals: Negotiating in the International Marketplace.* Boston: Houghton Mifflin.

Samuelson, Louis. (1984). *Soviet and Chinese Negotiating Behavior.* London: Sage Publications.

Schoonmaker, Alan. (1989). *Negotiate to Win.* Englewood Cliffs, N.J.: Prentice Hall.

Shenas, Delavar G. (1993). "A Comparative Study of Ethical Issues in International Business: The Case of American and Japanese Business Transactions." *International Journal of Management.* 10/1 (March): 39–46.

Smith, Raymond E. (1989). *Negotiating with Soviets.* Washington, D.C.: Institute for the Study of Diplomacy, Georgetown University.

Stewart, Sally, and Charles F. Keown. (1989). "Talking with the Dragon: Negotiating in the People's Republic of China." *Columbia Journal of World Business.* (Fall): 68–75.

Swierczek, Fredric William. (1990). "Culture and Negotiation in the Asian Context." *Journal of Managerial Psychology.* 5/5: 17–25.

Tung, Rosalie L. (1989). "A Longitudinal Study of United States-China Business Negotiations." *China Economic Review.* 1/1: 57–71.

Tung, Rosalie L. (1984). "Handshakes across the Sea: Cross-Cultural Negotiating for Business Success." *Organizational Dynamics.* 23/3: 30–40.

Tung, Rosalie L.(1983). "How to Negotiate with the Japanese." *California Management Review.* 26/4: 52–77.

Tung, Rosalie L. (1982). *Business Negotiations with the Japanese.* New York: Lexington Books.

Tung, Rosalie L. (1982). "U.S. China Trade Negotiations: Practices, Procedures and Outcomes." *Journal of International Business Studies.* 10/3 (Fall): 25–37.

Uchendu, Victor C. (1968). "Some Principles of Haggling in Peasant Markets." *Economic Development and Cultural Change.* 16/1: 37–49

Van Zandt, Howard F. (1970). "How to Negotiate in Japan." *Harvard Business Review.* (November/December): 45–56.

Walsh, Kevin J. (1993). "How to Negotiate European-Style." *Journal of European Business.* 4/6 (July/August): 45–47.

Warrington, M. B., and J. B. McCall. (1983). "Negotiating a Foot into the Chinese Door." *Management Development.* 21/2: 3–13.

Weiss, Stephen E. (1994). "Negotiating with the Romans—Part 1." *Sloan Management Review.* 35/2 (Winter): 51–62.

Weiss, Stephen E. (1994). "Negotiating with the Romans—Part 2." *Sloan Management Review.* 35/3 (Spring): 85–97.

Weiss, Stephen E. (1993). "Analysis of Complex Negotiations in International Business: The RBC Perspective." *Organization Science.* 4/2(May): 269–282.

Weiss, Stephen E. (1987). "Creating the GM-Toyota Joint Venture: A Case in Complex Negotiation." *The Columbia Journal of World Business.* 22/2: 23–37.

Wells, Louis T. Jr. (1977). "Negotiating with Third World Governments." *Harvard Business Review.* 55 (January-February): 72–80.

Withane, Sirinimal. (1991). "Technical Rationality vs. Consensual Rationality: The Dynamics of International Business Dealmaking." *Collective Negotiations.* 20/2: 145–158.

Wright, P. (1981). "Doing Business in Islamic Markets." *Harvard Business Review.* 59/1: 34.

Index

About the Authors

DONALD W. HENDON is President of Business Consultants International, a management consulting and training firm. Dr. Hendon has been a Professor of Marketing at several universities in the United States, Canada, Australia, and Mexico for over 26 years, and has published several books, including *Classic Failures in Product Marketing* (Quorum, 1989).

REBECCA ANGELES HENDON is Assistant Professor, Management Information Systems at Azusa Pacific University.

PAUL HERBIG is Assistant Professor of Marketing, the Graduate School of International Trade and Business at Texas A&M International University. Professor Herbig has worked on marketing management and product management with major international corporations, and is widely published in international business. His books include *The Innovation Matrix* (Quorum, 1994), *Innovation Japanese Style* (Quorum, 1995), and *Marketing Japanese Style* (Quorum, 1995).

DATE DUE			